THE KOREAN WAR

THE KOREAN WAR

A 25-YEAR PERSPECTIVE

Edited for
The Harry S. Truman Library Institute
for National and International Affairs

by

Francis H. Heller

THE REGENTS PRESS OF KANSAS
Lawrence

Photographs Courtesy of The Harry S. Truman Library

Library of Congress Cataloging in Publication Data

The Korean War.

Includes index.
1. Korean War, 1950-1953—United States—
Addresses, essays, lectures. 2. Truman, Harry S., Pres.,
U. S., 1884–1972—Addresses, essays, lectures. I. Heller,
Francis Howard. II. Harry S. Truman Library,
Independence, Mo., Institute for National and
International Affairs.

DS919.K67   951.9'042   77-4003
ISBN-0-7006-0157-0   *ap678*

Contents

Illustrations

Preface

This book is the record of a conference convened in early May 1975 by the Harry S. Truman Library Institute for National and International Affairs. It was the ninth, and in many ways the most ambitious, conference staged by the Institute since its establishment in 1957.

The Harry S. Truman Library Institute was formed to lend support to the Truman Library and to promote its interests. The Library itself is, of course, maintained and operated by the National Archives with federal funds. But these funds are not available for the promotion of research and the development of the Library as a major research center. It was President Truman's wish at all times that the library that bears his name and houses his papers should serve scholarly inquiry, and he encouraged the creation of the Institute as a means to channel private support to the advancement of the Library's use by scholars and students. Throughout his life he took an active part in the affairs of the Institute; routinely, he donated to the Institute whatever fees he received for lecturing and speaking engagements. Following his example, a number of his friends and associates have made generous gifts to the Institute, and over five thousand persons, from all walks of life and all parts of the country, contribute annually to the Institute through its Honorary Fellows Program.

Since the Library opened its doors for research in 1959, the Institute has given nearly 250 grants to scholars working in the Truman period. In addition, it undertook two special research projects of its own. Every other year the Institute recognizes an outstanding book on the Truman

PREFACE

period by the award of the David D. Lloyd Book Prize. Its conferences, held on the average of every other year, have generally been designed to focus attention on the potential of the Truman period as a research field and of the Truman Library as the major resource center for such research.

The 1975 conference on "The Korean War: A 25-Year Perspective" represents a departure from this format. The effort here was to bring together as many of the major actors in the events as possible, to hear their recollections, and to have them interact with scholars who had studied the period. Regrettably, financial considerations compelled limiting the conference to Americans. Among those who had participated in the events a few were unavailable for reasons of illness or conflicting engagements, but those who attended contributed generously, both in the formal setting of the conference and informally.

In selecting participants from the academic community the organizing committee started from the assumption that it was not attempting to compete with traditional scholarly meetings. The principal purpose was not to have historians discourse with other historians but to stimulate discussion between participants in and students of history. Because the committee did not conceive of the conference as a gathering of scholars only, it did not prescribe the form of written contributions it invited. Thus, contributors were free to employ footnotes or to omit them. Professor Leopold's survey of the literature (Chapter 6) is so comprehensive that it seemed superfluous to add bibliographical references at other points.

The only paper in this volume not actually presented and discussed at the conference is Professor Simmons's essay, "The Communist Side" (Chapter 5). In the early planning stages the organizing committee considered including a session on the Korean War in foreign perspectives. When time pressures supervened the committee decided to ask Professor Simmons's permission to include his paper in the proceedings anyhow, and he generously agreed. The committee believes that "The Communist Side" adds an important perspective to this discussion of the Korean War.

Also included in this volume are two addresses delivered, as part of the conference but to a larger, general audience, by W. Averell Harriman and Clark M. Clifford, two distinguished public servants who worked closely with President Truman. Their observations, though cast in a tenor somewhat different from that of the conference proper, served to highlight this retrospective gathering.

In the belief that readers might find it useful, a chronology of the Korean War—drawn largely from David Rees's *Korea: The Limited War*—has been included.

PREFACE

The concept of the conference originated with the staff of the Harry S. Truman Library. Its execution would have been difficult at best had it not been for the assistance of Dr. Benedict K. Zobrist, director of the Library (and secretary of the Institute), and of John Curry and Elizabeth Costin of the Library staff. Patti Deiter and Barbara Heacock deserve high plaudits for their skillful handling of the typing chores.

To my fellow directors of the Harry S. Truman Library Institute I extend my thanks for their unstinting support, both of the conference and in the preparation of this book.

May 1976   Francis H. Heller
Lawrence, Kansas

Conference Participants

Lucius D. Battle, Senior Vice President, Communications Satellite Corporation, Washington, D.C. (1950: Special Assistant to the Secretary of State.)

Ronald J. Caridi, Assistant to the Vice President for Academic Affairs, Trenton State College, Trenton, New Jersey.

Clark M. Clifford, senior partner, Clifford, Warnke, Glass, McIlwain & Finney, Washington, D.C. (1950: Special Counsel to the President.)

J. Lawton Collins, General, U.S. Army (retired), Washington, D.C. (1950: Chief of Staff, U.S. Army.)

Robert Dallek, Professor of History, University of California, Los Angeles, California.

Robert H. Ferrell, Professor of History, Indiana University, Bloomington, Indiana.

Norman A. Graebner, Edward R. Stettinius Professor of Modern American History, University of Virginia, Charlottesville, Virginia.

Robert Griffith, Associate Professor of History, University of Massachusetts, Amherst, Massachusetts.

Ernest A. Gross, partner, Curtis, Mallet-Prevost, Colt & Mosle, New York and Paris. (1950: Deputy U.S. Representative to the United Nations.)

Alonzo L. Hamby, Associate Professor of History, Ohio University, Athens, Ohio.

PARTICIPANTS

*W. Averell Harriman, former Governor of New York, Washington, D.C. (1950: Special Assistant to the President.)

*Francis H. Heller, Roy A. Roberts Professor of Law and Political Science, University of Kansas, Lawrence, Kansas.

Roger E. Kanet, Associate Professor of Political Science, University of Illinois, Urbana-Champaign, Illinois.

Lawrence S. Kaplan, Professor of History, Kent State University, Kent, Ohio.

Richard W. Leopold, William Smith Mason Professor of American History, Northwestern University, Evanston, Illinois.

Harry J. Middleton, Director, Lyndon Baines Johnson Library, Austin, Texas.

John J. Muccio, Clinton, New York. (1950: Ambassador to the Republic of Korea.)

*Charles J. Murphy, attorney, Washington, D.C. (1950: Special Counsel to the President.)

Richard E. Neustadt, Professor of Government, John F. Kennedy School of Government, Harvard University, Cambridge, Massachusetts. (1950: Special Assistant to the President.)

Forrest C. Pogue, Director, Dwight D. Eisenhower Institute for Historical Research, The National Museum of History and Technology, Smithsonian Institution, Washington, D.C.

Matthew B. Ridgway, General, U.S. Army (retired), Pittsburgh, Pennsylvania. (1950: Deputy Chief of Staff, then Commanding General, Eighth Army, in Korea.)

Richard H. Rovere, writer and editor, New York.

Robert R. Simmons, Assistant Professor of Political Studies, University of Guelph, Ontario, Canada.

*John W. Snyder, Washington, D.C. (1950: Secretary of the Treasury.)

Edmund Wehrle, Professor of History, University of Connecticut, Storrs, Connecticut.

Theodore A. Wilson, Professor of History, University of Kansas, Lawrence, Kansas.

John E. Wiltz, Associate Professor of History, Indiana University, Bloomington, Indiana.

*Benedict K. Zobrist, Director, Harry S. Truman Library, Independence, Missouri.

OBSERVERS

Daniel H. Bays, Assistant Professor of History, University of Kansas, Lawrence, Kansas.

OBSERVERS

Eliot Berkley, International Relations Council, Kansas City, Missouri.

*Thomas C. Blaisdell, Jr., Emeritus Professor of Political Science, University of California, Berkeley, California.

Martin Blumenson, Professor of History, The Citadel, Charleston, South Carolina.

*Charles F. Brannan, former Secretary of Agriculture, Denver, Colorado.

*Philip C. Brooks, former Director, Harry S. Truman Library, Sun City, Arizona.

*Girard T. Bryant, educator, Kansas City, Missouri.

*Rufus Burrus, attorney, Independence, Missouri.

Soon Sung Cho, Professor of Political Science, University of Missouri, Columbia, Missouri.

James L. Collins, Jr., Brigadier General, U.S. Army (retired); Office of the Chief of Military History, Washington, D.C.

Warren Cohen, Professor of History, Michigan State University, East Lansing, Michigan.

Doris M. Condit, Historical Office, Office of the Assistant Secretary of Defense, Washington, D.C.

Robert J. Donovan, Associate Editor, *Los Angeles Times*, Los Angeles, California.

*Anne K. Eaton, Northfield, Ohio.

India Edwards, Palm Desert, California.

John G. Fowler, Jr., Lieutenant Colonel, U.S. Army; U.S. Army Command and General Staff College, Fort Leavenworth, Kansas.

Lawrence Gelfand, Professor of History, University of Iowa, Iowa City, Iowa.

*Georgia Neese Clark Gray, former Treasurer of the United States, Topeka, Kansas.

*Richard S. Kirkendall, Executive Secretary, Organization of American Historians, Bloomington, Indiana.

Philip Lagerquist, Chief Archivist, Harry S. Truman Library, Independence, Missouri.

Chae Jin Lee, Associate Professor of Political Science, University of Kansas, Lawrence, Kansas.

*Robert J. Massman, construction executive, Kansas City, Missouri.

*Joseph J. McGee, Jr., insurance executive, Kansas City, Missouri.

Richard D. McKinzie, Professor of History, University of Missouri, Kansas City, Missouri.

Billy Mossman, Center of Military History, Department of the Army, Washington, D.C.

*James C. Olson, Chancellor, University of Missouri, Kansas City, Missouri.

OBSERVERS

Neil H. Petersen, Chief, Western Branch, Foreign Relations Branch, Department of State, Washington, D.C.

Daniel J. Reed, Assistant Archivist for Presidential Libraries, National Archives and Records Service, Washington, D.C.

*Carleton F. Scofield, Chancellor Emeritus, University of Missouri, Kansas City, Missouri.

Lynn L. Sims, Command and General Staff College, Fort Leavenworth, Kansas.

*Mack E. Thompson, Executive Director, American Historical Association, Washington, D.C.

---

* Member, Board of Directors, Harry S. Truman Library Institute.

Chronology

1945: August-September

By agreement of the Allies, Japanese forces north of the 38th Parallel surrender to Soviet forces, those south of the 38th Parallel to American forces.

1946: March

A Joint (U.S.-U.S.S.R.) Commission to work out trusteeship proposals for Korea is deadlocked.

1947: February

Korean People's Republic established north of the 38th Parallel.

September

At the request of the United States, the United Nations assumes responsibility for further efforts to unify Korea. United Nations Temporary Commission on Korea (UNTCK) established but is boycotted by Soviet-bloc nations and refused entry into North Korea.

Joint Chiefs of Staff recommend withdrawal of American troops from Korea.

1948: May 10

Elections in South Korea under UNTCK supervision.

August 15

South Korea proclaimed as Republic of Korea; Syngman Rhee is president.

September 9

North Korea proclaimed as Democratic People's Republic of Korea; Kim Il-song is premier.

CHRONOLOGY

December

Russian troops leave North Korea.

1949: February

General MacArthur urges prompt withdrawal of American troops in Korea.

June 29

American troop withdrawal from Korea completed.

1950: January 12

Secretary of State Acheson, in a speech to the National Press Club, places Korea and Formosa outside the U.S. defense perimeter in the Pacific.

June 25

North Korean forces—100,000 men with 150 Russian-built tanks—invade South Korea.

At U.S. request, the U.N. Security Council meets, calls for a cease-fire and North Korean withdrawal to the 38th Parallel. U.N. members are called upon to render assistance.

June 26

General MacArthur is directed to use air and naval forces to assist Republic of Korea (ROK) forces south of the 38th Parallel. He is also ordered to send the Seventh Fleet to the Formosa Straits to prevent Communist action "that might enlarge the area of conflict."

June 27

U.N. Security Council votes for an international military effort to assist South Korea.

June 28

Seoul falls to the North Koreans.

June 30

Truman authorizes MacArthur to use ground forces under his command (i.e., four divisions in Japan) in Korea.

July 1

First American combat units arrive in Korea.

July 13

Eighth Army headquarters (Lt. Gen. Walton H. Walker) established at Taegu, South Korea.

July 31

First reinforcements arrive from continental U.S.

MacArthur, without authorization from Washington, flies to Taipei for conferences with Chiang Kai-shek.

August-September

Defense of the Pusan perimeter.

CHRONOLOGY

August 6–9

Averell Harriman, special assistant to the president, in Tokyo for talks with MacArthur.

August 17

MacArthur sends message to Veterans of Foreign Wars convention; Truman orders message withdrawn.

August 29

British Twenty-seventh Infantry Brigade joins U.S. and ROK forces.

September 6

Eighth Army headquarters withdraws from Taegu to Pusan.

September 12

Gen. George C. Marshall appointed secretary of defense, replacing Louis Johnson.

September 15

Successful surprise landing at Inchon. Simultaneous breakout from the Pusan perimeter.

JCS directive to MacArthur on operations north of the 38th Parallel.

September 27

Seoul recaptured. General collapse of North Korean army.

Second directive to MacArthur on operations in North Korea directs that "no non–South Korean forces" are to be used in the provinces bordering Chinese and Russian territories.

October 7

U.N. Assembly votes to support unification of Korea.

First U.S. troops cross the 38th Parallel.

October 15

Truman and MacArthur meet at Wake Island.

October 19

North Korean capital, P'yongyang, falls to Eighth Army.

October 26

U.S. reconnaissance unit reaches the Yalu river.

First indications of presence of Chinese troops in Korea.

November 7

North Korean radio announces Chinese "volunteers" have entered the war.

November 24

MacArthur starts new offensive to reach the Yalu River in force; encounters heavy Chinese opposition.

November 28

MacArthur reports, "We face an entirely new war."

December 5

P'yongyang evacuated by U.N. forces.

CHRONOLOGY

December 6

Joint Chiefs of Staff direct clearance by Washington of public statements by theater commanders.

December 16

President Truman proclaims a state of emergency.

December 23

General Walker killed in jeep-truck collision; he is replaced by Lt. Gen. Matthew B. Ridgway.

December 31

New Chinese offensive begins. Ridgway orders withdrawal to a line seventy miles south of the 38th Parallel.

1951: January 4

Seoul again occupied by North Koreans.

January 12

General Collins, army chief of staff, and General Vandenberg, air force chief of staff, fly to Tokyo for policy discussions with MacArthur.

January 25

Allied counteroffensive begins.

February 13

General MacArthur issues statement critical of Washington's policy.

March 7

Second such statement ("Die for a tie").

March 14

Seoul recaptured by the allies.

March 20

Proposed peace statement sent to MacArthur who issues own statement of terms for a cease-fire.

March 27

Allies recross 38th Parallel.

April 5

MacArthur letter criticizing administration policy is read in the House of Representatives by Joseph W. Martin, minority leader.

April 11

President Truman relieves General MacArthur of his commands, replaces him with General Ridgway.

April 22

Chinese spring offensive starts; U.N. forces hold.

May 3

Senate committee hearings on MacArthur's recall open.

May 16

Second Communist spring offensive starts, produces only minor penetration with extremely high casualties.

CHRONOLOGY

May 22
Allied offensive begins; furthest advance reached in July.

June 1
Secretary Acheson indicates a cease-fire in the vicinity of the 38th Parallel would be acceptable.

June 23
Soviet U.N. ambassador, Jacob Malik, urges discussions leading towards a cease-fire and withdrawal of forces from the 38th Parallel.

June 29
General Ridgway is instructed to broadcast a message to the Communist command to initiate cease-fire talks.

July 2
Communists agree to a meeting at Kaesong.

July 8
Liaison officers from the opposing sides meet at Kaesong.

July 10
First meeting of full delegations.

October 25
Cease-fire talks transferred to Panmunjom.

November 12
General Ridgway orders an end to offensive action.

November 27
Agreement reached on line of demarcation.

1952: May 7
Cease-fire talks stalemated over issue of repatriation of North Korean and Chinese prisoners.

October 8
Plenary sessions recessed due to continuing failure to reach agreement on POW issue.

October 24
Presidential candidate Eisenhower pledges that, if elected, "I shall go to Korea."

November 4
Dwight D. Eisenhower elected president of the United States.

December 2–5
President-elect Eisenhower in Korea.

1953: February 2
President Eisenhower "unleashes" the Seventh Fleet: it will no longer prevent Chinese attacks from Taiwan on the mainland.

March 5
Death of Joseph Stalin.

CHRONOLOGY

April 2
Deadlock on POW repatriation partially resolved.
April 20
Operation "Little Switch": exchange of sick and wounded.
April 26
Plenary sessions resume at Panmunjom.
June 18
President Syngman Rhee unilaterally releases POWs who did not wish to
be repatriated.
July 27
Armistice agreement signed at Panmunjom.

THE KOREAN WAR

1

Introduction

On more than one occasion during the years after he left the White House, Harry S. Truman said that he regarded the decision to resist aggression in Korea as his most important decision as president. He believed firmly, as he wrote in his *Memoirs*, that "if South Korea was allowed to fall Communist leaders would be emboldened to override nations closer to our own shores. . . . If this was allowed to go unchallenged it would mean a third world war, just a similar incident had brought on the second world war" (2:333).

Certainly the American public agreed at the time. Russian intransigence had been evident in many places, most dramatically in Berlin. Most Americans believed that the Communist take-over of mainland China was a massive demonstration of the Kremlin's expansionist designs. Disclosures of Soviet spy activities within the United States had added to the popular perception of Moscow as the aggressor. The dramatic suddenness of the North Korean attack reminded many of Pearl Harbor—then, less than nine years ago. The president's decision made sense to most of his countrymen.

But the war in Korea did not become a popular war; its conduct was soon the subject of acrimonious, often partisan debate. More recently, against the backdrop of a much longer, much costlier (and much more unpopular) war in Asia, some have been heard to say that Korea and Vietnam were one of a kind—or at least that Korea paved the way for Vietnam. Some comments to this effect will be found in the pages of this book.

Of the rewriting of history there is, of course, no end. Human memory being what it is, events of the past may be recalled quite differently by different participants—indeed the same participants' recollections may come to vary over time. The problems this creates are encountered not only in history writ large, but also in our daily lives and private interactions. Some events, of course, can be established beyond doubt: President Truman did, on such-and-such day, at such-and-such time, sign such-and-such document. Though, as the discussion in this volume of the Wake Island meeting between Truman and MacArthur demonstrates, even such seemingly unequivocal occurrences as when an airplane arrived can become matters of dispute. Where contention really arises, however, is in the interpretation of events. If President Truman signed the document, why did he sign it? Are the reasons given the true reasons, or the sole reasons? Were there other motives?

I recall that, in the course of preparing his memoirs, Mr. Truman had the temporary assistance of an academician (now long deceased) who exasperated the former president by his persistent quest for hidden motives. As Mr. Truman related it: "I kept telling the professor that my reasons were straightforward and simple, and he kept telling me they had to be devious and complicated." But to most people who have faced the necessity of decisionmaking, the complexities that others may perceive—especially after the fact—are often not even apparent. They see a problem and they act on it. This, at least, was President Truman's approach. In a multitude of ways, his memoirs bespeak the uncomplicated, direct approach that was so typically his. What to do about aggression in Korea was, as far as he was concerned, never in doubt. During the war's later phases he would be harshly criticized for not giving free rein to an imperious general's perceptions of strategy. Again, Truman had no doubt about the correctness of his position.

As Averell Harriman points out more than once in the proceedings of this conference, we shall—in all likelihood—never see what the Kremlin's archives hold (or, for that matter, Peking's or P'yongyang's). Thus, it is relatively easy to argue that Stalin or Mao or Kim would or would not have done this or the other. Our wisdom is limited to what we know now. Mr. Truman's, Stalin's, Mao's, Kim's, MacArthur's wisdom, at that particular time, was considerably more confined. One may wish that Stalin's thoughts were on record and available but they are not. Mr. Truman's thoughts, as he recalled them, are recorded in his memoirs —presumably more accurately and more reliably than Merle Miller's rendition in *Plain Speaking*.

In these conference proceedings, men who were close to Mr. Truman at the time record their recollections. They call up their memories of what they heard the president say and what they saw him do. They

INTRODUCTION

bring back what they themselves said and did, and what others said and did. Of course, it is not as if this were the first occasion for recollection in twenty-five years. Some have recorded these memories in books; others have given their recollections before committees of Congress (most notably, the MacArthur hearings). Yet bringing these points of view together around a conference table added a further dimension. Take, for example, the matter of Acheson's speech to the National Press Club. Lucius Battle, who was Acheson's personal aide at the time, relates details of the circumstances. Ernest Gross contributes insights on the statement's reception at the United Nations. Others on the panel stress the fact that what Acheson said had been formulated in the councils of the government (with General MacArthur's concurrence) at least eighteen months earlier.

It was not the purpose of the conference to produce new and startling revelations. What was hoped for was that the interaction of participants in the events, both among themselves and with the academicians present, would serve to recreate the momentous days of 1950–52 and that the meanings of those events would be highlighted and explored.

It seemed logical to invite the participants to address themselves in one session to the impact of the Korean War on America's foreign relations and in another session to the domestic response to the same events. For each of these two sessions an invited paper served as the point of departure for discussion. But during both sessions—the papers notwithstanding—the discussion turned to foreign relations as the focal topic. Does this imply that, after twenty-five years, the Korean War is remembered mostly as a world event, less so as an American event? Speaking to this point, Richard Rovere observes that, in general, what happened twenty-five years ago has ceased to be an event and has become history. A generation that has not experienced the event cannot perceive it except as history. Where, then, does the Korean War stand in history?

The participants in our conference did not raise that question in so many words yet it runs through much of their discussion. To the older generation, those who had a share in the affairs of 1950–52, Korea was both *sui generis* and critically important. To the younger persons present, Korea was something that happened before Vietnam—and the possible relationship (or contrast) between the two emerged more than once as the discussion progressed. (The conference met only a few days after the fall of Saigon; Vietnam may have been more on people's minds than might have been the case several months later.)

While President Truman ordinarily categorized Korea as his most important decision, he usually grouped it with other events in his administration, each of which he also considered critical: the decision to come to the aid of Greece and Turkey; the promulgation of the Marshall Plan; the determined challenge to the Soviets' blockade of Berlin. To Mr. Truman these were turning points in preserving the predominance of Western values in the world. But until North Korean troops crossed the 38th Parallel in force in June 1950, the American response to Communist pressures had been in money, supplies, and advice—not in the use of military power. To Mr. Truman, to his associates, and to a large part of the American public in 1950, the importance of Korea was that it demonstrated to the world America's willingness to take this critical next step: to use force if it was needed to repel force. Theirs was a state of mind not unlike that expressed by John F. Kennedy, two presidential terms later: "We shall pay any price, bear any burden, meet any hardship, support any friend, oppose any foe to assure the survival and the success of liberty."

But if this was the prevailing attitude at the beginning it soon changed, especially after the entry of the Chinese produced "a new war." Would the American people have reacted differently if MacArthur had not promised to "have the boys home by Christmas?" To what extent, in other words, were the American people victimized by the syndrome of "unfulfilled expectations"? Once the daring operation against Inchon had succeeded, was there a euphoric assumption that the end was, in fact, a matter now clearly within our (i.e. American) control?

What if ———? Historians will have ample opportunity to raise that question, not only in their quest for motives but also in examining alternative courses of action. A few such questions are, in fact, raised in these proceedings; they evoke the important reminder from General Ridgway that there is always a difference between capabilities and probabilities, between assessing what could happen and what is likely to happen. It is a distinction of critical importance but one all too often forgotten.

Consider, for instance, Battle's and Harriman's comments on the decision not to seek a Joint Resolution from Congress in support of the initial decision to intervene. As Battle, in particular, tells it, the issue was decided on the basis of an estimate of what might happen in Congress. General Ridgway's observation aims at decisionmaking in the military realm; obviously, it is equally applicable to the political arena. Perhaps, however, lack of appreciation of this fact is one reason why the domestic aspects of the Korean War have received less attention than its international ones.

Another reason may well be found in the discussion of whether the war was a "traumatic" experience for the American people. The prevailing view seems to be that it was not. If there was a domestic event related to the war that appears to be vividly remembered by contemporary members of the public, it is General MacArthur's return and especially his address to the joint session of Congress. But any discussion of this episode quickly turns from domestic considerations to strategic decisions. The general himself had, after all, conceded the president's right to relieve him: what he challenged, and what therefore can be debated, is whether the president's or the field commander's strategic concept should prevail.

David Rees subtitled his book on Korea "The Limited War." To the extent that MacArthur highlighted the issue, the question of whether a major power could, in fact, fight a limited war in the twentieth century may well be a crucial matter. Earlier in these pages it was argued that Korea marked the acceptance by Americans (or, at the very least, by their leaders) of a resort to military force, if necessary, to contain what appeared to be a sustained expansionist drive on the part of the Soviets. As the Korean War continued, there emerged a critical corollary: resort to only as much military force as necessary for containment. This was a formula that required more than drive and desire: it called for discipline and self-control, qualities not characteristically predominant among people accustomed to having their own way.

Mark Roelofs has written about *The Tension of Citizenship*, that uneasy balance in a democracy between a citizen's commitment to his society and his desire to be left alone. Typically, Americans have accepted the first in time of clear crisis and insisted on the latter whenever they have not felt the impact of crisis conditions; they have been uncomfortable when asked to place themselves somewhere between these two extremes. Yet this is precisely the posture of sophistication and discipline which a limited war demands. The Korean War may not have been a trauma for Americans but it certainly subjected them to strains and stresses unlike any they had previously experienced.

By comparison, the Great Depression and World War II had been easy to cope with. One can, of course, write about the years from 1941 to 1945 in terms of conscientious objectors and "relocated" Japanese-Americans or describe the depression from the vantage of those few who were not drastically affected by it, but for most Americans both periods were marked by national objectives that were easily understood and shared by most. Korea required a more complex understanding—and in the process it ushered in a need for political maturity of a kind not called for before.

It is well to recall that when President Truman made his decision to come to the aid of the Republic of Korea, less than five years had elapsed since the end of World War II hostilities, less than twenty years since the depression had ended—less time than separates us today from June 1950. Most Americans were still under the sway of these two momentous events and of the direct, uncomplicated approach the nation had taken then. It had been "give us work" in one case, "let's beat Hitler and Tojo" in the other. Now it was, "We will resist aggression but we will not be drawn into a larger war"—a "yes-but" formula not nearly as easily assimilated. For the average citizen, this was not the way crises had been faced before; it added significantly to the "tension of citizenship."

What is suggested here is that the Korean War, whatever else it was or did, had a significant dimension in social psychology because it affected Americans as citizens even more than as persons. That assertion may well be incapable of empirical proof. It is advanced here because it appears to offer one explanation for the tendency of the conference participants to slight discussion of the domestic impact of the war in favor of the issues of world affairs and strategic choices.

The Korean War, as Professor Kaplan demonstrates, moved America's perspectives in Europe to a level of avowedly military priorities. The quantum jump that put the United States in combat in Korea placed American divisions in combat readiness within the NATO framework. Meanwhile, as Professor Wiltz shows, daily life at home underwent some changes, but the war's impact was not anywhere near that of World War II. As Professor Leopold indicates in his comprehensive review of research done and to be done on the Korean War, the attention of the scholarly community has focused largely on the military scene and on the Truman-MacArthur controversy. This is, of course, by no means unusual: the "big" events are recorded, discussed, analyzed (and reanalyzed) while subtle changes in societal texture and social perspective await later discernment.

We are just beginning to look at the depression and the Second World War with this kind of attention to the impact on people's thought and behavior. It may well be, as far as Korea is concerned, that the time to do likewise has not arrived, that more of what Professor Leopold identifies as outstanding work needs to be accomplished before we can answer the question: "What did the Korean War mean for the American people?"

Today, our response to that question would still be tentative; at best, it might be descriptive. By contrast, President Truman's actions have been detailed by himself and by others; the generals and the diplomats (at least a fair number of them) are on record. Historians and political scientists can move—and, of course, already have moved—to the next step and attempt analysis. Thus, the state of our knowledge may also

INTRODUCTION

explain why the conferees preferred to talk about Korea as a world rather than a domestic event.

There is, therefore, more to be said about the Korean War than was said by those assembled in Kansas City in May 1975, nearly twenty-five years after the event. There is still need for further research, as Professor Leopold and others clearly suggest. There are dimensions of analysis that have been barely attempted: Mr. Keyserling's observations on economic policy may serve as just one striking illustration. There is much to be learned yet about the other side; Professor Simmons's essay provides a good example.

The twenty-fifth anniversary is, of course, always a suitable event to observe. In some ways, though, twenty-five years afford deepened perception but they do not mark the point for a summing up. To reach that point, whether in the life of humans or of nations, more time must elapse. It is hoped, however, that the record of a preliminary assessment of the kind attempted here will be useful to more definitive efforts yet to come.

2

From Where I Stood:
A Panel

HARRY J. MIDDLETON (chairman): The task assigned to our panel is not to cover the entire Korean War but to take advantage of the special knowledge and insights of the panel. Consequently, some phases of the war, although important, will appear to be slighted, but I hope we can cover at least four major aspects. First, the beginning—that is the prewar period up to and including the outbreak of the war. Second, the early phase of the war—up to the entry of the Chinese forces. Third, the "new" war, which began with the entry of the Chinese. And fourth, the situation involving General MacArthur.

Going to the first of those, the prewar period and the outbreak of the war, we should begin with a question about the use of the 38th Parallel as the dividing line in Korea.

GEN. J. LAWTON COLLINS: This was actually decided by Dean Rusk and [Colonel Charles H.] "Tip" Bonesteel, an army officer who was with him at the time of the discussion as to where the dividing line should be drawn. It happened that there was one map available and Bonesteel noted that the 38th Parallel just about split the country in two. They had only a few minutes to make the recommendation. You will find a detailed statement of it in my book *War in Peace Time* [pp. 25, 26].

The interesting thing was that they hit on exactly the same line that the Japanese and the Russians had picked much earlier as a dividing line between their spheres of influence in Korea.

MIDDLETON: It is always interesting after something as dramatic as the outbreak of a war occurs to look back and see whether there were

10

signs that pointed to its happening. I want to ask Ambassador Muccio if he could see that war was about to occur.

AMBASSADOR JOHN J. MUCCIO: I think the several sources of intelligence available to us gave us a pretty good picture of what was going on in the North. There were as many incursions from the South into the North as there were from the North into the South. That is something that the press of the United States did not say too much about.

Beginning in February of 1950, the North Korean military was coming back from China as units. Up to that time there had been occasional individuals and small groups, but no units coming back. Now they brought in air power and also new tanks. We had a pretty good estimate of what was going on, but there was no determination as to whether this was more of the same kind of posturing that the North had been carrying on for several years, or whether they really intended to use the new material and new units they brought in, and if so, when. I felt that if the Communists were anywhere near as intelligent as we credited them with being, they would not use force because the South had many weaknesses.

I would also say that the intelligence in the North, about what was going on in the South, was even worse than our intelligence. With good intelligence, when they slammed across the 38th Parallel, they should have been in Seoul that same night [Sunday]; they did not get into Seoul until Wednesday morning. I attribute that in part to the weather: it rained cats and dogs the morning they crossed the parallel. Also, the South Koreans had broken up two guerrilla networks which the North had set up, one in the Seoul area and one in the Chola provinces. I think that agents in the South simply failed to report that defeat to their superiors in the North. They just did not dare report that the South Koreans had smashed these two networks. When they came across the parallel, the plan was to get Seoul, capture the government, and there would be an end to the South Korean governmental structure. In this they failed.

MIDDLETON: Mr. Battle, in January of 1950 the secretary of state made a speech in which he defined America's defense line in the Far East. It was a line that generally has been reported as excluding Korea. After the invasion by the North Koreans some critics reported, and have continued to report, that Mr. Acheson's speech was a signal that the United States did not intend to defend any incursion by the North Koreans into South Korea. Could you shed any light on that speech and what you considered to be its significance, or the circumstances of it?

11

THE KOREAN WAR

AMBASSADOR LUCIUS D. BATTLE: I think it is important to understand the context in which this speech was made and the moment at which it was made. A great deal has been written about this speech, a lot of it utter nonsense. The atmosphere, the climate are important. It was a period in which the China lobby was really beginning to rise in power and influence; the Hiss case was all over the press; and charges of treason, communism, whatever, were rampant in the city of Washington. China had just—as the China lobby put it—been "lost" by us. Of course, it was never ours to lose, but that subtlety seems to have escaped a few people; and there was a great deal of talk that seemed to point the finger at the State Department and the administration. They were expected to have a big, broad, new policy to change the whole course of a century in a very short time. It was against this background that Dean Acheson was scheduled, unfortunately, to make a speech at the National Press Club. I helped a good deal on this speech, as did Dean Rusk, Walt Butterworth, and others. We were all looking for a sweeping new policy—but that did not come easily, perhaps because none was really available at that moment. I did a draft, so did Rusk and Walt and others; all of them were pretty bad. The evening before the speech we all went over to Dean's house and spent many hours preparing for that address to come the following day.

The tradition of the Press Club is that nothing is off the record, but you don't have to have a prepared text. At the end of the evening—it may have been partly because he was sick of us and sick of the whole thing—Acheson said, "I've really had enough. I've listened to you all and there's no speech here. I'm going to do it on the basis of notes." Then, by himself, with the advice and help that we had already given him, he prepared his outline, staying home to work on it the following morning. I talked to him a couple of times during the morning; the speech was at lunchtime.

We went to the speech. As Acheson says in his book, some people thought it was brilliant, others thought it was controversial—depending partly on how they felt about him. I thought the speech was extremely well received at the time. Then, although there was no text, I had the task of trying to figure out what we would release. Of course, the speech was on tape and, as any statement made in that manner, some of it was not precise grammatically. I asked several people to go over the draft transcript.

The point that later became controversial was really not noticed. Walt Butterworth observed that Secretary Acheson had been a little bit optimistic about one of the provinces in China. A couple of points of that sort were made by those who looked at the draft, but no one said anything about the perimeter. It was, after all, precisely what General MacArthur had said approximately a year earlier, coming, I think, in a slightly different geographical context. The main impact, nevertheless, was about the same. MacArthur's statement attracted very little attention and, indeed, Dean Acheson's statement, at that time, attracted very little attention. That came later. The first real attack on it that I recall came right after our entry into Korea; it was heavily partisan, led by Bob Taft on the floor of the Senate. The enthusiasm in Congress and elsewhere with respect to our initial entry into Korea was somewhat lessened as time went on and interest in the so-called perimeter drawing intensified, depending on how well things were going in Korea and on how much of a hot political issue someone thought he had.

I do not think we can ever know, really, to what extent that statement was a major factor. It was *a* factor—possibly—to be taken into account with other issues, other bits of intelligence, other things that the other side might have had. My own guess is that there was about to be a test, somewhere. It happened to come there, perhaps in lieu of other places.

MUCCIO: There was nothing in Acheson's speech of January 12, 1950, that was not in the study made by the NSC and approved by the president as NSC 7–1 in 1947.

BATTLE: I think that's absolutely right.

MUCCIO: The Communists knew about that, unless they are dumber than we think they are.

GEN. MATTHEW B. RIDGWAY: I want to address myself to one thing on which my memory is very clear. The Joint Chiefs of Staff made a recommendation to the president in September 1947 (three years before the outbreak of the Korean War) which included the statement, "From the standpoint of military security, the United States has little strategic interest in maintaining the present troops and bases in Korea." Dean Acheson's statement of January 1950 merely gave voice to a policy which his president had already approved. That policy had been recommended by the four great military leaders—Leahy, Eisenhower, Nimitz, and Spaatz—which made it doubly understandable that the president gave it his approval.

GOV. W. AVERELL HARRIMAN: I think you have to go back to the beginning of the difficulty, which was in the talks during World War II. President Roosevelt spoke several times to Stalin about Korea and, of course, Stalin had agreed at Yalta that a trusteeship should be established

13

for Korea in which different countries would be involved. Then, when it came to the division, of course, the Russians refused to cooperate, as they did in all other cases around the world. Look at Khrushchev's book: I think he is correct in saying that Stalin armed the North Koreans. The Russians certainly had their officers there who trained the North Koreans. Whether or not they stayed—I have been told that they were taken out—I don't know, but it all really started with the Russian intransigence in not permitting Korea to be unified. Certainly Stalin gave Kim the nod to go.

Whether the general attitude of the United States towards Korea was caused by that, how much the North Koreans knew about the Joint Chiefs of Staff's recommendation, or the other statements, one cannot tell. The Acheson speech was only one of the statements that was made. I defended it on a political basis in the campaign in '52 when the Democrats were attacked. On the other hand, one cannot tell about a statement made by a secretary of state, or a particular phrase that may have been used. We shall never know; we'll never see the archives of the Kremlin.

I have always been inclined to think that Stalin was fairly cautious in military action, as shown by the fact that, when the North Korean invasion did not work, he stayed out. There are failures others can tell about. Mr. Gross probably can tell us more about why the Russians stayed out of the United Nations Security Council at that time. My own guess has always been that they figured that while the United Nations was debating, Stalin would have corrected this particular situation by unifying Korea through the action of the North Koreans, an effort he certainly stimulated.

It is very hard to tell why Stalin was so keen about South Korea, but he was very keen to get a zone of occupation. He wanted Hokkaido and told me so on several occasions; I think, if it had not been for some of the things we did in Moscow, he might have got it. But in any event, he did not get it, and his failure to get Hokkaido may have been one of the reasons for his moving in Korea. Acheson's speech was one of the things which made Stalin, I think, believe that we would not intervene militarily. Now perhaps you can tell us, Mr. Gross, why they stayed out of the Security Council just at that time, because that is a very important subject and it was very fortunate from our standpoint that they did.

AMBASSADOR ERNEST A. GROSS: I want to add that, as far as signals to the Russians were concerned, I was always struck by the fact that in 1949, when the Korean aid program legislation was before Congress—

FROM WHERE I STOOD

I happened at that time to be assistant secretary in charge of congressional relations and so I spent a lot of time on the Hill—we had particular difficulty in interesting the Foreign Affairs Committee of the House to make a substantial appropriation for Korean aid. According to my best recollection—although these sessions were normally executive sessions—both the Department of State and the military, particularly the military from the strategic point of view, expressed the opinion that Korea was indefensible. (I remember one bit of testimony on this before the committee.) If there were to be a determined assault in the peninsula, it would not be strategically defensible. Although there was considerable surface aid for the Korean people and although the establishment of a free and independent unified Korea was the U.S. policy and also the United Nations policy, nonetheless, there was not any indication shown by Congress that the United States had all that much priority to accord to Korea. I do not think that one has to look at words and phrases in one speech—even by the secretary of state—for signals, because that record, I think, will bear me out.

Governor Harriman has made an important point indeed with reference to that Press Club speech by Secretary Acheson. That speech did not write off Korea—quite the contrary. It pointed out that the defense perimeter was a strategic island chain which was of such paramount concern to the United States that we would unilaterally defend it if necessary. The defense of the integrity and independence of the countries of mainland Asia, on the other hand, was a matter of common concern, of collective concern, and a responsibility for the United Nations.

In January, after I had gone up to the U.N. with the U.S. mission, Acheson's speech was very widely discussed among the delegations. I remember this very well; and I remember talking about it with the then secretary general of the U.N., Trygve Lie, because he was interested in developing U.N. programs of aid. He was extremely impressed by that reference in the secretary's speech that these other areas, the mainland areas, were responsibilities of the international community.

BATTLE: I would like to make two points here. First, after this became a controversial speech—much later, after things began to go rather badly in Korea—Dean asked me once, "Get the text and let's look at it again. What did I say?"

I got the statement and here is the key phrase, which I think when one reads it it holds up rather well. He said, "Should such an attack occur"—that is an attack outside the perimeter—"the initial reliance must be upon the people attacked to resist it, and then upon the commitments of the entire civilized world under the Charter of the United Nations, which so far has not proved a weak reed to lean on by any people who are determined to protect their independence against outside aggression."

Dean immediately said, "Well, that's exactly what we did. I think it holds up pretty well."

MIDDLETON: The invasion took place on June 25. Mr. Muccio, would you tell about the events from the point of view of one who was there—the color and the flavor of it?

MUCCIO: Well, it is generally known that they smashed across the 38th Parallel in three places and landed on the east coast, way below the 38th Parallel, and also came across on the Ongjin peninsula. The South Koreans had been clamoring for air defense potential and we never got around to doing anything about it. We never gave Korea any more than small arms and defensive items, and they really had nothing to get at the planes and nothing to get at the tanks that the North Koreans used.

HARRIMAN: Was it not true that as a matter of policy—I wasn't involved in this, but I understood that it was a matter of policy—there were those who were afraid the South Koreans might attack and, therefore, we would only give them so-called defensive weapons?

MUCCIO: President Rhee had a very unrealistic attitude towards that whole issue. He thought that the people in the North were waiting for him to arrive on a white charger, that they would all get up and acclaim him, and that Korea would be unified. And, as I mentioned earlier, as many incursions north took place as incursions across the 38th Parallel into the South. That tied our hands, for there was a danger that the aggression would occur from the South.

COLLINS: You must also remember what the situation was in Europe during this same period. And you must remember that the amount of money given for defensive weapons *anywhere* to the military services was very, very low. The Joint Chiefs were faced with deciding whether to put what little money we had into an outpost that we recognized was not of vital importance to the United States in contrast to the much more important area in Europe, which was also being threatened by the Communists. This was constantly one of the major factors. Furthermore, when we made the decision (which was a political decision supported by General MacArthur) to withdraw our forces from Korea in the first place, back in 1947, it was decided that the only force that should be organized was a constabulary force for internal security. That is all General MacArthur could have supported. He had said he did not have the material, either in manpower or in physical materiel, to fight a major war in Korea, and so the decision was made with two factors in mind: first, the availability of funds; and second, the relative importance of Korea in contrast to Europe.

MIDDLETON: I am going to exercise the prerogatives of a chairman and move ahead. The word went from Seoul to Washington and then from Washington to Independence where President Truman was; President Truman returned to Washington. President Truman's *Memoirs* tell us what was in his thoughts.

Secretary Snyder was in St. Louis at the time. President Truman called to tell him what had happened and that he was going to stop in St. Louis, pick him up, and take him back to Washington with him. So, as far as I know, Secretary Snyder was probably the person who was the closest to President Truman at that time, and I think it would be of great interest to get his recollections of what President Truman's mood was, and what his conversation was, on that flight back to Washington.

SECRETARY JOHN W. SNYDER: Mr. Truman did not tell me anything about the developments in Korea until I saw him on the plane. I had gone to St. Louis to attend the opening of a Belgian exhibition at the request of Ambassador Silvercruys, and was staying over a day or two and had planned to go back Sunday to Washington. On Sunday morning, June 25, I received a call from Mr. Rowley of the Secret Service saying that the *Independence* was going to set down in St. Louis at around two o'clock that afternoon and that the president wanted me to go back to Washington with him.

I was there; the plane came in a minute or two after 2:00 and I got aboard. The first thing the president said to me was, "We're in trouble, I think." Colonel [Rufus] Burrus, who is also here, was aboard the plane; he was catching a ride back to Washington where he was stationed then. After I had greeted him, the president said, "Sit down, I've got some duties to attend to here." He said, "I want to talk to the press." He called in the few journalists on the plane and that was the first I heard about what had happened. He told them that the North Koreans had crossed the 38th Parallel in what appeared to be much greater force than they had made in previous attacks across the line, that he had very little detailed information, and he was giving out no statements until after he had arrived in Washington and learned in greater detail what had really happened.

He was cautious about giving the press anything before he got to Washington and got the latest news. He had waited until after we were airborne from St. Louis before he said a thing to them about it, and he had not said anything to me about it either. But then he immediately

President Truman discusses the invasion of South Korea with newsmen at the Kansas City airport—June 25, 1950.

had the radio man get in touch with Secretary Acheson to tell him our time of arrival and to ask him to invite all those at the Blair House conference to stay for dinner that evening. Then the president sent a message to Claunch, his maitre d' at Blair House, telling him to fix up a dinner for twenty to twenty-five people. He said to me, "This will be an opportunity to test out how quickly he can assemble a proper meal in time of emergency."

We then went back into his quarters on the plane, and he said, "I don't know how serious this is. They seem to think that it is rather serious in Washington." He said Secretary Acheson had called him the night before. It is interesting that you [Middleton] said that this started on June 25; actually it was June 25 in Korea, but it was June 24 in this country on Saturday, when Acheson first called President Truman. It was June 25 when Mr. Truman flew to Washington from Kansas City. Acheson had called him again that morning and told him it was rather urgent that he come on back.

The president said, "I'm so puzzled about this. We've been discussing this back and forth. I really don't know just how much the Russians are in this. We know that the North Koreans had training and they have been amply supplied—the Russians have supplied tanks and airplanes and pilot training, but I still know that there's an awful lot of manpower there of the Chinese that might be available in case some of this develops seriously." And he said, "It concerns me a great deal and I'll be most anxious to get back and get all of the diplomats and the defense people together and put this together and determine how serious this is." He said, "Because if it *is* serious, then this is going to be the testing point for our United Nations agreement of protection against invasion of a member country." He said, "Suppose it is serious, what do you think the Treasury will have to do promptly?"

Well, I said, "Mr. President, the first thing is we must stop an effort in Congress that is underway right now to cut back on the excise tax assessment," and I added that we should get that stopped until we could find out how serious it was. The second thing I suggested we ought to do was to call in the budget. (We had just finished the budget presentation for 1951, and that had just been settled a few days before.) I felt certain we ought to take another look and review the budget. "The next step," I said, "is that we should immediately start studies as to what kinds of increases we may need in present taxes and what new taxes, if this is a grave matter."

He said, "I agree with you, and you and I have agreed on that right along. We must see to it, if we possibly can, if this is a serious encroachment, that we are sound in our tax approach and in our budgetary operation, that we give extreme care to try to avoid excessive deficits." And he looked at me ruefully and said, "You and I both have seen two world wars started on less causes."

When we landed in Washington, the president's plane was met by

Secretaries Acheson and Louis Johnson, James E. Webb, and two or three others. I had to go by the Treasury Department to pick up a document for the president and met them at Blair House. When we arrived there every one of the group summoned was present. The president had cocktails served out on the veranda in the back of Blair House. He said, "Now, I don't want anyone"—one or two had started to make remarks—"to talk about this matter until after dinner when the servers have all withdrawn. Then we can take up the discussion."

We soon finished our drinks and had dinner. I must tell you one thing that to me has always been most significant, and it is particularly so in light of subsequent events. President Truman said that he and Dean Acheson had discussed how sorry they were that Averell Harriman was in Paris working on the Marshall Plan. The president spoke of Harriman's experience with the Communists, his knowledge of their thinking, his vast world experience, his extreme help during the war and the subsequent days. The president said, "I wish we could have him back here." Acheson said he would call and ask Harriman if he would come.

Mr. Truman said, "Oh, he won't give up an ambassador's job to come back here and fight with you cabinet members." And then he said, "Do you suppose if I made him my special assistant he would take it?"

Acheson said, "I don't know, but I could ask him."

The president said, "Will you do it?"

Well, subsequently it turned out that Dean did call the governor and he was delighted; he really wanted to come. So, the next morning, the president himself called him and, sure enough, on Wednesday Governor Harriman showed up as special assistant to the president.

Did I get that about right, governor?

HARRIMAN: No. I called the president and said, "Mr. President, you may be a little short-handed." I don't know whether there were any talks about my coming back before, but the first that I knew about it was when I called the president and he said, "Yes, why, I would like you to come back," and he asked, "How soon can you get here?"

I said, "Well, I'll leave this afternoon." So I left on four hours' notice.

SNYDER: That proves my point exactly, that the governor was an invaluable man whom we needed and one who was willing to come and take on a tough job.

The first thing I did the following morning [Monday] was to go up on the Hill and talk to Chairman Doughton, to Chairman Maybank, and to Scott Lucas. Sam Rayburn wasn't there, so I talked to McCormick. I explained to them that this was coming off, that we didn't know the extent of it, and that the president was probably going to call them down so he could talk with them personally. But we would like to hold up on the excise tax bill revision that was before Congress.

Later, when we found out it was really serious, within sixteen months we passed three tax bills that had a gross tax collection of a little over $15 billion a year. We started promptly to try to help rebuild the funds that we could use for these purposes as a member of the United Nations team, because as I remember, Mr. Truman kept calling it a police action for quite a while—a United Nations police action. We did take that prompt step, though, to get taxes in motion and Congress cooperated splendidly.

MIDDLETON: Even before the meeting that the president had in Blair House, the U.N. Security Council had been requested to call an emergency session and it did so.

Now, Mr. Gross, we come to the question: Why was the Soviet Union not present at the critical meeting of the Security Council? You have written about this in your book, and you have stated that it was deliberate and also that it really didn't make any difference.

GROSS: Well, the Soviet delegate walked out of the U.N. Security Council meeting—it happened to be the very first meeting of the Security Council I ever attended as U.S. delegate—on the announced basis that the Security Council was illegally composed because the Chinese people were not properly represented. China, as a permanent member of the Security Council, had to be properly represented—and that meant represented by the People's Republic—or the Security Council itself was an invalid body and not in conformity with the U.N. Charter. That was the essence of the speech the Soviet delegate made, and then he got up and walked out.

That incident took place almost six months before the outbreak of the Korean War: later there was considerable speculation as to why the Soviets had chosen that particular time to leave. Many months later, I asked Mr. Malik (who was then, as he is now again, the Soviet representative to the U.N.) point blank why it was. They had participated in the work of the Security Council by that time for about four years. All that time China was represented by what he then called the Kuomintang clique. His answer was very curious. It was the only time that I ever heard a Russian actually use the expression "dialectical materialism." At that time, he explained, the character of the United Nations organization had changed and it obviously bore on the relationship between the Soviet Union and China. My own feeling was—and this is purely speculation—that the Soviet government considered it more important at the time, in terms of its relationship with China, to take that stance and to insist that China should be represented in the United Nations by the Communists. The Chinese themselves were taking it very seriously, as Chou En-lai made clear repeatedly.

I also think the Soviets felt they had very little, if anything, to worry about. They did not anticipate that the Security Council would take action. I am certain that they were surprised when it did and that they then began to look for a suitable opportunity to come back. And despite the dialectical materialist explanation, such as it was, they waited for the first reasonable, plausible opportunity to come back, which was when their turn came on the rotation basis for the Soviet representative on the Security Council to serve as president. When that month came, the Soviet representative showed up, took his seat, and called the meeting to order. It was just as if he had always been there in terms of the climate or the atmosphere which he created. So I feel that the Soviets were caught by surprise, on June 25. The action having been taken, they wanted to get back in. Despite their vehemence in arguing that the Security Council was illegally composed in the absence of Chinese Communist representation, they did come back in when it was their turn to preside, on August 1, 1950.

I referred to the fact that the Soviet Union's absence from the Security Council was not decisive. Obviously, they would have used the veto had they been there, and there would not have been any Security Council resolutions. But it is a matter of fact that on that morning of June 25, I went to see the secretary general and his assistant and his counsel, and we discussed the possibility that the Soviet representative might come back and sit in the Security Council at the afternoon meeting of June 25. We agreed that if that happened, and if the Security Council became muscle-bound by a Soviet veto, then an emergency special session of the General Assembly would be convened, if necessary within forty-eight hours. Of course, at that time the "Uniting for Peace" resolution was not in existence; that was not adopted until later that year. But what the U.S. delegation and the secretary general agreed upon was that the Assembly was master of its own rules and, if an emergency special session were needed, it could waive its rule on the amount of notice required to call a special session. That move was contemplated but it turned out to be unnecessary. It was for that reason that I said the United Nations would not necessarily have been stymied by the Soviet presence.

FROM WHERE I STOOD

HARRIMAN: But it would have been delayed, of course.

GROSS: For forty-eight hours, yes.

MIDDLETON: After that, the United Nations called for a cease-fire, which North Korea ignored. Two days later the United Nations asked all member nations for help and asked the president of the United States to appoint a commander for the U.N. forces. President Truman had already ordered American ships and planes to help the South Koreans; two days later he ordered American ground forces into action.

Right here, it seems to me, history turns on two very important points about the commitment of force. One is the decision to use force, the other is the decision to limit force, which prevailed throughout the war.

General Collins, Gen. Thomas Power, who was then vice-commander and later commander of the Strategic Air Command, wrote a book in the mid-1960s [Design for Survival] in which he said that the United States came close—and close was his word—to using the atomic bomb during the Pusan perimeter period. In his book he said, "I had been ordered to have SAC units stand by for such action."

The way he presented it seemed to bypass the normal kind of contingency planning. I have never seen any reference to the possible use of the atomic bomb in any other place. Would you like to say anything about this?

COLLINS: I do not recall that this question ever was raised. So far as I know, we never gave any consideration to the use of the atomic bomb in Korea.

MIDDLETON: Now to the early phase of the war. The first unit committed to action was the Twenty-fourth Division from Japan, joined shortly by the First Cavalry Division, the Twenty-fifth Division, with air force and navy support, under the command of Lt. Gen. [Walton H.] Walker. For a period from June through August, General Walker's command retreated to a five hundred square-mile beachhead around the port city of Pusan, in the southern part of the peninsula. General Collins, in a letter to me, wrote: "It seems to me that the least understood and appreciated aspect of the Korean War was the part played by General Walker in the withdrawal to and defense of the Pusan beachhead." General Collins, would you expand on this?

COLLINS: The major point I want to make here is that General Walker was not a popular man, either publicly or, frankly, within the army. But his handling of the defense of the Pusan perimeter was masterly.

One of the tough things to do is to shift reserves, particularly when you have practically no reserves. Walker did a magnificent job, in my judgment, with the Twenty-seventh Infantry, with the Fifth Regimental Combat Team under Johnny Throckmorton, and with the First Marine Brigade in shifting these three units, as needed, to meet the persistent attacks of the Communists against the Pusan perimeter.

If we had not been able to hold the Pusan perimeter we would have had to withdraw from Korea and I think that Walker deserves credit for the fact that he was the man who was really responsible for finally holding the Pusan perimeter.

MUCCIO: I would like to point out General Walker's unique qualities for that particular situation; also Air Force Gen. "Pat" [Earle E.] Partridge's. The two worked hand-in-hand, day in and day out during that very, very dire period. They saved us. I would also like to add that the one satisfaction I had in Korea was to see the magnificent caliber of men who had been selected and came to the fore during World War II. They were still at the peak of their physical and mental vigor. The leadership we had in Korea was magnificent.

MIDDLETON: Soon after the invasion, General MacArthur, as he wrote about it later, using the withdrawal down to the southern end of the peninsula to gain time, contemplated a turning movement, as he put it, deep into the enemy's rear and flank. That plan—which he reported he thought about as he stood on the banks of the Han River, soon after the North Koreans had invaded—materialized into what we know as the Inchon invasion, an amphibious attack on the port of Inchon on the coast of Korea, near Seoul, which turned the tide of the war.

Now there were many arguments against the Inchon plan. The histories recount that almost everybody advised General MacArthur against Inchon. In late August two members of the Joint Chiefs of Staff went to Tokyo to discuss it with General MacArthur, and General Collins was one of those two.

General Collins, would you desribe your meeting with General MacArthur?

COLLINS: The only question that Forrest Sherman, who was chief of naval operations, and I, as chief of staff for the army and executive agent for the Joint Chiefs of Staff, had was not so much about the concept of an envelopment around the left flank, but about the exact spot of the landing, and then the conditions under which it was to be done and the timing. General MacArthur was a much older, much more experienced man than any of us. We were relative youngsters on the JCS at that time. We could get no details from MacArthur as to what these plans were. The navy was very skeptical about it and the marines were very skeptical about it, because of the tremendous tides in that area and the very narrow waterways that lead up to Inchon. So, finally, not getting any details from MacArthur, the Joint Chiefs decided to send us over to see what we could find out in the way of details. We did question MacArthur about it; he defended his position, and ultimately the Joint Chiefs, after we had gotten his plans, gave approval; the plan was approved then by the president. That's the gist of it.

HARRIMAN: This plan was approved by the president and the Joint Chiefs on August 9.

RIDGWAY: I know that I was one of the many General Collins refers to as being opposed to this plan when I went out there, but the magic of General MacArthur's presentation convinced me, as I think it did the others who were present. When Lauris Norstad and I came back to Tokyo from a quick inspection trip to Korea, I sat up all night trying to summarize our views and compose a little, condensed memorandum. I gave it to Governor Harriman on the plane before we got back to Washington, and it had his approval. I think you transmitted the president's answer, but that in essence was the basic approval to which General Collins has referred.

MIDDLETON: A history, compiled by the United States Navy shortly after the Korean War, states that at some meeting at which two members of the JCS were present, General MacArthur said that he recognized that it was a 5,000-to-1 gamble but that he was willing to take the chance.

HARRIMAN: I think we ought to really get down to what happened. General Ridgway and I were both there, and we both know what happened. General Norstad and General Ridgway were going to the Far East. I decided that as assistant to the president I should go with them, and the president approved. I asked the president if there were any messages he wanted me to give to General MacArthur, and he said, "Yes, I want you to give him two." One was: "I want him to stay clear of Chiang Kai-shek and not to get us into war with mainland China"; the other was: "I want to find out what he wants and, if it's at all possible to do it, I will give it to him."

So we went. I had a long talk with MacArthur and he told me he would accept the first proposition although I had the impression that he did not really agree with it. The next day we (Ridgway, Norstad, and I) went to Pusan and spent the day. We met with Ambassador Muccio and came back the same day. The following morning, which I think was August 8, MacArthur presented to us in his brilliant manner the program for the Inchon landings. We had known something about it, but I guess we all thought it was impossible because of the tremendous tides. The three of us were enthralled by General MacArthur. He had a specific number of troops he needed and that schedule was given us. We returned to Washington about the time that Mr. Truman got to his office in the morning. I went directly to see him about seven o'clock in the morning and told him of the recommendation which General Ridgway and General Norstad were going to make to him. I described MacArthur's plan to him and he said, "You better get over to the Pentagon as fast as you can and talk to Johnson and to Bradley."

I had a fast breakfast and shaved and I guess it must have been between half past nine and ten o'clock when I got to the Pentagon. Louis Johnson said to me, "What the hell have you been doing to the president?"

I said, "What do you mean?"

"He's been calling me up every fifteen minutes to know what the decision is."

In any event, the Joint Chiefs made this decision and within twenty-four hours the president approved it that following morning.

The Joint Chiefs of Staff recommended it and the president approved the plan in principle. Then the details were worked out, and of course, it was a tremendously ambitious plan. MacArthur had his view which was that the North Koreans had to be defeated and defeated fast. He did not think that the Russians or the Chinese would come in, but he knew all the risks. It wasn't 5,000 to 1, but it was surely a military risk that he was ready to stake his whole life's reputation on.

RIDGWAY: It was a brilliant concept and magnificently executed, attended with a great deal of luck, which is essential to any successful campaign.

MIDDLETON: Shortly after the successful invasion of the port of Inchon, the Eighth Army broke out of its perimeter around Pusan and the forces linked up and soon were poised at the 38th Parallel. And now one of the critical decisions of the Korean War was debated and reached: the decision to cross the 38th Parallel. To what extent was it a military decision, to what extent was it a political decision?

COLLINS: The Joint Chiefs felt that if we were required to stop at the 38th Parallel, nothing would have been done to solve the real problem.

In other words, if you stopped at the 38th Parallel, then the North Koreans, supported by the Chinese and the Russians, could once again attack when they were ready to. The 38th Parallel had no defensive merit whatsoever; therefore, General MacArthur recommended that he be permitted to go on. The Joint Chiefs supported his recommendation that we continue the attack, at least to a point where a good defensive line could be held.

MIDDLETON: Once the decision was made on a military basis to cross the 38th Parallel, what about a consideration of stopping at a defensible line that perhaps might have approximated the cease-fire line we eventually settled for?

COLLINS: There was no specific thought of that at all, as a matter of fact, and General MacArthur wanted to press on right up to the Yalu. When the authority was given to General MacArthur to cross the 38th Parallel, there were certain limitations placed on him. One specific limitation was that he should avoid approaching too close to the Yalu; another was that no non-ROK troops—that is, no American troops and none of the United Nations troops other than ROK—were to go up all the way to the Yalu. These were two of the limitations placed on General MacArthur after crossing the 38th Parallel.

But the United Nations had passed a resolution which supported the effort to create a unified Korea. General MacArthur took advantage of this later on, in defending his action and going right up to the Yalu, because he thought that the only way to get a unified Korea was to defeat the North Korean forces and the Chinese forces in the field.

GROSS: That was a basic resolution which stated the aims of the United Nations, which included—as had been the aim of the United Nations since 1946—that there should be a free, unified, independent Korea, with democratic institutions and a government selected by popular plebiscite under U.N. supervision. That was the program. But it was never the U.S. position, as relayed to us at the U.S. mission to the U.N., that it was the purpose of the United States (or of the United Nations, as far as we were concerned) to unify all of Korea by force. It was explicitly stated to us, by instructions from the State Department, that this was not our intention.

This is a very, very important point. The mission had instructions, dated December 20, 1950, from the secretary of state, but drafted, we understood, by Dean Rusk. They stated: "Our objective in Korea has never varied from that of the U.N. resolutions, the establishment of a unified, independent and democratic country." We had hoped, and still hoped, to bring that about by peaceful means under U.N. procedures. Neither we nor the United Nations were committed to bring it about by whatever force would be required. The memorandum went on to say, "The enemy is now in fact capable of preventing a U.N. military success in all of Korea." That was from the Department of State on December 20, 1950.

We felt at the U.N., with all respect to MacArthur, that MacArthur had distorted the resolution to justify an action which shocked everybody at the U.N.

BATTLE: I think the great weakness of the U.S. government's position at the time was that it wasn't clear. It wasn't clear to those of us within the government and I doubt it was totally clear to MacArthur. Certainly he had the option of saying that it was not. There were political considerations, there were military considerations, and there were a vast number of other considerations, including a groundswell in the press asking why MacArthur was being held back, why he was not being permitted to cross the Yalu. A lot of this was artificial, but it was still in the press, and it was causing a good deal of concern.

I saw the instructions that went to MacArthur. I was in New York with Dean Acheson at the time Dean Rusk brought them up. I was a brash young man of thirty at the time, and I argued that they weren't clear at all, that there ought to be a limit put on him, and that you couldn't let him cross the 38th without a clear definition of objectives.

HARRIMAN: I would like to dispute that. General Collins would say they were clear as could be.

COLLINS: Well, MacArthur was authorized to cross in order to defeat the North Korean forces in the field, but, as I have said, limitation was put on him that he would not go close to the Yalu and that he would not use any non-Korean troops anywhere close as a matter of policy.

HARRIMAN: And he broke those instructions.

COLLINS: And he broke those instructions, no doubt about it. He did it by saying that the JSC had not, in so many words, said that he was *not* to do what he was doing. In my judgment, there was no question but that he violated the idea behind those instructions, and I so testified.

HARRIMAN: And of course, that was all due to the fact that the Chiefs had a much greater concern about the possibility of a Chinese intervention than General MacArthur did.

FROM WHERE I STOOD

COLLINS: That's right.

HARRIMAN: General MacArthur's intelligence was entirely different or else—as I always thought—there was confusion in his own intelligence.

COLLINS: Yes, [Maj. Gen. Charles H.] Willoughby, his G-2, was wishy-washy—back and forth as to whether he thought that the Chinese were going to come in or not come in. There's no question about it; he gave MacArthur, in my judgment, poor G-2 intelligence.

MUCCIO: In that regard: I went to Wake Island and Dean Rusk came up to me afterwards and said, "John, you had better come back to Washington and discuss the post-hostilities set up in Korea."

I was summoned back to Washington about ten days later and spent eight days in Washington and at the United Nations. On my way back, I spent three and a half hours alone with MacArthur, talking, discussing things that had developed in Washington. Before I left he said, "John, I want you to know that we're poised to take off"—it was about November 17—"around the 20th. It may be delayed a few days." He went on, "My intelligence reports that twenty-five thousand Chinese have crossed the Yalu, but there cannot be more than thirty thousand—otherwise we would know about it."

My God, in that one sector alone there were ten times the Chinese, and over at the Chosin Reservoir there was another quarter million Chinese. Our intelligence at that particular time was terrible.

MIDDLETON: The Chinese entered; there was another American withdrawal. In December 1950, General Walker was killed, and the day after Christmas General Ridgway took over that command. The story of General Ridgway's assumption of command of the Eighth Army is the kind of thing that has not too many parallels in military lore. I think the simplest thing is to ask you, General Ridgway, how did you do it?

RIDGWAY: Well, that was a military task and I think it would bore this audience to go into detail on it. It was purely a soldier's task to take a dispirited and badly handled army, poorly supplied, and fire them up. They had neglected the elemental principles of reconnaissance and terrain appreciation. The first thing was to restore the confidence of the leaders themselves and then of the troops in their leaders. The very first task, of course, was to visit my corps commanders and then the division commanders, including the ROK division commanders, in their own field. I made them brief me on their own ground, and from that I could detect immediately whether they knew what the situation was, what the degree of confidence or lack of it was, and make an assessment. It had to be a rather rapid one. Within forty-eight hours I had visited all three corps commanders—two American commanders and the one ROK commander—and all of their division commanders, except the one way over in the east near the Sea of Japan. They were badly under strength; their spirit was low.

By my own combat experience, I think, I could tell immediately the general state of morale of a unit as soon as I entered its area. You talk to enlisted men and you either get no response or a reluctant, surly answer. It was perfectly evident, with their depleted strength, their present spirit, and this great ice-clogged river as wide as the Potomac at our backs, that if the enemy made an attack—and I assumed it would come on New Year's Eve, which it did—we would jeopardize the safety of all of the troops north of the river, the Twenty-fourth and Twenty-fifth Divisions. We had only the very weak First Cavalry Division in a blocking position to the rear. So, I ordered the evacuation of Seoul.

MIDDLETON: There have been a good many references and allusions already to General MacArthur's conduct. Let us look at three important areas: his differences with the administration; his relations with the Joint Chiefs of Staff; and his somewhat special relationship with General Ridgway.

A critical point in the administration's relationship with General MacArthur was the trip that Governor Harriman made, with General Ridgway accompanying him, which has already been discussed. I would now like to ask Governor Harriman to assess the events of that trip.

HARRIMAN: As I have already said, I reported to the president that General MacArthur had said that, as a soldier, he would accept the president's orders; but MacArthur had a very strong view that he wanted to support Chiang Kai-shek or anybody who was ready to fight Communists; he even wanted to get Chiang Kai-shek's air force to attack the mainland. That was one of the things he proposed. I told him he could recommend that to the president; I would certainly oppose it. But the importance of this trip was that the decision on the Inchon landings came out of it.

We should talk about the president's trip to Wake Island on which I have a little piece of information that is unique in a way, and which I think it is very important to get on the record. The idea that there was disagreeable talk between the president and General MacArthur is not true. I am utterly convinced there were no disagreeable words spoken between the two men.

I have some pencil notes made at the time which I have since found and which I will read; they are very short. General MacArthur arrived,

FROM WHERE I STOOD

I think, the night before. I arrived at Wake Island on the plane before
the president's. I was a good friend of General MacArthur's going back
to the days when he was superintendent of West Point. I will read
from my notes:

> On landing at Wake Island, I walked toward General MacArthur's quarters
> to talk with him. He met me halfway. He asked me, "What is this meeting
> about?" I told him the president wanted to discuss with him how political
> victory in Korea could be attained, now that MacArthur had won the
> brilliant military victory. Also the Japanese peace treaty, and all matters
> affecting the Far East. He seemed relieved, saying, "Good, then the presi-
> dent wants my views?"
>
> I said, "Yes."
>
> After a word or two of greeting to General Bradley and Secretary Pace, who
> then had come up, I had a further talk. He [MacArthur] took my arm and
> walked towards the President's incoming plane. I explained to him the strong
> support the President had given to him in the operation. MacArthur said

National Park Services, Abbie Rowe

President Truman, returning from Wake Island, is met by Averell Harriman, George
C. Marshall, Dean Acheson, John Snyder, Frank Pace, and Gen. Omar Bradley—
October 18, 1950.

that though the action was now successful, he, MacArthur, had taken a grave responsibility. I pointed out perhaps the President, at least equally, had taken a grave responsibility in backing him.

After the meeting was over, I again saw MacArthur. He said that he was very much impressed by the president; newspaper accounts and articles had not done him justice. So MacArthur expressed a high regard. He referred to what he had said to the president at the meeting, that no commander in history had received such support by all agencies in Washington as he had, and agreed that this comment should be given to the press.

I want to say that there was not a single ugly word spoken between the two men, and the president ended the meeting saying that he had a decoration to give to General MacArthur. The president said, "It's been a most satisfactory meeting, we've covered a great deal of ground."

The details of that meeting, of course, did cover a great deal of ground, but this idea which is being spread today that the row between the president and General MacArthur started at Wake Island has absolutely no foundation whatsoever.

MUCCIO: I was MacArthur's guest on that plane trip to Wake Island and back again. In fact, I had spent the night in the same bungalow with him on Wake Island because the accommodations there were so limited.

His plane arrived about six o'clock the night before. Merle Miller's book [*Plain Speaking*, pp. 293–94] is completely wrong on that. There was no jockeying in the air as to which plane would come down first.

On the way back, MacArthur and I sat and discussed details of what had happened at Wake Island. There was no acrimony evident in his position. He was in a much better mood on the way back than he was on the way down.

HARRIMAN: It is quite true that the president did ask General MacArthur—and it was very much on the president's mind—about the Chinese. General MacArthur did assure the president that in his judgment they would not come in, that they did not have enough strength to cross the Yalu, but that if they should try to come across, it would be a bloody slaughter.

MUCCIO: "The bloodiest slaughter in history," MacArthur said.

HARRIMAN: I don't think he went quite that far, but he may have. I'm being very conservative in my statements.

CHARLES S. MURPHY: General MacArthur did go that far; he was the most persuasive man I think I ever saw. He said that his view on this did not rest on intelligence as to the intentions of the Chinese but on his intelligence and knowledge of their capabilities. He said that they could not effectively intervene. He did say that it made him sick to think of the way the bodies would be piled up and the slaughter that would occur.

HARRIMAN: Well, I remember his saying (though it's not in the record), "I know the Chinese and they'll never attack, but should they attack it will be ———," and then this remark about a bloody slaughter.

MIDDLETON: General MacArthur, in the hearings which followed the president's relieving him from his commands, testified to the effect that he was not aware of any differences between him and the Joint Chiefs of Staff. Could I ask you to comment on that, General Collins?

COLLINS: He certainly should have known that there were differences of opinion, because we had warned him about the possibility of the Chinese. There is no question, in my judgment, that General MacArthur knew that the Joint Chiefs did not want him to go right up against the Yalu and that he also knew he was not to take any non-Korean troops up against the Yalu.

HARRIMAN: Isn't it true that the Joint Chiefs were very gravely concerned about the Chinese moving in, and that MacArthur brushed it off?

COLLINS: We were gravely concerned, and, as I said earlier, I think he had faulty intelligence and grossly underestimated the threat from China.

HARRIMAN: My impression was that MacArthur was impressed with the fact that the Chinese had never fought. He had seen the Chinese, and they had never fought during his experience in China. He did not place much confidence in their ability to fight, which was one of his great miscalculations.

MUCCIO: I think that came to a great degree from Willoughby.

HARRIMAN: Willoughby's intelligence may have been wrong, but General MacArthur's knowledge of the Chinese was obsolete.

GROSS: Obviously, this had a profound effect at the United Nations. The nations with troops in Korea—with whom, of course, we were in constant touch daily and really hourly during that period (principally through Dean Rusk in Washington and then through our mission in New York)—were expressly advised that the U.N. forces would stop on the southern borders of the northern tier of provinces in Korea and would not go into the northern tier of provinces. I, myself, on instructions from the State Department, conveyed that statement to a number of delegations, including the British and the French, within a matter of days prior to the actual movement of the force up to the Yalu River. There was a profound shock at the United Nations as a result of that.

MIDDLETON: General Ridgway had the unique experience of being first, General MacArthur's subordinate, and then, his successor.

RIDGWAY: There is not much to say about my relationship with MacArthur that is not in my book. When I reported to General Mac-Arthur on the day after Christmas, he gave me one of his usual brilliant expositions of the situation as he saw it. I had been following this fourteen hours a day as General Collins's deputy in Washington in the Operations Division, so I was pretty thoroughly familiar with the situation, so far as one could know it from Washington. Now, as an airborne soldier, I believe in attack and I had the idea that, once I got into the field and if the situation was right, that is what I would want to do. So I asked General MacArthur, "If I find a situation, General, to my liking, would you object to my going on the offensive?" He said, "Matt, the Eighth Army is yours. Do with it what you like." Now, no field commander could ask for more than that.

COLLINS: I might add that this marked a decided change in the general relationship between General MacArthur and the commander in the field. General MacArthur had been exercising command over the Eighth Army and the Tenth Corps, which had landed on the east coast of Korea, from Tokyo.

Frankly, he did not have full confidence in General Walker. From a purely military point of view, in my judgment, one of the major mistakes General MacArthur made was to try to control from Tokyo the operations of the Eighth Army, on the west side of the peninsula, and the Tenth Corps, on the east side. When General Ridgway reported to him, MacArthur gave him the authority that in my judgment Walker should have had. If MacArthur did not have sufficient confidence in him, he should have relieved Walker.

I might also say that General Ridgway has been very modest in what he achieved. He was the man who turned this thing around, there is no question about it. The Eighth Army was a badly defeated army, its morale was zero, practically, and Matt Ridgway turned that around. I do not think he has ever been given enough credit for what he achieved after taking command.

HARRIMAN: This has never been said, but I do not see any reason why it should not be said. After this trip in August 1950, General Norstad and I recommended to the president that General Walker be relieved and that General Ridgway be appointed in his place. This was on August 9, and if that had been done, what General Collins has described would have been very different.

I do not know if you remember, General Collins, but I made that recommendation to the president and he said, "Talk to Bradley about it," and I do not know whether Bradley reported to you about it.

COLLINS: No, it was not brought up before the Chiefs. I had talked with General MacArthur, however, about the possibility of Walker being killed in action. With all his faults, he was up front all the time. It happened that he was killed in an automobile accident, but I had talked with General MacArthur personally about a successor, and I had also recommended Matt Ridgway to take over the Eighth Army when and if anything happened.

RIDGWAY: You all held that out on me. I never knew this until now.

3

The Korean War and U.S. Foreign Relations: The Case of NATO

Lawrence S. Kaplan

For President Truman, self-conscious about his role in history, the invasion of South Korea on June 25, 1950, was a landmark that would affect the future of America and of the world. He never saw it otherwise. On his flight back to Washington from his brother's Missouri farm that fateful day, he reflected on the meaning of the news from Korea. As he reported in his memoirs, he recalled the 1930s. If the invasion "was allowed to go unchallenged it would mean a third world war."[1] In interviews with Merle Miller years later he repeated those sentiments. "The flight took about three hours, and on the way I thought over the fact that what the Communists, the North Koreans, were doing was nothing new at all . . . Hitler and Mussolini and the Japanese were doing exactly the same thing in the 1930s. And the League of Nations had let them get away with it. Nobody had stood up to them. And that is what led to the Second World War."[2]

The crisis convinced Truman that a worldwide Communist conspiracy had operated in Korea and would manifest itself elsewhere. This conclusion placed China under Soviet direction, and thus made subsequent isolation of the People's Republic an integral part of American foreign policy. To contain China and ultimately to return Chiang Kai-shek to power, the administration had to reorder its affairs in Southeast Asia. The cautious efforts to disengage the United States from France's struggle in Indochina gave way to gradual but increasing American entanglement in the area. ANZUS and SEATO and bilateral alliances with Korea, Formosa, and Japan all followed. The American commitment to South Vietnam thus became a heritage of the Korean War.

36

THE WAR AND U.S. FOREIGN RELATIONS

The heritage in Europe has proved no less clear. The vague commitment of American assistance to Western Europe in the event of attack and the lip service paid to mutual support of the many councils established by the Atlantic alliance became specific guarantees of American involvement as the treaty was transformed into a military organization capable of defending Europe on the ground against attack from the east. If the Russians could act through the North Koreans or the Communist Chinese, they could also employ East Germans as their surrogates. To deter such a threat, a rejuvenated NATO, under American generals, divided Europe into defensible regions, lobbied successfully for inclusion in the alliance of nations on the flanks of NATO (such as Greece and Turkey), and pressed Europeans and Germans to accept the Federal Republic of Germany as a partner in the war against Communist expansionism.

Firm in its belief that no negotiation with the enemy was possible, the United States, during the years after 1950, undertook relentless combat against a conspiratorial enemy whose power seemed enormous, whose appeal was insidious, and whose control centered in Moscow. There was no room in this evaluation for possibilities of diffusion of power or division of nations within the Communist world; nor was there any role for neutrals of the Third World. For at least a decade under the Truman and Eisenhower administrations, and to only a slightly lesser extent under the Kennedy and Johnson administrations of the 1960s, the pattern set by the Korean War endured with few changes. Neither Stalin's death in 1953 nor rebellion on the other side of the Iron Curtain in 1956 nor increasing instability in Soviet-Chinese relations nor the growing power of the nonaligned countries during the 1960s changed America's outlook on the world fashioned in the Korean War. Stopping the advance of the North Koreans seemed to have been the challenge the nation required to institutionalize the Truman Doctrine, to make credible our professed assumption of world leadership. According to Charles E. Bohlen, "It was the Korean War and not World War II that made us a world military-political power."[3]

These observations may or may not be considered pejorative. If the judgment of the wisdom of American behavior since 1950 rests on exorcising the fears which moved Truman to action, his decisions served America and the "free world" well. Despite the abortive attempt to unify Korea late in 1950, American involvement assured the independence and territorial integrity of the Republic of Korea. Fragile as any armistice must be, the arrangements at Panmunjom in 1953 remain in effect today. The promise was kept. Moreover, the policy of containment succeeded. Neither the Soviet Union in Europe nor Communist China

37

in Asia attempted subsequently to invade territories officially under the protection of American commitments. And the United Nations, although sometimes a reluctant partner in the Korean enterprise, gained power and prestige in peacekeeping that made 1950 as much a landmark in the history of that organization as it has been in American history. Enhancement of the General Assembly's influence, with the aid of Acheson's "Uniting for Peace" resolution of September 1950, remains a factor to be reckoned with by superpowers a generation later.

This benign assessment of the effect of the Korean War has often been accompanied by an assumption that the war was a Communist test of America's leadership and that the fate of the world hung on passing that test. The sense of trial was no simplistic notion of the president's. It was shared widely by the pundits of the day—Hanson E. Baldwin of the *New York Times* and Joseph and Stewart Alsop of the *New York Herald Tribune*.[4] European leaders agreed. Foreign Minister Robert Schuman of France was quoted as saying, "Thank God, this will not be a repetition of the past."[5] Prime Minister Clement Attlee of the United Kingdom observed "that the Korean attack was not an isolated episode. It showed that communist forces were prepared, if occasion offered, to resort to war."[6]

American policymakers, reviewing the events of that month, not only subscribed to this opinion but showed pride in America's responses. Dorothy Fosdick of the State Department's Policy Planning Staff admitted that the initiative was on the other side, partly because of American errors of statecraft. "But in foreign policy just having the initiative is no virtue. . . . Far from being ashamed that we came into that war to *defend* Korea, that was the right way to come in."[7] Ambassador W. Averell Harriman was "convinced Stalin directed the attack on South Korea and did not think that we would intervene except to protest to the United Nations."[8] The swiftness and forcefulness of American action threw the Russians off balance. Even such statesmen as Bohlen and George F. Kennan, who had deep reservations about United States conduct of the war, were relieved at the American reaction. They had no doubt of Soviet involvement. It would be "childish nonsense" to believe otherwise, as Bohlen put it.[9] Whether or not America's actions were in the best strategic interests of American forces was immaterial. The contest between the Soviet Union and the United States was not over position, but over the steadfastness of America's commitments.

Over the years, particularly in the last few years, questions have been raised concerning the whole range of activities identified with the Korean War. Some of them had appeared at the outset of the conflict, mostly from Republican critics. For Sen. Robert A. Taft, the war was too convenient a vehicle for the enlargement of executive power; for Sen. Arthur H. Vandenberg, the Korean debacle was the result of the failure of the administration to manage a bipartisan program in Asia as it had in Europe. "For some unaccountable reason, we pursued an opposite course in the Far East."[10] While Vandenberg did not proceed in the same letter to account for the "unaccountable," he did so by implication. Others were more direct in blaming Secretary of State Dean Acheson for announcing to the Russians in a speech six months before the attack that the American defensive perimeter in Asia excluded Korea. Disregarding evidence that Gen. Douglas MacArthur had expressed much the same view of American responsibilities in the area, the isolationist opposition attributed responsibility for the war to the weakness of Democratic policy in Asia. The "loss" of China was linked to the war in Korea.

Although criticism mounted during the early 1950s as events unfolded in Korea, Republican critics at the outset supported both the war and the assumption of Soviet involvement. It did not matter whether the Russians or the North Koreans had given the signal for invasion; the latter were armed and trained by their patrons. If the North Koreans acted on their own initiative, the Soviets accepted the war on the assumption that the United States would not intervene. Thus, the mystery of the Soviet boycott of the United Nations Security Council at the moment of attack becomes explicable. In fact, this explanation seemed to satisfy Bohlen and Kennan as well, neither of whom believed the invasion was part of any Communist master plan at that time.[11]

In light of the national revulsion against the Vietnam War, it is hardly surprising that revisionist scholars and observers would find a different meaning in the origins and outcome of the Korean War. If it did not become a major preoccupation of the "new left" during the 1960s, the relative neglect of Korea was probably due to the attention given the Cold War's beginnings in World War II, when the drama of initial Soviet-American division was higher and the documents describing it, more readily available. First in the field were the speculations of I. F. Stone, centering on the aggressive stance of President Syngman Rhee of South Korea and his possible collaboration with American leaders. By provoking the North Koreans to attack, Stone argued, Rhee could engage the United States in his plans for unification of the country under his control. The fact that Secretary of Defense Louis Johnson and Ambassador John Foster Dulles had visited Rhee in Korea and MacArthur in Japan a week before the outbreak encouraged speculation about a Korean axis with the Pentagon or with Republican anti-Communists, smarting over Chiang's failure in China.[12] Stone pointed out that leading

Chinese Nationalists, intimate with the China lobby in the United States, had made a fortune in the stockmarket in soybean futures during the summer of 1950.[13] Was it luck or advance information about war in Korea that accounted for the financial coup?

The revisionists of our own time, however, have moved well beyond Stone. Intriguing as the Stone scenario is, there are more attractive targets than the China lobby and its connections. The temptation to identify an imperialist first cause more central to American polity, although not necessarily less sinister, was too great for most present-day revisionists to resist. The tragedy of the Vietnam War deserved roots commensurate with the devastation it was to create. Soybean speculations would not serve.

The well-publicized NSC-68 document of April 1950 filled that function perfectly. The timing of the paper was just right: it was presented six months after the Soviet's successful testing of its atomic device and two months before the Korean War. While it has been widely discussed and carefully analyzed, it remained officially classified until February 1975, and hence an object of continuing suspicion. Could this document be the key to the meaning of the Korean War, and so to the events of the past quarter-century? Circumstantial evidence permitted such conclusions. The Truman administration, worried about the implications of the Soviets' possession of nuclear weapons for the defense of NATO, required information from experts about the price to be paid for security in Europe; NSC-68 provided the answer.

Actually, NSC-68 was less formidable than its critics believed. It was essentially a comprehensive general statement of America's present military position as of 1950, with recommendations for improving it. Under the leadership of Paul Nitze, chairman of the Policy Planning Staff of the State Department, the National Security Council examined the extreme steps of a preventive war and of withdrawal of all forces to the Americas. It rejected both. It looked at the current modest effort of military assistance to NATO and to other friendly nations and found them inadequate. The planners concluded that only rapid expansion of the American military forces would permit the United States to deal with the Soviet Union from a situation of strength. No other situation would impress the Communists. The planners determined that in peacetime 20 percent of the gross national product could be expended without disrupting the economy and urged the raising of $50 billion immediately, almost four times the budget of fiscal year 1950.[14]

There were differing opinions within State over NSC-68 between Nitze on the one hand and Bohlen and Kennan on the other. Bohlen and Kennan feared that publication of the document would scare the administration and Congress into giving a dangerous priority to nuclear weaponry. Another difference developed between the State and Defense departments. While the former spoke of a budgetary increase from $13 to $35 or $50 billion, the latter, presumed major beneficiary of the funds, would settle for a mere $5 billion.[15] It seems to be a nice piece of irony that the Joint Chiefs of Staff emerged as more modest in their appetite than the State Department's policy planners.

The nuances of these internal debates were essentially irrelevant to critics who could make causal connections between a declared need for increased military expenditures and a war crisis two months later which justified those expenditures. Until June 25, the administration had not acted on advice of the National Security Council. The military assistance program continued at its leisurely pace; the North Atlantic Council meeting of May 1950 exuded no sense of urgency in its communique; and when war broke out, a modest Defense Department budget proposed for fiscal year 1951 had not yet been accepted by the Senate. Perhaps the reluctance of Defense spokesmen to talk of increases in the manner of their State Department colleagues was a reflection of Secretary of Defense Louis Johnson's sensitivity to the cost-consciousness of Congress. Was the disregard for NSC-68 a sign that the administration had recognized its inability to realize the document's aims?

If so, the Korean War, by design or by accident, served to put NSC-68 into immediate operation. Acheson himself may have been pointing to this result elliptically when he observed in his memoirs that "events in Korea had broken the inertia of thought on many critical matters. . . ." His biographer, Gaddis Smith, found NSC-68 to be "a thoroughly Achesonian exposition"; and Ronald J. Stupak has identified the secretary of state as "instrumental in operationalizing NSC #68, the theoretical foundation for rearming the United States when the Korean conflict erupted."[16] That the war unleashed the ambitions of an aggressive secretary, a veritable "commissar of the Cold War," as Ronald Steel has called him, was obvious also to Gabriel and Joyce Kolko. They noted, in the apparent conflict over funds between the civilian and military representatives, the greater martial ardor of civilians whose "desire . . . to spend money as a tool of foreign economic policy . . . was scarcely comprehensible to the docile military men."[17]

All the elements of a plot were present. Even if no direct connection can be made, critics found that policymakers were able to manipulate the situation once it occurred, to push America into a massive armament program for itself and its allies. To win votes in Congress and the approval of the public, they had to raise the Red Scare at home and abroad. The Korean War was their instrument. Richard J. Barnet asked rhetorically how men who could use words with the precision of Acheson could be so imprecise in speaking of a "red tide."[18]

The facts cannot be denied. The Korean War did alter the direction of American foreign policy in such a way that the recommendations of the NSC paper of April 1950 were approved during the summer of that year. It is the interpretations of those facts that are so difficult. Was the attack on South Korea an act comparable to Pearl Harbor, something to have been anticipated and prepared for? The answer is clearly negative. And like charges about the responsibility for that disaster, could the policymakers be associated with its planning as well as with the exploitation of its results? Gen. George C. Marshall, a participant in both events, was not the target of suspicions in 1950 as in 1941. Dean Acheson, a more likely candidate for such accusations (as the comments above indicate), was never seriously affected by them. The revisionist attack on this aspect of Korea never captured popular or congressional imagination. Rather than interpret American behavior at the outbreak of war as a product of cold-blooded imperialistic planning, David McLellan and John Reuss suggest persuasively that Truman's foreign policy would be better explained "in terms of leaders faced with desperate and compelling choices, forced to act under circumstances of greatest uncertainty, and acting while straining to avoid plunging the world into a new maelstrom."[19] This approach to the problem is applicable to the United States reaction to the invasion of the Republic of Korea.

The second revisionist argument over Korea is more compelling, if only because the policymakers have frequently raised it themselves: namely, the validity of the imagery of falling dominoes. The Korean War, they claim, forestalled the disaster that would have resulted from successive losses of peoples and territories to Communist control. Minutes of the president's meeting with congressional leaders two days after the North Korean attack reveal his warning: "If we let Korea down, the Soviets will keep right on going and swallow up one piece of Asia after another. We had to make a stand some time, or else let all of Asia go by the board. If we were to let Asia go, the Near East would collapse and no telling what would happen in Europe." Lloyd Gardner quoted this statement from the George Elsey Papers in the Harry S. Truman Library to demonstrate how aware the administration was of the importance of a stand in Korea.[20] Yet, given Truman's frequent public pronouncements, there seems little need to take an unpublished statement from the archives to confirm what the president had proudly proclaimed. No taint of conspiracy clings to it.

There are other uses to which the domino principle may be put. Rather than preventing a chain reaction, as Truman and Eisenhower interpreted it,[21] observers can find the dominoes falling from events set in motion by the Korean War. Indeed, the decision on Korea could explain all events of the next twenty-five years. Stephen Ambrose found that America's conviction that a Communist conspiracy underlay actions of North Koreans meant that all national liberation movements would thereafter be labeled Russian proxies. "This view in turn allowed the Americans to dash into Lebanon at President Eisenhower's orders, to attempt by force, with President Kennedy's approval, to overthrow Castro, to intervene in the Dominican Republic at President Johnson's command, and most of all to involve this country in Vietnam."[22]

There are shortcomings to this application of the metaphor. The politician or historian can be hypnotized by the picture of dominoes falling one after another along a straight or even a twisted row. That these dominoes can be transferred to historical events beyond a limited span of time is doubtful. While American foreign policy was deeply influenced by the choice to fight in Korea, it need not follow that the row of dominoes is falling today or had just completed its run in the disengagement from Vietnam in 1973. Are the actions of statesmen of one generation fully binding on those of another? Even if events impose constraints on later policymakers, there comes a time when decisions are made independently of the falling of the first domino. The dominoes Truman had in mind were limited in time and space to a few years in Europe, from 1936 to 1939 or 1941. Policies carried out during the Kennedy, Johnson, or Nixon administrations, or even during the Eisenhower administration, had a life of their own. Determinism as an explanation of policymaking has distinct limits.

This essay assumes that vibrations from the Korean War may be felt in 1975, but that the war is neither the dominant influence in the shaping of American foreign policy today nor responsible for the direction foreign policy has taken in this generation. Rather, it is a milestone in the evolution of American diplomatic history, a turning point that led to events most clearly identifiable in the period immediately following the war, during the Truman and first Eisenhower administrations.

The most direct result was the treaty with Korea reversing the 1948 decision to leave Korean defense to the United Nations. Similarly, the Japanese peace treaty, completed in 1951 without Soviet participation, included provisions for protection which reflected the Korean conflict. The elaborate network of bilateral and multilateral mutual defense pacts, culminating in the Southeast Asia Treaty Organization in 1954, developed from a need to prevent another Korea. The embrace of Chiang Kai-shek might have occurred simply on the strength of the Communist victories in 1949, but the Korean experience solidified the emotional and political

ACME Newspictures—UPI

French soldiers form part of the United Nations force in the Wonju area—
January 22, 1951.

bond between the Nationalist government on Taiwan and the United States.

Although it was not immediately embodied in a treaty, American perception of the French struggle in Indochina underwent major change as a result of the Korean War. Prior to the conflict, it was at least theoretically possible that the Pentagon would not have acted on information transmitted to Secretary Johnson in April 1950 that deterioration of the French military position in Indochina would increase without American aid.[23] Or, at least, it would not have been offered unless France made greater efforts to appease nationalist sentiment in the colony and work toward eventual independence. After June the fear was that a French withdrawal from Indochina would endanger the American effort in Korea. The Pentagon Papers emphasized that "holding the line in Southeast Asia was essential to American security interests."[24] Conceivably, the French role in NATO would have permitted France to manipulate American sentiment in Indochina even without the war in

Asia. But it is clear that the vision of Communist aggression in the Korean peninsula extended without serious reservations to the Indochinese peninsula. When France evacuated Indochina in 1954, the United States did not join the exodus. Protocols to the SEATO treaty covering Laos, Cambodia, and the "free territory under the jurisdiction of the State of Vietnam" centered on the belief of Secretary of State Dulles that Korea and Indochina were the "two flanks, with the principal enemy—Red China—in the center." They both had to be preserved.[25]

It is Europe rather than Asia, however, where the impact of Korea may best be observed. The changes there were more profound, and the ultimate consequences probably more important. The mutual defense pacts in Asia had a negative objective of forestalling a replication of the event. Granted that there was hope of a prosperous democratic republic flourishing in the Republic of Korea or of a counterrevolution in China springing out of revival of spirit in Formosa, the purpose was to rectify the mistakes of Korea by inhibiting the Communist world from initiating new tests. If such were attempted, American power would prevail through the alliances established for East Asia. There was a rigidity both in purpose and in results.

While many of the same purposes underlay American policy toward Europe in the wake of the war, the nature of problems there provided the occasion for imaginative changes both within the Western European community and between the United States and its NATO allies. Recognition that a divided Germany, like a divided Korea, created conditions for East Germans to perform the role of North Koreans led not simply to strengthening forces or writing more treaties or consigning more funds, as was the case in Asia; it transformed the Atlantic alliance. The United States found itself shedding the substance as well as the language of isolationism, and the Federal Republic of Germany found a way to become assimilated into a new Europe. The election of Eisenhower in 1952 ratified this new course of American foreign policy.[26]

To effect such vast changes in European-American relations demanded diplomatic skills of the highest order. They required American policymakers to deal with a domestic isolationism that blamed defeat in Asia on Communist influences in the Truman administration. The apparent failure of American policy in China permitted McCarthyites to use the language of anticommunism, which the administration itself had employed to win popular support for controversial projects in the past. Propelled by Sen. Joseph R. McCarthy's rhetoric, more genuinely isolationist spokesmen, such as Robert A. Taft and Kenneth Wherry, attacked the administration for wasting funds abroad and for accumulating executive power in Europe at a time when the stake for America was in Asia.

Simultaneously, the administration had to face a resurgent neutralism in Europe. The events in Korea disturbed and confused Europeans. On the one hand, the NATO partners knew that the forces available to them could not stop a Soviet invasion and that the efforts hitherto expended in NATO were insufficient to deter attack in the immediate future. On the other hand, they feared that a rapid military build-up could undo the benefits of the Marshall Plan by upsetting their national economies and provoking the very invasion they wished to deter. The relief most Europeans felt over the vigor of America's response to invasion in Korea was mitigated by a suspicion that traditional American priorities in Asia would divert American attention from Europe. Even if Europe remained America's first commitment, would errors of judgment exhibited in managing China's position on Korea be repeated in Europe? The singlemindedness of America's pressure for a German contribution to Europe's defense raised deep suspicions about the qualities of American leadership at a time when to Europeans the memories of Nazi bestiality were still so vivid.

The Truman administration had a formidable task in Europe. The surmounting of most of these obstacles provides a tale that has been neglected so far in the historiography of American foreign relations. There are few heroes or villains in it. The details dwell mostly on mistakes, misunderstandings among the parties, and particularly on the arrogance implicit in America's insistence upon accepting responsibility. Europe, for its part, was frequently jealous of American power, resentful of pressures, and selfish in its use of benefits gained from the alliance.

The day-to-day reading of relations gives the impression that frenzied activities following the outbreak of the Korean conflict widened the gap between Europe and America. From the perspective of a generation later, this view is misleading. A climate of cooperation was created in a few years' time in which symbols of national sovereignty withered and new institutions of an integrated Europe blossomed. Not all have survived; not all have been in the interest of the United States, or in the interest of its allies, or in the interest of détente with the Soviet Union. But for the short run, the changes within NATO from 1950 to 1955 brought a sense of security that manifested itself in the economic expansion and political integration of Europe during the next ten years.

Less than fifteen months before the Korean War it seemed that the signing of the North Atlantic alliance by twelve member nations would resolve America's intentions toward Europe. The signature of the United States on the Treaty of Washington on April 4, 1949, meant that Europe could count on American support should an act of aggression be made against any of the partners. By so notifying a potential aggressor, it was expected that there would be no repetition of the experiences of World Wars I and II when the aggressor did not know America's position. The pact existed to deter such an event. And it seemed to work.

The Russians called off the Berlin blockade and the Federal Republic of Germany came into being five weeks after the treaty was signed. A military assistance program of more than $1 billion, most of it scheduled for NATO allies, had been introduced in Congress almost immediately after the treaty had been ratified in the summer of 1949. By October the mutual defense assistance bill became law, and during the course of the winter of 1949–50 the United States completed a series of bilateral agreements with NATO beneficiaries under Article 3 of the treaty. Within the first year of NATO's history a web of regional planning groups serving the North Atlantic Council had been established under Article 9 of the treaty. The heart of military planning was in the Standing Group of the Military Committee of NATO, composed of representatives of the United States, the United Kingdom, and France. Guiding this steering committee were two other institutions established in October 1949: the Defense Financial and Economic Committee and the Military Production and Supply Board. Respectively, they would study the financial effect of expanded military efforts on each country and recommend measures to increase available supplies.

Most of these accomplishments were published in the communiques of the North Atlantic Council but few of them were meaningful, and all the participants in the organization at the time knew their deficiencies. The language of cooperation and mutual support was a spindly bridge between promise and fulfillment that could never have borne the weight of a serious challenge from the Soviet Union. American military aid was slight and exceedingly slow in coming.

Congressional limitations helped to account for the sluggish pace. The Mutual Defense Assistance Act of 1949 prevented the president from initiating assistance until he was able to state that it would fit into the integrated defense aid of the North Atlantic area, and this could not be done until bilateral agreements were completed between the United States and each beneficiary. This process took time. Given the obstacles, the official signing on January 27, 1950, of agreements with the NATO allies deserved more than the simple ceremony it received. The first shipment left American ports in March, accompanied by appropriate fanfare. By April 6, according to the first semiannual report of the

MDAP, only $42 million of the $1.3 billion authorized had been obligated.[27] That figure reached $52 million by June.

The activities of the Military Production and Supply Board and the Defense Financial and Economic Committee were as sluggish as the flow of military aid. Little serious evaluation of national capacities for sacrifice was made. Nothing beyond a vague Medium Range Defense Plan, calling for positions to be held at the Rhine, was introduced without expectation of its being realized. The short-range plan involved only procedures for evacuating occupation troops.[28] The NATO machinery was of little help. Committees met in London, Rome, or Paris, without coordinating their activities. The foreign, defense, and finance ministers who headed them were too busy with their normal duties to care about the trappings of NATO.

It may be that the air of illusion surrounding the new organization was the product of calculation, not of accident or incompetence. The defense of Europe perhaps would stem from the American nuclear umbrella spread over the NATO allies. Military planning and military assistance, therefore, were psychic props to complement European recovery and to provide justification to the American public for American protection of Europe. At the hearings on extending the military assistance program into 1950, Secretary Acheson justified assistance on these grounds.

> The whole purpose of the Marshall Plan and of the North Atlantic Treaty was to prevent war and to preserve peace and the environment of peace which comes from an unwillingness of a potential aggressor to take a chance. Now, that is being successful. We are getting in Europe the economic, spiritual, moral, social strength which will lead them and in company with us, to create the adequate defense so that it will become less and less and less probable that anyone will want to take a chance of aggression in that area.[29]

This is not to say that the administration did not expect efforts in rearmament, in troop commitment, even in specialization within a collective defense plan to be made by the allies. America's own involvement depended on Europe's partaking in the enterprise. But the efforts, all told, were intended to be modest, in keeping with the fiscal conservatism of Congress as well as with European fears that diversion of the economies into military channels would dislocate the economic growth carefully nurtured under the Marshall Plan. The shift from civil to military production could create shortages in critical materials, set off an inflationary spiral, and, in general, jeopardize rather than enhance European security. Politically, even a hint of a German role in European defense, which would follow from a massive effort, would alienate public opinion among the allies. As it was, Communist workers in France and Britain announced their intentions to prevent the unloading of the few military supplies that were to arrive in Europe during the spring of 1950.[30] Not a Soviet invasion, then, but the instability of the European partners was the primary NATO concern prior to the Korean crisis.

Even with the careful handling of the NATO publics, the organization remained fragile. Neutralism was not just a Communist device. On the first anniversary of the signing of the North Atlantic Treaty, a dynamic young French journalist, Jean-Jacques Servan-Schreiber, writing for the influential *Le Monde*, aired a point of view shared by many friends of the alliance.[31] He wondered about its purpose. If it was to instill a sense of security in Europeans by giving them the means to defend themselves, it had not succeeded. Should a war break out, Servan-Schreiber claimed, the combined forces of America and Western Europe could not stop it. And if a genuine effort were made to build an imposing military machine in Europe, the ensuing destruction of European economies would turn victory over to the Soviet Union in the Cold War. He raised the question of American isolationism and suggested that it should not be discounted as a factor in American behavior. Perhaps a neutral stance and accommodation with Russia should be the alternative. This was not Servan-Schreiber's preference. Indeed, he urged a unification of Europe and the vitalizing of the organs of NATO. He articulated a mood which NATO planners had to take into account.

Beneath the public posture, uneasiness within NATO over Soviet possession of nuclear weapons was growing, even as the original assumptions of the treaty continued. NSC-68 was a measure of this distress. Recommendations that Europe make the financial sacrifice required by building European armies could trigger neutralist sentiments, identified by Servan-Schreiber, into an open and violent rejection of NATO. These sentiments would invite the wrath of senators already disposed to write off the military assistance programs as a trickle that would become a flood of dollars from the American treasury, and end with American entanglement in a foreign war brought about by the accumulation of arms. Small wonder that the paper was kept under wraps.

The administration's dissatisfaction manifested itself in guarded statements about the importance of increased European contributions and in its active support of ways to make NATO more efficient. Acheson admitted to the Foreign Relations Committee a few weeks before the Korean War that "we are a long way from having an adequate security force for the North Atlantic Treaty, and I think that all the members have got to face the fact that unless there is a very considerable change in the international climate and actions of certain other powers, we may have to put more, rather than less effort into the defense field."[32] That all was not well with the variety of NATO committees was the message of the North Atlantic Council's communique from London a month before, which announced appointment of deputies to each member's council representative under a permanent chairman to provide continuity and direction to NATO's mission. Charles M. Spofford was the first chairman.

The disparity between public statements about NATO and private sentiments was sharpest over the sensitive issue of a German contribution. A year before, when the North Atlantic Treaty was debated before the Foreign Relations Committee, it was understood that the dismantling of German industry would be "complete and absolute" and that any "discussion of including West Germany in the pact is not possible."[33] The language remained much the same more than a year later when Acheson repeated assurances to the House Foreign Affairs Committee, deliberating on an extension of the Mutual Defense Assistance Program, that the demilitarization of Germany continued. "There is no discussion of anything else. That is our policy and we have not raised it or revalued it."[34] Technically, the secretary of state was correct. In fact, on every level of government in the United States and among the allies, the place of Germany in the defense of Europe was the subject of intense concern and discussion, although it did not reach the stage of policy.

The Germans had been among the first to press for clarification of their position. If there should be war in Europe, where would it be fought and how? In December 1949, the West German government asked formally what plans were being made for its defense in event of a Soviet attack. It feared that NATO would make only a token effort to halt an invasion at the Elbe and then move back to the Rhine. Given the projection of military plans during the winter of 1950, these questions were to the point. Chancellor Adenauer, lacking facilities of a foreign office, later confessed to using press interviews to broadcast his alarm.[35] While opposing German rearmament, he insisted that if German troops were to be summoned, they should function within "the framework of the army of a German federation." So the *Cleveland Plain Dealer* reported on December 3, 1949. Here was an offer of German assistance on terms that could destroy the Atlantic alliance.

The insufficiency of the Medium Term Defense Plan, particularly the pessimism over defending the European heartland, alarmed the Dutch and Danes as well as Germans. Dirk Stikker, foreign minister of the Netherlands, claimed to be shocked by the allied strategy of 1950 which was based on defense of the Rhine-Ijssel line.[36] It implied that the northern provinces of the Netherlands as well as German lands east of the Rhine were expendable. The desperate condition of the twelve divisions at NATO's disposal in Europe also moved military spokesmen to consider a German contribution. Even Gen. Pierre Billotte, France's former representative on the military committee, could not envisage a defense of Europe in March 1950 without German rearmament.[37]

Position papers within the State Department concerning the Council of Foreign Ministers' deliberations on Germany pointed in the same direction. As early as November 1949, one of them urged the secretary to point out that "the German problem must be viewed and dealt with in the total context of general developments. It cannot be isolated. What we do in Germany must not be dictated by considerations of what the Germans demand, or even of our respective national interest, but by a fair appraisal of the indispensable requirements of the Western community of free peoples."[38] While admitting the need to display sensitivity to the feelings of European victims of the Nazi experience, it suggested that Americans could bring "a certain detachment to the treatment of German problems which is difficult for other people to attain." But it is clear that such sensitivity as American diplomatists could muster had to be balanced against the danger of inaction in the face of intolerable Russian behavior by its "puppet German regime in the East."[39]

These State Department documents were classified until 1974. There were signals in all major newspapers in the form of rumors and denials by the NATO allies to alert any observer that, whatever the official line, the status of Germany was changing with the intensification of the Cold War. Pressures for ending the dismantling of plants, for close economic integration of Germany into Western Europe, and for admission of West Germany into the Council of Europe were staples of the Department of State's behind-the-scenes recommendations. France's response was expressed in the Schuman Plan, the European Coal and Steel Community, which would interlock German and French heavy industry in a supranational structure. This Europeanizing of German power, in which Italy and the Benelux countries were represented, was a means of controlling West Germany, rebuilding Europe, and appeasing America's concern for integration.

Despite the Schuman proposal of May 1950, the meeting of the North Atlantic Council did not face up to what the United States regarded as the most urgent forms of Franco-German collaboration: a sizable, integrated army and the use of German men and material. No mention of Germany appeared in the council's communique. The most that was done to prepare the public for change was an announcement by the Big Three foreign ministers in a precouncil session that spoke of the gradual integration of Germany into a "European community."[40] The statement was conspicuously silent on military contributions, despite concern for the growth of paramilitary troops in East Germany, manifested in a joint protest to the Soviet Union by the three other occupying powers a week later. Such was the situation within NATO on the eve of the Korean War.

The effect of that conflict on the organization of NATO was immediate and mixed. Europeans breathed a sigh of relief "almost as palpable as a rush of fresh wind on a sultry day," as Anne O'Hare McCormick of the *New York Times* expressed it.[41] But while the NATO partners observed that the United States did not abandon Korea to the Communists, they feared the consequences of actions in the Far East. Conceivably, the dynamics of conducting a war, combined with the tradition of "Asia first," could turn American attention from Europe and leave it more exposed to military danger than before.

Germany understandably became the first focus of Western attention. Adenauer claimed to believe that "Stalin was planning the same procedure for Western Germany as had been used in Korea."[42] The NATO leaders agreed. What had been nervous glances at East German police forces a month before were nightmares of invasion in July. A divided Germany, with the preponderance of military strength on the Communist side, could lead to an even greater disaster for the West in Europe than had occurred in Asia.

The specter of sixty thousand East German paramilitary troopers, backed by twenty-seven Soviet divisions in the eastern zone, facing twelve badly equipped and uncoordinated NATO divisions, galvanized American planners. The unspecified target date of a "progressive build-up of the defense of the North Atlantic area" (to use the language of the council's May communique), along with the assumption that present resources were sufficient "if properly co-ordinated and applied," yielded to a demand for massive armament immediately throughout the alliance.[43]

There was no question in Congress that the current military assistance bill was inadequate. The president's request for an additional $4 billion in aid met no serious opposition. Emotions of the moment swept away all previous caveats about the program which had limited military aid. In executive session Sen. Henry Cabot Lodge, Jr., spoke of the "mortal peril" of Europe and need for creating a NATO force of fifty divisions.[44] By September the president announced plans to reinforce American troops in Europe. It was obvious that the powerful American war machine, which had been mobilized with such effective results in World

War II, was poised to come to the aid of its NATO partners. The United States would keep the promise of the North Atlantic Treaty.

Such gratification as Europeans felt over the stirrings across the Atlantic had to be weighed against the price they would have to pay for America's bounty. Congressional inquiry into the administration's plans left no doubt that the cost would be high. At the hearings on supplemental appropriations, the legislators kept pressing witnesses to tell them exactly what expenditures would be made by the allies for the common defense, how many troops they would raise, how much sovereignty would be relinquished to produce a genuinely integrated European army. Most explicit was their demand to include Germany in the rearming of Europe; their impatience with evasive answers on the German question was rarely concealed. It seemed illogical to them that any credible plan for the defense of the Continent could be made without a German contribution. It also seemed unfair for Europeans and Americans to provide manpower and equipment to protect German territory without Germany sharing in the common sacrifice.

Given the NATO partners' ambivalence on the German question, it is hardly surprising that Acheson and Johnson had difficulty countering congressional queries. When Senator Wherry asked the secretary of state how effective the rearming of France and other Western European countries would be if Germany remained unarmed, Acheson responded that "a program for western Europe which does not include the productive resources of all the countries of western Europe, which included Germany as well as France, and includes the military power of all western Europe, which includes western Germany as well as France, will not be effective in the long-range political sense. Therefore we must include them both."[45] Sen. Homer Ferguson wanted to know specifically if Germany, then, was to be rearmed under NATO supervision; Acheson had to answer no. Germany was not included in the current NATO defense plans.[46] It was difficult for the secretary of state to admit that there was no real defense without a German role, but that there was no immediate intention of bringing Germany into the defense program. It was a little less difficult for the secretary of defense, because contradictions in their testimonies seemed less evident to him than to Acheson.[47]

The European allies listened to these debates unhappily. Although both the initial relief over American response to the North Korean invasion and the fear of American neglect of Europe had dissipated, new concerns replaced the old. The sense of imminent disaster had receded when the Russians did not take credit for the Korean operation or open a German front. Relaxation rather than intensification of efforts was the mood of late summer, particularly in September after General MacArthur reversed the tide of Communist advances in South Korea. In this mood, American demands for arming Germany and for diverting their economies into military channels sounded to many Europeans more menacing than potential Soviet aggression.

Of all the European allies, the French were most directly involved and most emotionally upset by the German issue. Their sentiments had to be taken into account and harmonized in some fashion with the American conception of NATO, or the alliance would collapse. There was some evidence of a drift toward the inevitable, even if grudgingly. On July 25, France withdrew its objections to German industries manufacturing war material for NATO consumption. A month later the ministry was willing to allow German police to be used as a surrogate military arm in the event of an emergency. Was this an opening toward the acceptance of a reconstructed Germany?

Chancellor Adenauer thought it signaled a lowering of French resistance to change.[48] His optimism was buttressed by Winston Churchill's resolution in August at the assembly of the Council of Europe in favor of "the immediate creation of a unified European Army, under the authority of a European Minister of Defense, subject to proper European democratic control and acting in full cooperation with the United States and Canada."[49] In this setting the Allied high commissioners asked Adenauer to offer a German view of European security. In one memorandum dated August 29, the chancellor returned to a pre-Korea problem, proposing a West German police force equal in size to the East German paramilitary groups. He responded to the new circumstances by recommending a reinforcement of Allied troops in Europe and a provision for German military units within a European army. A second memorandum expressed expectations that the occupation of Germany would end and equality of status be offered in return for the German contribution to the common defense.[50] Adenauer commanded more than Churchill's support for his views. Stikker had spoken out a month before, stating his personal belief in the need for German rearmament.[51]

The extent of France's acceptance both of a rapid increase in its own rearmament and of a German share in the new Europe defies quantification. Sentiments of leading opinionmakers appeared favorable. Servan-Schreiber, who had spoiled the first anniversary of NATO with his impious reflections on the state of the alliance, had abandoned whatever interest he may have had in France standing aloof from the Soviet-American rivalry. He urged a single armed force in Europe with contributors served by a permanent Marshall Plan. Such measures as Premier Pleven had proposed to increase France's arms budget were clearly inadequate, according to Servan-Schreiber, no better than a symbolic gesture—like sending an escort vessel to the Korean conflict in place of divisions.[52] Raymond Aron's language was less picturesque, but his recommendations for France's future were equally explicit. Countering this advice was the voice and influence of the prestigious *Le Monde* and of its editor, Hubert Beuve-Méry. Their search for a course that would spare France the psychic cost of a German army and the economic penalties of a massive armament program revived neutralist tendencies.[53] Beuve-Méry evoked the memories of two world wars to ask if the price of liberation once again might not be too high to pay. Would NATO forces, even after their reconstruction, stand fast at the Elbe or at the Rhine?

It was just this kind of questioning that invited doubts among American and British leaders about France's contribution, even if the German issue could be resolved. Suspicions based on France's large Communist bloc and on French behavior in 1940 were rarely articulated, but they were always just below the surface; and at the hearings on critical issues of NATO, congressmen occasionally aired them. The British journal, *Spectator*, did raise the question boldly in an article entitled, "Would France Fight?" The author comforted himself and readers with reflections on the rational quality of the French character as well as on the initiative France had demonstrated through the Schuman Plan.[54]

No matter how many reservations the allies may have had about the direction of Franco-German relations, they had no choice except to maximize every positive sign they could find in the Pleven ministry. The Schuman Plan seemed to open the way to other kinds of European cooperation and fitted the American interest in a unified European response. Schuman was personally willing to incorporate German units into a European army.[55] France recognized that American dollars, and even increased American troops in Europe, would be insufficient to assure Europe's defense. Manpower was a vital need, and the thirty-six divisions planned for 1955 were required in 1952. The most France spoke of during this period was equipping fifteen divisions on the condition that American supplies and finances be commensurate with these efforts.

Nothing was plainer in the late summer of 1950 than that the fifth session of the North Atlantic Council in New York would center on the *quid* of an integrated European army with a German component in exchange for the *quo* of continuing American assistance. The consequence for Europe would be a severe strain on national economies and a direct confrontation with the German question. Results of a study by the Council of Deputies of the Medium Term Defense Plan, on the strength of new estimates of needs and capabilities, pointed to no other conclusion. The American divisions would not be sent into a vacuum or into an allied military system in which each partner was not matching sacrifices.

Despite an abundance of advance signals, the formal American proposal, made by Acheson on September 12, 1950, in preliminary meetings of the Big Three foreign ministers, emerged as the "bomb in the Waldorf."[56] The impact of the proposal was explosive. But if it was a bomb, it was more a time bomb than a grenade lobbed into a startled assemblage of diplomats. It had been ticking for weeks and had been inspected from all sides by the concerned parties at the Waldorf. The components of Acheson's proposals were familiar. He asked for ten German units of divisional strength under a unified command—a plan in apparent harmony with ideas coming out of Paris. An arrangement of this sort would bind American and British forces more firmly to those of their Continental allies.

If the image of a bomb is applicable, it would be in the rigid linking of an integrated command with German involvement. The message was clear: American troops and American aid were contingent on NATO's accepting a German contribution. This single package, as Dean Acheson has pointed out, was largely the work of his colleagues at the Pentagon.[57] It had its attractions. The new organization of NATO and the special provisions to eliminate an independent German force were intended to allay fears of a full-blown German army. But the French reacted as if an American Cadmus was sowing dragon's teeth along the Rhine. Could a thin NATO frame contain marching Germans?

France's position was adamant. Jules Moch, the minister of defense and an implacable foe of German rearmament, left no room for doubt. Schuman, who had professed to be personally in favor of the American plan, cited Moch and President Vincent Auriol as blocks to France's approval of the plan. Although Moch admitted that Acheson did not seek an autonomous army for the Germans, he objected to the integrated arrangement. It would be along the lines of Marshal Foch's authority during World War I. In effect, then, it would be a national army, as the American Expeditionary Force had been, and this was wholly unacceptable to a body of Frenchmen wider than Moch's Socialist constituency.[58]

Schuman argued the case for France before the North Atlantic Council more diplomatically than Moch had done. He raised objections to immediate German rearmament. They ranged from a denial of the assumption that German rearmament would result in increasing the total resources of NATO to doubts about the legality of incorporating West German units into a European defense force and the plan's probable rejection by the German and French public. In a major appeal to his allies, Schuman did not demand that they renounce the issue. "I do not decline to do this. What I cannot do, what my government cannot do, at the present time and under the present circumstances, is to reach a premature decision on this problem. Such a decision might, besides, be fatal if it were to become known."[59]

However gracefully Schuman expressed his government's position, it amounted to a rejection of the American proposal. The stance was not surprising; Acheson had anticipated it even as he admitted the logic of the Pentagon's position. In bowing to Pentagon demands, he followed a course which he later claimed was "largely my own fault."[60]

What is more surprising was the council's endorsement of the Pentagon's position. There were misgivings about the dangers of political extortion from the Germans, as the West bid for their help. Bevin warned against NATO putting itself "in a position of approaching the West Germans as a suppliant."[61] At the same time he saw no alternative. According to the Dutch foreign minister, "In spite of the atrocities inflicted by Germany on the Netherlands some 80 percent of the Dutch Parliament would probably accept the proposals made . . . by the United States."[62]

After consulting with Lester Pearson of Canada and Halvord Lange of Norway, Stikker took the lead is pressing for a German share in European defense plans. Although his two colleagues wanted to defer action until the Big Three had been apprised of their sentiments, Stikker had Acheson's blessing in developing his argument around a "forward strategy" for NATO, in which Germany would participate "in the proper way and at the proper time."[63] The communique ending the New York meetings reflected the stalemate created by France, but it also reflected the pressures being placed on France. It endorsed the defense of Europe as far east as possible, and promised to examine "the methods by which Germany could most usefully make its contribution" to that defense.[64]

Despite frustration over France's veto, the council meetings in New York generated changes that pushed NATO along new paths. Self-conscious about its isolation, France looked around for means to appease the allies by giving at least the illusion of an invitation to Germany. Even as the meetings were underway, Jean Monnet, the father of the Schuman Plan, was at work on a design to provide a Franco-German connection in the military sphere, analogous to the Schuman Plan in the economic. Or so Joseph Bech, the foreign minister of Luxembourg, told Acheson.[65]

There was a break in the American position, as well, shortly after the council adjourned. The resignation of Secretary Johnson, an enemy of Acheson's (whose conduct the latter asserted "had passed beyond the peculiar to the impossible"), permitted new initiatives.[66] George C. Marshall succeeded Johnson as secretary of defense on September 21 and immediately reopened channels between the State and Defense Departments. Acheson was able to assert that German participation would follow the creation of the unified command. By establishing the structure, with its prominent American component, the French would have time to become accustomed to a German military presence.[67]

It was in this new context that the French unveiled their Pleven Plan on October 24, 1950; under it the NATO European partners would pledge a special European force to the supreme command, with its own staff system under a European minister of defense. When this army of potentially one hundred thousand men came into being, German contingents would function at the battalion level. The National Assembly applauded. American applause was more subdued, barely a murmur of appreciation for the initiative the French had taken. Privately American diplomatists were dismayed. They felt the French had floated a plan that was fashioned to antagonize Germans, by consigning them to an inferior status, and that would do little for European defense in the immediate future.[68]

The council of deputies never approved the Pleven Plan. It is unlikely that the French even had meant it to be more than a vehicle to delay the painful issue of German rearmament. If so, it worked magnificently. The art of diplomacy in blurring the sharp lines of confrontation was fully practiced over the next four years, as variations on the theme of an integrated army followed, one upon another.

In November 1950, the deputies, looking for some measure of progress to report at the next council meeting in Brussels in December, devised the Spofford Compromise between the American wishes and the French offer. The French scrapped the requirement that German contingents join the force only after the European army had been formed and agreed to accept combat teams at regimental strength in place of battalions. The German soldier in a European uniform would never exceed 20 percent of the total force and would serve side by side with Belgians and Italians, all similarly cloaked in a European command under a European defense minister. The minister, in turn, would receive instructions from a supranational council of ministers responsible to a European parliamentary assembly.

The German response to the variety of proposals concerning their role was uneasy at best. Social Democrats complained both of the encouragement rearmament would give to German militarism and of the perpetuation of the division between East and West Germany it would foster. Adenauer was always more optimistic. To him, the European defense force meant opportunity to enmesh Germany permanently in the Western community so that it might not be a danger to itself or to others. At the same time the chancellor insisted that any arrangement demeaning to Germany's status in Europe would make mere cannon fodder of its troops. The Brussels meeting addressed many of these concerns by announcing appointment of a supreme allied command. It would have a German representative, pointing the way to political roles in the future for a rehabilitated Germany.[69]

The North Atlantic Council sessions at Brussels set the stage for a conference in February 1951 to develop the European army, and the European Defense Community was a product of these deliberations. For the next two and one-half years there was a painful process of formulating terms of the treaty, protocols of British and American relations with the community, as well as revision amendments, interpretations, and guarantees before the treaty was ratified. The EDC's members finally signed it in May 1952; the United States Senate approved the protocols in July 1952; more than two years later, on August 30, 1954, the French National Assembly ended debate on ratification of the EDC and scuttled the community.

It is a tale of failure. Was it also an elaborate French hoax? Acheson's sardonic comments in *Present at the Creation* suggest a measure of American suspiciousness from the start. John Foster Dulles's anger and shock over the French legislature's action in 1954 reflects betrayal and disillusionment. By a vote of 88 to 0 on July 31, 1954, the Senate urged the president to give the Federal Republic full sovereignty unilaterally if France did not ratify the EDC. By their behavior, the French had demonstrated no intention of submerging French troops in a European army or of accepting German troops alongside their own.

Yet the experience of France and its neighbors in experimenting with a European Defense Community left its mark. Europe would not have accepted Germany as a NATO partner in 1951; it was prepared to do so in 1954, after failure of the EDC. How much the educational campaign of the preceding three years helped the success of the imaginative Eden proposals associating Germany with NATO through the Western European Union is impossible to say. One can observe that after the Korean War began, West Germany's status underwent visible change. It was no longer an enemy under Allied occupation, but a full member of the Council of Europe. The high commissioners became ambassadors as the Federal Republic achieved much of the acceptance abroad that Adenauer had hoped would come from a commitment to Western Europe. EDC may have had only a shadow life for three years, but it helped stimulate a solution to the German problem which Europeans, still traumatized by World War II, might not have found otherwise.

NATO might have collapsed in 1950 had France not made a pretense of responding to the conditions the United States placed on continuing assistance and association with Europe. The Pleven Plan legitimized both the decision to reinforce American troops in Germany and the appointment of an American, Gen. Dwight D. Eisenhower, as the first supreme Allied commander. These actions took place at the very time China's entry into the Korea War had focused almost all of America's attention on Asia once again. Without the earnest of European cooperation provided by the French plan, a reinvigorated American isolationism might have realized the NATO countries anxieties about American intentions toward NATO.

As it was, criticism of Secretary Acheson had mounted steadily over the year, beginning with McCarthy's unverified charges of Communist officials in the State Department. Senator Wherry had demanded the secretary's resignation on August 7. Five days later, four of the five Republican members of the Senate Foreign Relations Committee, joined by Taft, accused Acheson and the president of having invited the Communist attack on South Korea. As Acheson left for the Brussels meeting in December, a congressional caucus of Republicans of both houses asked Truman to remove the secretary. Citing Lincoln's defense of Seward, the president publicly and pointedly rejected the criticism.[70]

Eisenhower's appointment opened a great debate that became the major test of the alliance in its early years, but the administration stood firm. Congressional restiveness over the Truman-Acheson leadership, combined with the latent power of an isolationist suspicion of Europe and traditional concern with the Far East, could have wrecked the ambitious plan to transform the North Atlantic Treaty into a military machine buttressed by a visible American presence in Europe. No matter how illusory, the reconciliation of France and Germany within a Europe that was integrated economically and militarily was the requisite for an American commitment. The policy succeeded under the most adverse of circumstances, when the war in Asia was going badly and the isolationists' attack going well. It stood even the climactic moment in April 1951, when a vengeful MacArthur came home to a hero's welcome.

Even before Congress held hearings on the assignment of ground forces to Europe, former President Herbert Hoover had raised the standard of a "fortress America." Beyond helping Europe with some material assistance, he urged the United States to let that continent alone. The alternative, he said, would be destruction for the entire West.[71] Earlier in December, former Ambassador Joseph P. Kennedy had contrasted the might behind the Iron Curtain with the fatal deficiencies of the West. He told students at the Law School Forum of the University of Virginia that entanglement with Europe and Asia "is suicidal. It has made us no foul weather friends. It has kept our armament scattered over the globe. It has picked one battlefield and threatens to pick others impossibly removed from our sources of supply. It has not contained Communism. By our methods of opposition it has solidified Communism. . . ." The only sensible course was to remove Americans from Korea and from Europe. If the consequence should be triumph of communism in Western Europe, it would be a short-lived triumph; eventually Europe would follow the path of Tito in Yugoslavia and break loose from Soviet control. But whatever happened there, America's concerns should be with problems in its own hemisphere.[72]

The "great debate" began auspiciously enough for the administration. Despite the unbuttoned rhetoric of these elder statesmen, Acheson claimed that the debate opened in a deceptively amicable atmosphere when the congressional foreign affairs committees met on December 22 to hear him report the results of the Brussels conference. It went well. He spoke of Eisenhower's new responsibilities, of a new Defense Production Board to advance the industrial capacities of the allies, and of the apparent consensus on Germany's future position in Europe's defense. "Nothing sweetens relations between the Secretary and his guardian committees like a little success."[73]

The affability, however, did not last long. Taft, one of the thirteen senators who had voted against the North Atlantic Treaty, raised his voice in the Senate on January 5, 1951. While he did not call for abandonment of Europe, he argued against both military assistance and the dispatch of troops. Assumption of the new role in NATO, Taft argued, would enmesh America in the toils of Europe and increase presidential power. Commitment of troops to Europe should follow, not precede, development of Europe's ability to defend itself, and the numbers should be a token in keeping with "the general spirit of the Atlantic Pact"; otherwise, we might be inciting the Russians to war. In the meantime, Taft charged, the president had no authority to send troops to Europe without congressional approval.[74] Having unburdened himself of his feelings that excessive presidential power and commitments to Europe were harmful to the national welfare, Taft finally voted for the assignment of troops, since congressional approval would be required for specific numbers at specific times in the future.

Dislike of executive domination obviously had a higher priority in Taft's thinking than worry over American membership in NATO, and much of this same spirit pervaded other isolationist criticism in the Senate. The danger of provoking the Soviets to a militant response diminished if such provocation was undertaken by congressional rather than presidential authority. The Wherry Amendment of January 8, providing that "no ground forces of the United States should be assigned duties in the European area for the purposes of the North Atlantic Treaty pending the formation of a policy with respect thereto by the Congress," was the most dramatic attempt to limit the president's power at this time.[75] General Eisenhower's report on his tour of NATO capitals on January 23 provided the occasion for a joint session of the Senate Foreign Relations and Armed Services committees to examine Wherry's call for hearings on the question. They took up most of the month of February.

Military spokesmen carried the bulk of the administration's case before the committees. While Eisenhower addressed himself to the measures European countries were taking to arm themselves, Secretary of Defense Marshall emphasized that NATO was providing exactly what the Congress had demanded: a plan for defense of the North Atlantic area. Whether it would succeed depended on support from the United States. Eisenhower and his staff could be only as effective as the means they had to execute their commission. The abilities of the supreme Allied commander were beyond question; the intentions of Congress were the nub of the problem, according to the secretary of defense.[76] When Sen. William Knowland asked Marshall why the pledge of assistance made in the treaty was not a sufficient earnest of America's intentions, Marshall replied that it had helped morale before the Korean War. "Now we have to meet the situation where they are under duress, are under a continuous threat and a very terrible threat." More was needed.[77] Mindful of the overwhelming share assumed by the United States in the current war, Knowland suggested that American soldiers be limited to a specific percentage of the total manpower needed. Marshall opposed this approach, commenting that it might hamper military movements. "Korea happened to be right close to Japan, where we already had divisions overseas on the ground. The conditions are quite different from those in Europe."[78]

Acheson reinforced Marshall's argument. He pointed out the diminishing usefulness of retaliatory air power as a deterrent to Soviet aggression. Although air power still had value, the United States must use the time now available to build its ground forces and those of its allies. The balanced collective force was a matter of immediate urgency, since it would serve notice that would prevent a repetition of the Korean experience. That invasion had awakened Americans and Europeans to more than just "the possibility of bold, naked aggression by the Soviet Union itself . . . we have seen recent examples of another form of Communist aggression through a satellite."[79]

Arguments in the Senate seesawed back and forth. The Korean example registered with the senators, who were less inclined to let the issue of executive power go unchallenged. Sen. Bourke Hickenlooper dismissed Acheson's attempts to cite court decisions granting presidential authority over commitments of troops abroad, despite the secretary's appeal to "an unbroken practice from the very first days of the Republic."[80] Hickenlooper noted instead the inconsistency with the promises Acheson had made at the hearings on the North Atlantic Treaty in 1949. When he had asked if Article 3 of that treaty would

ACME Newspictures—UPI

U.S. infantrymen move into the Naktong River area as South Korean women and children flee from the Communists—August 11, 1950.

obligate the United States to provide troops as part of developing the allies' capabilities to resist aggression, Acheson in 1949 had given a clear, absolute "No." The only response the secretary could make in 1951 was that he had not changed his view. Conditions had changed making troops necessary irrespective of the claims of Article 3.[81]

Acheson found some comfort in the Republican ranks, notably support from Senator Lodge and Gov. Thomas E. Dewey of New York. The latter cited the time limit of February 2, which Wherry had placed in his resolution, as congressional meddling in the delicate area of executive prerogatives. There was a major distinction, Dewey insisted, between a congressional voice in provision of funds for military aid to the alliance and in sending soldiers to the European theater. The fact that the deadline date had passed over three weeks before the time Dewey was testifying indicated the absurdity of a deliberative body attempting to perform functions of the executive.[82] Wherry's resolution failed. So did Taft's effort to postpone sending troops until the allies had reached an agreement on the nature of their international army.

The upshot of the Senate hearings was a resolution approving Eisenhower's command and accepting the dispatch of four additional American divisions to Europe. The resolution also required that no more than the four divisions be sent "without further Congressional approval, and that the Joint Chiefs of Staff certify that the allies were making appropriate progress in collective defense before soldiers left the United States."

Strings attached to the troop assignment demonstrated that the administration's battle with Congress had not ended. In fact, a case may be made that the Congress had won its fight to limit executive prerogatives.[83] Its resolution was in keeping with the spirit of the Bricker Amendment to the Constitution, then threatening to hobble executive agreements with foreign powers.

But what was noteworthy about the outcome of the great debate was not restraints on the president or suspicions about NATO's value or anger over delays in securing German contributions, but that all of these factors weighed so lightly in the final balance. Despite the reverses in Korea, the Senate helped the administration endorse the Atlantic alliance and change the course of NATO. The victory was of Eisenhower's European orientation over MacArthur's Asia-first fixation, as Gaddis Smith has observed. "After the winter outburst of 1950–51 the Truman administration did not again suffer a formidable Congressional attack on its European objectives."[84]

Reorganization of NATO made a visible difference in the West's relations with the Soviet Union during the next few years. The most obvious changes involved nations militarily important to the new operational commands established under the supreme Allied command in Paris. Greece and Turkey, on the southeastern flank, and Germany, in the center, joined the alliance to fulfill the new functions of NATO. The Balkan issue was easier to handle. Although the North Atlantic Council had rejected Greece's and Turkey's initial applications in September 1950, creation of a headquarters under Eisenhower made possible their membership in the alliance in February 1952.

Germany's participation in the alliance, as noted, was more difficult. In retrospect, it is obvious that despite all the pressures for immediate German rearmament, neither Americans nor Europeans assumed that it could be forthcoming immediately, nor that it was even necessary immediately. Congressional inquiries at the hearings on troop assignments, regarding many facets of American foreign relations, included surprisingly little examination of the Pleven Plan, the Spofford Compromise, or plans for the European army then underway. What NATO leaders wanted out of a solution to the German question was permanent engagement of the United States in the alliance. The European Defense Community was primarily a means to secure that end.

Reinforcement of the American military position in Europe in 1951 had replaced assurances which the treaty had supplied earlier and which the Korean War had damaged. The security of Europe during this period rested on the knowledge that an invader would encounter American soldiers and, hence, American involvement.[85] There was an oppressiveness about America's protection as impatience expressed itself periodically, even more vehemently under Dulles than under Acheson. Even so, Western Europeans at the time considered the benefits of the alliance worth the harassment and preachments they had to accept from American leaders in return.

The enormous publicity attending the military expansion of NATO held some of the elements of charade that were to reappear in discussions over Germany. The goals of military expansion were impressive. To defend the Continent from a major ground attack required some one hundred divisions, according to planners in 1951. Even with six American divisions in Europe, the gap was enormous. Twenty-five Greek and Turkish divisions on the southeast flank of NATO swelled the ranks numerically, but did little for the heartland of Western Europe where France and Britain presented few troops and Germany none, pending signing and ratification of the European Defense Community. The North Atlantic Council at its meeting in Rome in November 1951 decided to establish a force of forty-three divisions by 1954. Three months later the projected force levels reached their peak when the council at Lisbon approved plans for fifty divisions in 1952, seventy-five in 1953, ninety-six by 1954. Twelve of these constituted the German component within the EDC.[86] Acheson was sufficiently carried away by the new sense of purpose in the organization that he told the president, "We have something pretty close to a grand slam."[87]

The contrast between the exuberance of NATO leaders at Lisbon in February 1952 and the state of NATO preparedness in 1952 or 1953 or 1954 has led observers to write off NATO goals as a sham. By the end of 1953 there were no more than fifteen NATO divisions facing the Soviets in Germany. Although Roger Hilsman has argued that this was an impressive improvement over the previous year and that those divisions could obviate a surprise ground attack,[88] this was not the message heard in Europe or America at the time—or later. Failure of NATO to meet its reported plans became identified in the public mind with the collapse of the European Defense Community and the apparent willingness of the Eisenhower administration's planners to sacrifice expensive conventional forces for the promise of a cheaper deterrent, implicit in Dulles's talk of "massive retaliation" throughout 1953 and 1954.

Part of the difficulty stemmed from the relaxation among the European partners as the Korean War receded and as the American presence increased. Reasons for sacrificing men, money, and equipment seemed less compelling than the threat posed to their economies and societies by the NATO program. Rearmament had raised the cost of imported raw materials, already inflated by the Korean War. An increasing imbalance of payments accompanied inflation in domestic prices in most allied countries. According to the report of the Mutual Defense Assistance Program, prices of raw materials needed by European manufacturers rose 35 percent during the fifteen months following the outbreak of the war in Korea, while export prices in Europe rose only 12 percent.[89] American offshore purchases in Europe of products for U.S. forces were a welcome palliative, but insufficient.

The North Atlantic Council addressed the problem at its Ottawa meeting September 1951 by appointing a Temporary Council Committee, under Harriman of the United States, Sir Edwin Plowden of the United Kingdom, and Jean Monnet of France—the "three wise men" as they came to be known. The committee produced a plan of rearmament that could reconcile raising military expenditures in each member nation without reducing the standard of living in those countries. The method was to pay for new armaments out of more efficient production and, above all, out of future purchases the United States would make abroad.[90]

Sensible as the advice was, its delivery in December was unacceptable to the allies. Nor did it fit American plans; the new mutual security program, which had come into effect for fiscal 1952, subsumed economic assistance under a military rubric, to the disadvantage of European economies. Even a provision in the act allowing up to 10 percent of the total budget to be transferred from one category to another could not prevent the dislocation of European economies.[91] The communique at Lisbon announcing that "the Council took detailed and comprehensive action based on the recommendations of the Temporary Council Committee" had no more meaning than a reader wished to give it.[92]

Perhaps the excessive expectations derived from the loose figures or from temporary bouts of euphoria indulged in by even the most experienced statesmen helps explain the skepticism NATO accomplishments frequently evoked. The semiannual reports of the secretary of defense and of the Mutual Security Program, as well as the communiques of NATO council meetings and official accounts of the secretaries-general, tended either to overwhelm constituents with vague, optimistic generalizations expressed in cliches of the day or to bury them in statistics. Yet cliches can confirm successes as well as conceal failures; and statistics can test them.

Although the American military assistance which poured into Europe in unprecedented size may not have been enough to release counterpart monies among the beneficiaries or even to create the military machine anticipated, they made an impact. Quantitatively, the record of the translation of military aid into what the French called infrastructure— port installations, air bases, fuel storage facilities, pipelines, and signal communications systems to support NATO armies—is impressive. Only fifteen airfields operated in Western Europe when Eisenhower's SHAPE was established in 1951; eventually there were over one hundred such military air bases ready for use. Three hundred signal communications units were begun, from Norway to Turkey (although only half of them completed). More than thirty-five hundred kilometers of interconnected pipelines were started, designed to provide new methods of handling the enormous consumption of fuel by modern jet aircraft.[93]

Was all this information designed merely for the edification of legislators, particularly American congressmen? What the data cannot tell is the effect of these building programs on traditional conceptions of national sovereignty. When the reader's numbness wears off, he can look behind the statistics and see a genuine military interdependence in Western Europe growing out of these projects. Seaport facilities in one country include pipelines that cross into a second country's territory to serve air bases on the soil of a third country. There are political implications in the blurring of national boundary lines as well as military implications for defense of all the countries concerned.

THE KOREAN WAR

While France's departure from the organization ten years later suggests that the mutual dependence was not complete, progress toward the goal of a European community—politically, economically, and militarily—has been evident. By pressing for a unification of Europe to maximize the military and economic assistance the United States granted, American planners won more than was apparent at the time. That they may not have anticipated or approved all the paths taken by a revived Europe over the next two decades does not detract from the American contribution to that revival.

The impact of the Korean War on European-American relations may make that event, rather than the signing of the North Atlantic Treaty in 1949, the watershed of American isolationism. The conflict tested America's determination to turn away from the traditional abstention from European political affairs and from military obligations they might impose. Isolationist challenges erupted periodically during this period over a number of issues; they were all defeated. In the course of debates, great and small, during the first half of the 1950s, the idea of alliance took on meanings which may have been hoped for in 1949 but were never truly expected. The European infrastructure for NATO represented one measure of a new interdependence of the allies; American acceptance of status-of-forces agreements was another.

An optimistic interpretation of NATO changes need not rule out examination and judgment of flaws attributed to the alliance and to American leadership. There is little doubt that Acheson's emphasis on building situations of strength from which to negotiate ruled out any possible talks with the Soviet Union during this period. It precluded an appreciation of Soviet fears and needs and gave an unnecessarily harsh cast to the contest with the Soviet Union. American initiative locked the West into an inflexible stance. At the same time, American pressure forced the rebuilding of Germany, without sufficient empathy for the feelings either of the European allies or of the Germans themselves. By embracing Adenauer, American policy helped to ensure a division of Germany for a generation, with a vulnerable Berlin remaining a point of friction between East and West. America's political and military weight in Europe stimulated European anger and resentment, which may have been expressed in sublimated form by the Anglo-French Suez invasion of 1956 and, more candidly, by France's posture during de Gaulle's decade of power.

From another angle of observation, the rearmament of the Western European countries, particularly of Germany, may have been unnecessary—the result of America's misdirected initiative in anticipating a Soviet invasion that was never part of Soviet intentions. What point was there to build a military machine operating from the Arctic to the Caucasus if the Russians had no plans to push towards the Atlantic, or even towards the Mediterranean? This may have induced the Russians to establish a counter-NATO, the Warsaw Pact, after Germany entered NATO. Such was the essence of Kennan's warning about the rearming of Germany in the mid-1950s.[94]

Much of the foregoing evaluation, of course, is based on knowledge the historian today does not possess. He can manage to interpret the results of rigidity in the American position and of the pressures for militarizing NATO. He cannot judge the sources of Soviet conduct to learn if Soviet overtures to the West for settlement of the German question in 1952 were genuine. If so, were they a product of the success of NATO in forcing the Soviet Union to choose new means to effect their foreign policy? Was that policy built around neutralization of Germany for the sake of Russian security, or would a neutralized Germany lead to the dismantling of Western Europe? These speculations point to the larger question of whether the relative peace in Europe after 1949 was not the product of America's involvement in NATO.

While such questions can end only in uncertainty, other questions are susceptible to answers. The period from the outbreak of the Korean War to the signing of the armistice agreements three years later was a time of constructive diplomacy in Europe. NATO became a working alliance, if not of equals, at least of members among whom an informal consensus, the "NATO method," operated to secure collective decisions.

Some of the results of NATO decisions are easily quantifiable. The records reveal the dollars authorized, appropriated, and expended; airfields and headquarters buildings constructed; nationalities mixed in training exercises under a NATO regional command; and protocols to the original treaties affecting the sovereignty of member states. It is more difficult, but still possible, to conclude as Raymond Aron has done in his *Imperial Republic* that "the *European* diplomacy of the Truman Administration from 1947 to 1952 was correct; by this I mean that it offered the best means by which to achieve its aims: the reduction of the risks of war to a minimum, the promotion of the recovery of Europe within a climate of security, and the paving of the way for the reconciliation, cooperation, and even unification of the former enemies."[95] In retrospect, it is doubtful that any other approach would have yielded greater security or prosperity to the NATO allies.

I am reluctant to leave this subject without raising again the attractive metaphor of the falling dominoes. In examining the development of NATO in light of the Korean War, the emphasis has been on the short run. Where does the short run end and the long run begin? Where does one game of dominoes end and another begin? Or are events always to be considered part of a seamless continuum? It would be as unreasonable to blame President Johnson's errors in Vietnam on the Korean War's impact on American attitudes toward Indochina as it would be to blame Johnson's dismissal of the multilateral-force idea in 1964 on the 1950 decision of the North Atlantic Council to establish a unified European command. New situations created new possibilities for statesmen to move in more than one direction. The events of the 1960s and 1970s follow more from new arrangements of dominoes than from the one piece set in motion by the North Korean attack on June 25, 1950. If there was a long-range impact of that event, it was in the aggressive American acceptance of the challenge of leadership, particularly executive leadership, with its potential for abuse in domestic and foreign relations. For Europe, the result over the last twenty-five years has underscored the passing of the old tradition of isolationism.

NOTES

1. Harry S. Truman, *Memoirs*, vol. 2, *Years of Trial and Hope* (Garden City, N.Y.: Doubleday, 1956), p. 333.
2. Merle Miller, *Plain Speaking: An Oral Biography of Harry S. Truman* (Berkley Publishing Corp., 1973), p. 274.
3. Charles E. Bohlen, *Witness to History, 1929–1969* (New York: W. W. Norton, 1973), p. 304.
4. *New York Times*, June 28, 1950; *Washington Post*, July 5, 1950. See discussion of columnists' reactions in Alexander George, "American Policy-making and the North Korean Aggression," *World Politics* 7 (January 1955): 209–32.
5. Bohlen, *Witness to History*, p. 292.
6. Clement Attlee, *As It Happened* (New York: Viking, 1954), pp. 279, 280.
7. Dorothy Fosdick, *Common Sense and World Affairs* (New York: Harcourt, Brace, 1955), p. 48 (emphasis in original).
8. W. Averell Harriman, *America and Russia in a Changing World: A Half Century of Personal Observation* (Garden City, N.Y.: Doubleday, 1971), p. 55.
9. George F. Kennan, *Memoirs, 1925–1950* (Boston: Little, Brown, 1967), pp. 395–96, 497–98; Bohlen, *Witness to History*, p. 294.
10. Robert A. Taft, *A Foreign Policy for Americans* (New York: Doubleday, 1952), pp. 32–33; Arthur H. Vandenberg, Jr., ed., *The Private Papers of Senator Vandenberg* (Boston: Houghton Mifflin, 1952), pp. 543–44.
11. Kennan, *Memoirs*, pp. 524–25; Bohlen, *Witness to History*, p. 292.

12. I. F. Stone, *The Hidden History of the Korean War* (New York and London: Monthly Review Press, 1952), pp. 70–74.

13. Ibid., pp. x–xii; Stone broke the soybean story in the October 1951 issue of his *Monthly Review*.

14. See Paul Y. Hammond, "NSC-68: Prologue to Rearmament," in Warner R. Schilling, Paul Y. Hammond, and Glenn H. Snyder, *Strategy, Politics and Defense Budgets* (New York: Columbia University Press, 1962), p. 306; see also "NSC-68," A Report to the National Security Council on United States Objectives and Programs for National Security, April 14, 1950, p. 58ff, National Archives.

15. Hammond, "NSC-68," p. 319.

16. Dean Acheson, *Present at the Creation: My Years in the State Department* (New York: W. W. Norton, 1969), p. 425; Gaddis Smith, *Dean Acheson* (New York: Cooper Square, 1972), p. 161; Ronald J. Stupak, *The Shaping of Foreign Policy: The Role of Secretary of State as Seen by Dean Acheson* (Indianapolis: Odyssey Press, 1969), p. 36.

17. Ronald Steel, *Imperialists and Other Heroes: A Chronicle of the American Empire* (New York: Random House, 1971), p. 17; Joyce and Gabriel Kolko, *The Limits of Power: The World and United States Foreign Policy, 1945–1954* (New York: Harper & Row, 1972), pp. 508–9.

18. Richard J. Barnet, *Roots of War* (New York: Atheneum, 1972), p. 273.

19. David S. McLellan and John M. Reuss, "Foreign and Military Policies," in *The Truman Period as a Research Field*, ed. Richard S. Kirkendall (Columbia, Mo.: University of Missouri Press, 1967), p. 34.

20. Lloyd C. Gardner, "Truman Era Foreign Policy: Recent Historical Trends," in *The Truman Period as a Research Field: A Reappraisal, 1972*, ed. Richard S. Kirkendall (Columbia, Mo.: University of Missouri Press, 1972), p. 63.

21. "Domino" was applied first to Indochina in a press conference of President Eisenhower on April 7, 1954; see *Public Papers of the Presidents of the United States, 1947–1955* (Washington, D.C.: G.P.O., 1964), 1954, p. 383.

22. Stephen E. Ambrose, "The Failure of a Policy Rooted in Fear," *Progressive* 34, no. 11 (November 1970): 18.

23. U.S., Congress, House, *United States–Vietnam Relations, 1945–1967* (a study prepared by the Department of Defense for the House Armed Services Committee), 92d Cong., 1st sess., 1971, 1:5.

24. *Pentagon Papers* (Senator Gravel Edition), 4 vols. (Boston: Beacon, 1972), 1:83; see also statement on "domino principle" in NSC 124/2 in ibid.

25. Ibid., 1:85.

26. Norman Graebner offered a different view of the Korean War's effect on the election of 1952: "The tragedy of the campaign was that Eisenhower, who had been nominated to quell the neo-isolationist tendencies in the Republican party, had actually tightened the grip of such views on the party." *The New Isolationism: A Study in Politics and Foreign Policy Since 1950* (New York: Ronald Press, 1956), p. 109.

27. See William Adams Brown, Jr., and Redvers Opie, *American Foreign Assistance* (Washington, D.C.: The Brookings Institution, 1953), p. 482.

28. See Roger Hilsman, "NATO: The Developing Strategic Concept," in *NATO and American Security*, ed. Klaus Knorr (Princeton: Princeton University Press, 1959),p. 14.

29. U.S., Congress, Senate, Committees on Foreign Relations and Armed Services, *Mutual Defense Assistance Program*, Hearings, 81st Cong., 2d sess., June 2, 1950, p. 15.

30. Reports of Communist plans to stop shipments at French docks, *New York Times*, January 28, 1950; at British docks, ibid., April 26, 1950.

31. *Le Monde*, April 5, 1950.

32. Senate *MDAP* Hearings, June 2, 1950, p. 12.

33. U.S., Congress, Senate, Committee on Foreign Relations, *North Atlantic Treaty*, Hearings, 81st Cong., 1st sess., April 27, 1949, pp. 57–61, cited in Laurence W. Martin, "The American Decision to Rearm Germany," in *American Civil-Military Decision: A Book of Case Studies*, ed. Harold Stein (Birmingham, Ala.: University of Alabama Press, 1963), p. 646.

34. U.S., Congress, House, Committee on Foreign Affairs, *To Amend the Mutual Defense Assistance Act of 1949*, Hearings, 81st Cong., 2d sess., June 1950, p. 22, in Martin, "The American Decision to Rearm Germany," p. 645.

35. Konrad Adenauer, *Memoirs, 1945–53*, trans. Beate Ruhm von Oppen (Chicago: Henry Regnery, 1965), p. 267.

36. Dirk U. Stikker, *Men of Responsibility: A Memoir* (New York: Harper & Row, 1966), p. 297.

37. Peter Calvocoressi, ed., *Survey of International Affairs: 1949–50* (London: Oxford University Press, 1953), p. 155.

38. U.S., Department of State, *Foreign Relations of the United States, 1949*, vol. 3 (Washington, D.C.: G.P.O., 1974), p. 295.

39. Ibid., pp. 295–96.

40. Quoted in Martin, "The American Decision to Rearm Germany," p. 650.

41. *New York Times*, July 5, 1950.

42. Adenauer, *Memoirs*, p. 273.

43. "Final Communique," Fourth Session, North Atlantic Council, Lon-

don, 19 May 1950, in Lord Ismay, *NATO: The First Five Years, 1949–54* (Paris: NATO, 1955), p. 183.

44. U.S., Congress, Senate, Committee on Foreign Relations, *Reviews of the World Situation: 1949–1950*, Hearings, 81st Cong., 2d sess., July 24, 1950, p. 320.

45. U.S., Congress, Senate, Committee on Appropriations, *Supplemental Appropriations for 1951*, Hearings, 81st Cong., 2d sess., August 30, 1950, p. 285.

46. Ibid., p. 286.

47. Ibid., p. 287.

48. Adenauer, *Memoirs*, p. 273.

49. Quoted in Calvocoressi, *Survey of International Affairs: 1949–1950*, pp. 159–160.

50. Adenauer, *Memoirs*, p. 278 ff.

51. *New York Times*, August 2, 1950.

52. Harold Callender in *New York Times*, August 1, 1950.

53. *New York Times Magazine*, August 13, 1950.

54. *Spectator*, August 11, 1950, p. 169.

55. U.S., Department of State, *Summary Minutes, United States Delegation Staff Meeting*, NACO M-2, Fifth Session of the North Atlantic Council, September 16, 1950, Department of States files.

56. A description attributed to a member of the French delegations; see Martin, "The Decision to Rearm Germany," p. 650.

57. Acheson, *Present at the Creation*, p. 437.

58. *Summary Minutes*, September 16, 1950, Jules Moch, *Histoire du rearmement allemand dupuis 1950* (Paris: Robert Laffont, 1965), pp. 46–47.

59. *Statement Made by M. Schuman before the North Atlantic Council on September 16, 1950*, Verbatim Record no. 3, C-5-VR/3 (part), p. 6, Department of State mss.

60. Dean Acheson, *Sketches from Life of Men I Have Known* (New York: Popular Library, 1962), p. 29.

61. *Summary Record of the Second Meeting, Fifth Session, North Atlantic Council, 15 September 1950*, Summary Record no. 5/2, p. 3, Department of State files.

62. *Summary Record of the Third Meeting, Fifth Session, North Atlantic Council, 16 September 1950*, Summary Record no. 3, C5-R/3; p. 3.

63. Stikker, *Men of Responsibility*, pp. 298–99.

64. "Final Communique," Fifth Session, North Atlantic Council, New York, September 2 , 1950, in Ismay, *NATO: The First Five Years*, p. 186.

65. Acheson, *Sketches from Life*, p. 42.

66. Acheson, *Present at the Creation*, p. 441.

67. Ibid., p. 444.

68. Ibid., p. 459.

73

69. Adenauer, *Memoirs,* pp. 307–9; see also Robert McGeehan, *The German Rearmament Question: American Diplomacy and European Defense after World War II* (Urbana, Ill.: University of Illinois Press, 1971), pp. 67–74.
70. Acheson, *Present at the Creation,* pp. 362–66.
71. Herbert Hoover, "We Should Revise Our Foreign Policies" (December 20, 1955), in *Addresses Upon the American Road, 1950–55* (Stanford, Cal.: Stanford University Press, 1955), pp. 11–22.
72. Joseph P. Kennedy speech, December 12, 1950, quoted in *American Foreign Relations in the Twentieth Century,* ed. Manfred Jonas (New York: Thomas Y. Crowell, 1967), pp. 170–73.
73. Acheson, *Present at the Creation,* p. 488.
74. U.S., Congress, Senate, 82d Cong., 1st sess., pp. 54–61. See Acheson, *Present at the Creation* for commentary on Taft's speech of January 5, 1950; Taft, on the same theme, in *Assignment of Ground Forces of the United States to Duty in the European Area,* Hearings before the Committees on Foreign Relations and on Armed Services, 82d Cong., 1st sess., 1951, pp. 609–11.
75. S. Con. Res. 8, cited in *Assignment of Ground Forces,* Hearings, p. 555.
76. Statement by General Eisenhower, February 1, 1951, ibid., pp. 1–8; statement by Secretary of State Marshall, ibid., pp. 39–40.
77. Ibid., p. 67.
78. Ibid., p. 69; Henry A. Kissinger, in *Nuclear Weapons and Foreign Policy* (New York: Norton, 1969), p. 135, concluded that "the importance of forces ready to intervene rapidly was surely one of the lessons of the Korean War."
79. *Assignment of Ground Forces,* Hearings, p. 79.
80. Ibid., p. 93.
81. Ibid., pp. 109–11.
82. Ibid., pp. 555–56.
83. Taft claimed that "the Senate resolution and the concurrent resolution adopted by the Senate on April 4, 1951, was a clear statement by the Senate that it has the right to pass on any question of sending troops to Europe to implement the Atlantic Pact. . . ." See Taft, *A Foreign Policy for Americans,* p. 36; S. Res. 99, S. Con. Res. 18, *Congressional Record,* 82nd Cong., 1st sess., pp. 3282–83, 3293.
84. Smith, *Dean Acheson,* p. 252.
85. In an interview on March 24, 1972, Gen. Alfred M. Gruenther claimed that "the actual size of our force in Europe was not that important in our planning as long as it was large enough to show the Russians that we were serious in our commitment there through NATO." Quoted in Richard F. Grimmett, "The Politics of Containment: The President, the Senate and American Foreign Policy, 1947–1956" (Ph.D. diss., Kent State University, 1973), p. 138.

86. See Robert E. Osgood, *NATO: The Entangling Alliance* (Chicago: University of Chicago Press, 1962), pp. 83–87.
87. Acheson, *Present at the Creation*, p. 626.
88. Roger Hilsman, "NATO: The Developing Strategic Concept," pp. 22–23.
89. U.S., Department of State, *Building a Mutual Defense*, Mutual Defense Assistance Program, April 1, 1951–October 9, 1951, pub. no. 4473 (February 1952), p. 12.
90. Osgood, *NATO: The Entangling Alliance*, pp. 82–83.
91. See Brown and Opie, *American Foreign Assistance*, p. 554.
92. "Final Communique," Ninth Session, North Atlantic Council, Lisbon, February 20–25, 1952, in Ismay, *NATO: The First Five Years*, p. 191.
93. Ibid., p. 122.
94. George F. Kennan, *Russia, the Atom, and the West* (New York: Harper & Row, 1958), p. 87.
95. Raymond Aron, *The Imperial Republic: The United States and the World, 1945–1973*, trans. Frank Jellinek (Englewood Cliffs, N.J.: Prentice-Hall, 1974), pp. 50–51 (emphasis in original).

Comments

Robert Dallek

In his paper, Professor Kaplan reasonably argues that the Korean conflict had a substantial impact on American foreign policy. In Europe, he says, the war turned a fragile, vaguely defined North Atlantic Treaty Organization into a formidable alliance backed by specific American commitments. It put NSC-68 "into immediate operation," prompted the United States to pressure her European allies into accepting a major German military role in the alliance, and forced a successful confrontation with "Asia-first" isolationists who essentially wished the United States to continue its traditional aloofness from European affairs. Professor Kaplan also sees the war as having influenced American policy in Asia: it reversed the 1948 decision to leave Korea's defense to the United Nations; it fostered special provisions in the 1951 Japanese peace treaty for the protection of Japan; it led to an "elaborate network of bilateral and multilateral mutual defense pacts," including SEATO; and it solidified emotional and political ties between the Nationalist government in Formosa and the United States. All in all, though, Professor Kaplan sees the impact of the Korean War as more important for Europe. There, he concludes, "the changes were more profound and the ultimate consequences probably more important."

While Professor Kaplan is surely correct in saying that the Korean War significantly influenced American actions toward Europe, I would suggest that the conflict played an equally, if not more, important part in transforming American–East Asian relations. In the years between 1945 and 1953 American policy in Asia underwent a revolutionary change. Between the end of World War II and the close of the Korean fighting, the United States moved from friendship with China, enmity toward Japan, and limited interest in Korea and Indochina to antagonism toward China, amity with Japan, substantial involvement in Korea, and emerging commitments to Vietnam. While the Cold War and China's revolution were the primary causes of this change, the Korean War also played a major part. The onset of the Korean fighting not only pushed the United States into an unwanted involvement in that nation's affairs

76

COMMENTS

but also forced a shift in our China policy and a consummation of plans for Japan. Under the impact of direct combat with Communist China, hope for Sino-American friendship at the expense of the U.S.S.R. largely disappeared. Opposition to Peking's entrance into the U.N. and the 1954 defense pact with Taipei were legacies of the Korean War. Simultaneously, the Korean conflict spurred negotiations with Japan for the Peace and Security Treaties of September 8, 1951, and expanded American commitments to Indochina from a modest $15 million to a mutual defense assistance agreement in December 1950 and the Southeast Asian Collective Defense Treaty in September 1954.

Beyond all this, the Korean War also brought to an end America's traditional Open Door policy in Asia. For fifty years, the United States had spoken for "territorial integrity," nonannexation, and equal opportunity in Asia generally and in China specifically. While this was a policy with clearly defined ends, its hallmark was an absence of means. In China, in the face of European, Russian, and Japanese spheres of influence during the early years of the century, Japan's military conquests in the thirties, and a Communist take-over in the forties (which seemed to assure a monopoly of Russian influence), the United States continued to enunciate the principle of the Open Door but never advanced the means to make it work. The Korean War marked the point at which we broke with this tradition. For the first time in our history we entered a major land war in Asia, and what was once a policy chiefly of ends without means became a policy of means without clearcut ends. In Korea, for example, where we applied the military might shunned in the past, we vacillated between unifying North and South Korea and simply driving Northern forces from the South. As journalist Joseph Kraft has stated the point:

> It is possible to argue that the emphasis on force became so great that this country in some cases . . . over-reacted militarily and took on some unnecessary commitments. A case in point is the crossing of the 38th Parallel which eventually produced the Chinese intervention in Korea. Another was the commitment to defend, with nuclear weapons if necessary, the islands of Quemoy and Matsu. Whatever the case with these individual episodes, however, it seems to me inescapably clear that the military logic overshadowed all other American thought about Asia. Whereas the ends exceeded the means of American policy during the Open Door period, the means subsequently came to obliterate the ends.[1]

Two additional points. First, it seems reasonable to suggest that all these changes in American foreign policy—in Europe and Asia—could and would have taken place without direct American participation in the Korean fighting. Indeed, the strengthening of NATO, a German military contribution to the alliance, commitments to Japan, and mutual defense agreements throughout Asia could have formed a logical American substitute for fighting in Korea; and, given Moscow's generally cautious approach to the United States during these years, such steps would undoubtedly have deterred the Soviets from future adventures as much as direct action in Korea. Secondly, the Korean War not only had an impact on American foreign policy, it also revealed the fragility of this country's postwar internationalist consensus. Reared on a diet of what the historian C. Vann Woodward has called "free security" and easy victories over foreign adversaries, the United States was unprepared for the frustrations of a limited war. The tensions, recriminations, and assertions that in war there was no substitute for victory made clear that for all the new departures in American foreign policy after World War II, traditional isolationist assumptions continued to have a strong appeal in the United States.

NOTES

1. *Los Angeles Times*, February 10, 1967.

U. Alexis Johnson*

Professor Kaplan has done well to concentrate on NATO in his study, for it is all too often ignored by both Americans and Europeans that, except for Korea, NATO might well have remained a largely paper organization, without the will or the capability to defend its members' interests. I have often observed that whatever mistaken frustrations Americans may have with respect to their action in Korea, I am certain that those responsible for planning the aggression had no cause to congratulate themselves or give out any medals. Before Korea, the opportunities offered by a United States that was disarming itself and a divided Western Europe that was virtually defenseless must have been increasingly attractive to potential enemies. As Professor Kaplan ably points out, Korea was, in very considerable measure, responsible for the remarkable change that took place over a few short years with respect to the U.S. defense posture. The U.S. defense expenditures during this time more than trebled. U.S. ground forces were formally committed to

* Official duties prevented Ambassador Johnson's participation in the conference. He prepared this comment while serving as United States chief negotiator at the SALT talks in Geneva, Switzerland. During the Korean War, Mr. Johnson served, first, as deputy director, Office of Northeast Asian Affairs, Department of State, and later, as deputy assistant secretary of state for far eastern affairs.

COMMENTS

the land defense of Western Europe; the total armed forces available to NATO more than doubled in three years; and the indispensable participation of a free and vigorous German people was realized. Whatever the controversies, criticisms, and shortcomings of NATO may be, the indisputable fact is that in the intervening twenty-five years since Korea no NATO country has suffered invasion or attack. The added bonus of U.S. participation in NATO is that our own defense lines were, in effect, moved well beyond our shores.

I regret that the scope of Professor Kaplan's paper did not permit him to examine the impact on Asia of the action in Korea. The effect on Japan itself, as well as its relations with and confidence in the United States, is perhaps obvious. The effect on Chinese-American relations of the Chinese intervention into the war were, of course, profound. Directly related to this has been the effect on the status of Taiwan in relation to the Chinese mainland. Less obvious, but worthy of study, is the effect of the Korean War on the development of the Sino-Soviet schism. One hopes that some day we will have the material on which to base a better estimate of what effect the then-fresh memories of American action in Korea had on the situation in Vietnam. I have in mind especially the 1954 decision of North Vietnam and its supporters to agree to a cease fire at the 17th Parallel, rather than to pursue further their military advantage at that time.

Today, when no conscientious American can ignore the tragedy of Vietnam and Cambodia, it is perhaps not out of place to draw some lessons from the great success story of Korea. As Professor Kaplan notes, American involvement in Korea assured the independence and territorial integrity of the Republic of Korea. It bears underlining that the armistice arrangements with respect to Korea reached in 1953 remain in effect today. In the intervening years, the Republic of Korea has not only become self-supporting but has developed one of the most vigorous and dynamic economies in what we now call the less-developed world.

As far as Vietnam is concerned, it is my observation that those involved in the decisions after 1960 had the Korean experience very much in mind when it became clear that South Vietnam was being subjected to an armed attack from the North. Whatever the wisdom or lack of wisdom in the decisions taken with respect to American intervention into Vietnam, it is clear that as a people we did not heed, or deliberately chose to ignore, the Korean experience when seeking to bring that conflict to an end.

Certainly one of the reasons that the Korean Armistice of 1953 remains in effect is that some American military force has remained in Korea throughout this period as an earnest of our intent to friend and potential foe alike. To be sure, Vietnam is not Korea or vice versa; many factors contributed to the tragic collapse of South Vietnam. Among the negative factors, however, certainly must be counted the fact that our domestic situation prohibited us from maintaining a force in Vietnam that could act as an earnest of our intent. Furthermore, the enemy was assured by formal legislative action that it had nothing to fear from the United States—regardless of whatever actions it took, not the least of which were flagrant violations of formal agreements to which the United States was a party. This sad and sobering thought has had its effect on friend as well as foe; it is a lesson we should apply to our further application of diplomacy and its handmaiden, the proper use of military power.

Roger E. Kanet*

The standard American interpretation of the Soviet role in events leading to the outbreak of the Korean War in 1950 is stated quite succinctly in a recent study of the Soviet Union's foreign policy by Thomas W. Wolfe: "Undertaken apparently at Soviet initiative without due appreciation for its impact on the Western world—especially in the wake of China's succumbing to Communist power—the Korean War was viewed both in the United States and in Western Europe as the opening round of a new aggressive phase of Soviet policy, leading to a widespread belief that it might next be Europe's turn to be subjected to Communist military pressure."[1] Although, as we shall see below, there is significant evidence today to question this interpretation of the Soviet role in Korea, the second half of Wolfe's statement is strongly supported by the available historical evidence. United States decisionmakers and their counterparts in Western Europe did view the Korean War largely in terms of a continuation of aggressive Soviet behavior, as Lawrence Kaplan has argued in his paper. The Korean War did play an instrumental part in transforming NATO from a largely paper organization into an effective military force with substantial resources committed to the buildup of American and Western European military capabilities.

In the following pages I shall attempt to outline briefly the role of the Soviet Union in the outbreak of hostilities in Korea and during the early stages of the war itself. I will argue that, whatever Soviet goals might have been in June 1950, the Korean War actually resulted in two series of developments basically detrimental to overall Soviet foreign

* The author wishes to express his appreciation for comments by Donna Bahry on an earlier version of this paper.

COMMENTS

policy interests—one, its relations with the United States and the West; the other, its relations with the People's Republic of China.

Soviet goals during the years following the Second World War were based largely on security concerns and only secondarily on the desire to expand "international communism." In Eastern Europe, however, Stalin's conception of Soviet security interests resulted in the creation of regimes not only friendly to the U.S.S.R. but also ruled by Communist leaders totally dependent on the Soviet Union for their very positions. Almost all local Communists who had spent the wartime period in the underground were purged by 1950 and replaced by party officials who had returned to their native countries along with the victorious Red Army in 1944 and 1945. The economies of the East European states were tied to that of the Soviet Union in a series of trade agreements and "cooperative" economic ventures in such a way that Eastern Europe became, in effect, a source of capital for the reconstruction of the Soviet economy. In addition, the domestic socio-political systems established in the area were virtual carbon copies of that developed earlier in the Soviet Union.[2] In the areas along the southern rim of the Soviet Union, Stalin and his associates had attempted in the wake of World War II to expand their control into portions of Turkey and Iran.[3] The Communist-led guerrillas in Greece were also indirectly supported by the U.S.S.R.

The Soviet approach to security in Eastern Europe, their domination over the newly established Communist regimes, and their bellicose statements about the inevitability of a war between the capitalist West and the Communist East played a major role in American and Western European perceptions of the Soviet Union as an aggressive imperialist power, intent on conquering as much territory as possible. The Czechoslovakian coup in 1948 and the Berlin blockade of 1948–49 strengthened Western convictions that the U.S.S.R. was indeed about to initiate a policy of conquest and led directly to the creation of the North Atlantic Treaty Organization in 1949.[4]

The Communist victory in China in October 1949 was viewed by the United States as yet another part of the expansion of Soviet power and influence. As we now know, the relationship between the Soviets and the forces of Mao Tse-tung were not nearly as cordial during the Chinese Civil War as official statements of Chinese-Soviet friendship implied. Stalin, in fact, continued to recognize the government of Chiang Kai-shek until 1949 and cautioned Mao to work out some sort of compromise agreement with the Nationalists. Even after the Communist victory and the establishment of the People's Republic of China in October 1949, there were apparently differences between the leaders of the two countries.[5]

81

THE KOREAN WAR

The general guidelines of American policy had been set even before the outbreak of war in the Korean peninsula. By 1947–48 the United States, with the support of Western Europe, began laying the economic and military foundation for a policy of "containment." Large-scale economic assistance to reconstruct the Western European economies (in order to make the area less susceptible to internal Communist political activity), the creation of a common defense system in NATO, and a general effort to prevent additional Communist territorial expansion had already been initiated. In late 1949 President Truman instructed the secretaries of defense and state to reexamine our foreign policy objectives and priorities. The resulting analysis was based on an assumption of continued Soviet efforts at expansion; it called for a massive program of "rebuilding the West's defensive potential to surpass that of the Soviet world, and of meeting each fresh challenge promptly and unequivocally."[6]

At the time of the outbreak of the Korean War, however, the United States had not yet acted on the recommendations proposed in this report. As Paul Nitze, chairman of the group that wrote the recommendations, noted later, the Korean War played the decisive role in translating those recommendations into specific actions.[7] One important result of the Korean War, therefore, as Kaplan argues in his paper, was to provide the impetus for the global buildup of American and Western European military capabilities, including the creation of NATO as a real military force rather than a "paper" organization.

As we have already noted, the United States response to the attack on South Korea—along with much of the later Western analysis of the origins of the war itself—was based on assumptions that the Soviets controlled the North Koreans and that the attack was part of an overall Soviet plan for military expansion. In his recent study of North Korean–Chinese–Soviet relations during the Korean War, Robert Simmons has argued quite persuasively that this interpretation represents a serious oversimplification and ignores the role of domestic Korean political developments, both north and south of the 38th Parallel, in the outbreak of the war. His paper (Chaper 5) ably summarizes his argument.

Another indication that the Soviets may have been caught off-guard is that it was several days after the North Korean attack on the South before the Soviet Union officially supported the North Koreans' claim of self-defense. During the early weeks of the war, while the North Korean armies were moving steadily south against the outmatched South Korean and American troops, the Soviet Union provided both verbal and moral support for their allies. By September and October 1950, however, as United Nations forces under the command of General MacArthur pushed north and began to approach the Chinese and Soviet frontiers with

COMMENTS

Korea, the Soviet leadership faced a serious question. Should Soviet troops intervene, first, to support the North Korean regime, which was in the process of being totally annihilated, and second, to prevent the United States from approaching the Soviet border near Vladivostok? The Soviets refused to intervene, but by November the People's Republic of China, after several prior warnings, finally entered the war, sending thousands of "volunteers" to support the North Koreans.

It seems clear that the Korean War resulted in two serious, new problems for the U.S.S.R. First, as we have already seen, it added a degree of militancy to the United States containment policy and presented American leaders with congressional and public support for a major program of military rearmament, not only in Asia, but also in Europe. Why should the Soviets have run the risk of such a development by preparing North Korean forces for battle and by granting general approval for an invasion of the South? The influence of North Koreans seeking a reunification of their country under Communist con-

ACME Newspictures—UPI

Local livestock provide food and transportation for South Korean soldiers—
January 24, 1951.

83

trol does seem important, especially since the costs of reunification by military force appeared relatively small. Moreover, the creation of a unified Communist Korea would very likely have influenced internal political developments in Japan, suggesting to the Japanese that communism was the "wave of the future" in Asia. Finally, Soviet leaders seemingly anticipated no major response by the United States to a North Korean attack. The United States had not intervened on behalf of the Nationalist government to prevent the Communist take-over of China a year earlier; neither American forces in Korea nor the troops of the Republic of Korea were a military match for North Korean forces in 1950 and a military engagement could be relatively quickly and successfully concluded; and, finally, Secretary of State Acheson had seemingly placed Korea outside the U.S. defense perimeter in a major foreign policy speech in early 1950. The Soviets miscalculated, however, thereby exacerbating U.S.-Soviet hostility and lending strength to the anti-Soviet coalition which the United States was in the process of constructing.

A second important long-term effect of the Korean War on the Soviet Union was the creation of tensions in relations with its major ally, the People's Republic of China. The Soviet failure in the fall of 1950 to provide direct assistance to the North Koreans and the Chinese decision to intervene in the face of American troops approaching the Chinese border created several conflicts in the interests of the two Communist allies. Throughout the remaining months of the Korean War the Chinese bore most of the weight of the military action, while the Soviets merely provided military equipment—equipment not always of the highest quality and for which the Chinese were later required to reimburse the Soviets.[8] The Soviet failure to supply the Chinese adequately in a war which was obviously in the interests of both countries had a serious impact on Chinese attitudes toward the Soviet Union. The Chinese learned that Soviet interests came first in Moscow's foreign policy, and that the Soviets were quite willing to have allies fight their battles, if not to share the burdens of the battle. As a "senior Chinese official" informed the editor of the semiofficial Egyptian newspaper, Al-Ahram, in the spring of 1973:

> In the Korean War, we interfered in the fighting. When we interfered we found ourselves obliged to wait for help from the Soviet Union. The help was delayed at times. We felt torn apart and we suffered. Sometimes we were angry and we begged, but we had to tolerate it because we were on the battlefield and because the modern weapons came from the Soviet Union. The wise man also learns the lesson from the experience. We have learned an important experience.[9]

The Korean War seems to have played an important part in what Adam

Ulam refers to as the "psychological emancipation" of the Chinese from the Soviet Union.[10] The Chinese had their first real experience—to be supplemented by developments later in the fifties—of the Soviet refusal to provide real assistance.

In retrospect, the Korean War resulted in a serious setback to Soviet foreign policy interests, among the least of which was the defeat of the North Korean armies. Far more important was the fuel Korea provided for worldwide United States rearmament and for the gradual split that developed during the 1950s between the Soviet Union and the People's Republic of China.

NOTES

1. Thomas W. Wolfe, *Soviet Power and Europe, 1945–1970* (Baltimore: Johns Hopkins University Press, 1971), p. 26.
2. The exception to this entire process was Yugoslavia where Tito had come to power largely independent of outside Soviet support. By 1948 Soviet-Yugoslav relations were severed primarily as a result of the Yugoslav refusal to become a dependency of the U.S.S.R.
3. The Soviets demanded the "return" of two provinces in eastern Turkey and attempted to gain control over the Dardanelles. At the same time, they continued their wartime occupation of portions of northern Iran and supported the creation of Communist regimes in two Iranian provinces. These efforts eventually collapsed in the face of firm United States support for the pro-Western regimes in Turkey and Iran.
4. It should be noted that much of the United States policy during the immediate postwar period could definitely have been viewed in Moscow as hostile to the interests of the Soviet Union. Several recent studies of the period, while not presenting extreme revisionist arguments, do point to those aspects of American policy which antagonized the Soviets. See, for example: George C. Herring, Jr., *Aid to Russia: Strategy, Diplomacy, the Origins of the Cold War* (New York: Columbia University Press, 1973); Thomas G. Paterson, *Soviet-American Confrontation: Post-War Reconstruction and the Origins of the Cold War* (Baltimore: Johns Hopkins University Press, 1973); and Lynn Etheridge Davis, *The Cold War Begins: Soviet-American Conflict over Eastern Europe* (Princeton: Princeton University Press, 1974).
5. For example, Mao was in Moscow for two months before a Soviet-Chinese Treaty of Friendship, Alliance, and Mutual Assistance was signed between the two countries. In addition, the Soviets were willing to grant loans to China of only $300 million over a five-year period for the purchase of Soviet equipment and materials. See, for

example, O. Edmund Clubb, *China and Russia: The "Great Game"* (New York: Columbia University Press, 1971), pp. 381ff. Robert Simmons presents a plausible case that Soviet behavior in the U.N. in January 1950 actually hurt the chances of the People's Republic of China gaining membership. He notes that although Communist China was not given the Nationalist seat on the first U.N. vote, the chances for the P.R.C.'s being accepted in the near future were good. The Soviet walkout may well have been calculated to make Chinese admission a Cold War issue, thereby preventing the P.R.C. from gaining admission and maintaining Chinese dependence on the U.S.S.R. for representation in the world body. See Robert R. Simmons, *The Strained Alliance: Peking, P'yongyang, Moscow and the Politics of the Korean Civil War* (New York: Free Press, 1975), pp. 90–91.

6. Paul Y. Hammond, "NSC-68: Prologue to Rearmament," in Warner L. Schilling, Paul Y. Hammond, and Glenn H. Snyder, *Strategy, Politics and Defense Budgets* (New York: Columbia University Press, 1962), p. 307.

7. Paul H. Nitze, "The United States in the Face of the Communist Challenge," in *The Threat of Soviet Imperialism*, ed. C. Grove Haines (Baltimore: Johns Hopkins University Press, 1954), p. 374.

8. Most of the equipment provided by the Soviets was from surplus stock and obsolescent. In addition, weapons captured from Chinese units during the first six months of Chinese involvement in the war show that the overwhelming percentage of Chinese weapons were either of World War II Japanese origin or captured U.S. weapons— more than 68 percent of the weapons of the Third Field Army, which was in constant contact with U.S. forces, were of Japanese or American origin. See Simmons, *Strained Alliance*, pp. 180–81.

9. *Foreign Broadcast Information Service, Supplement* (Washington, D.C., March 7, 1973), no. 45. In the letter of the Central Committee of the Communist Party of China to the C.P.S.U. of February 29, 1964, it was noted that the loans from the Soviets, used to purchase the war material used in Korea, had to be repaid with interest by the export of Chinese foodstuffs and raw materials to the U.S.S.R.; see William E. Griffith, *Sino-Soviet Relations, 1964–1965* (Cambridge, Mass.: M.I.T. Press, 1967), p. 183.

10. Adam Ulam, *Expansion and Coexistence: Soviet Foreign Policy, 1917–73*, 2nd ed. (New York: Praeger, 1974), pp. 531–32.

Forrest C. Pogue

Because Professor Kaplan's paper deals in detail with only one phase of the Korean War's influence on the United States foreign relations, there is a tendency to overstress the direct influence of the war's

COMMENTS

impact on NATO development as opposed to other long-term influences. Despite the additional impetus given to the strengthening of the military containment of the Soviet Union in the West, one must not overlook the far more positive influence of Soviet activities in Western Europe—the Berlin Crisis, in particular.

On the other hand, it is important to emphasize the statement which Kaplan has quoted in his paper: "Korea has broken the inertia of thought on many critical matters." In this connection, note Acheson's statement in *Present at the Creation* that the Defense Department for some years had held that Europe could not be defended without the willing and active participation of Western Germany. The State Department lagged behind in this respect. Acheson notes that on June 5, 1950, he said that there was no American intent to stop German demilitarization. But Bradley takes a different view: "The need for increased military strength," he writes, "was in the air; it was given a fillip by the Korean attack."

The negative effects of the Korean attack are, at least partly, handled well in Kaplan's provocative and thoughtful paper. But it should be stressed that the United States commitment in Korea aroused many old fears concerning continued American aid to Europe. As in World War II, when Churchill feared lest massive U.S. arming of new divisions and the development of certain units would siphon off weapons which might be available to Britain, Western European countries feared that American interests would shift radically to the Far East at the expense of Europe's defense against the Soviet Union. There was also a hint of Churchill's old fear that Roosevelt was giving too much to China in the later reaction of the Western European allies over aid to Korea.

In the United States, the Korean crisis reawakened the scarcely dormant attack on the administration for the "loss" of China—the argument that a pro–Chiang Kai-shek policy would have settled the Communist threat in the Far East. The war helped to stir, in addition to the attack on Acheson and Truman, a virulent attack by a few extremist senators on General Marshall. This first took form as a result of the special legislation introduced in Congress to permit him as an army officer to hold the position of secretary of defense. Some opponents of the administration seemed to feel that they must reduce Marshall's stature if the Truman administration intended to continue to use his prestige to confront international and internal political problems. This was apparently what William Buckley had in mind when he wrote later in *McCarthy and His Enemies* (p. 392): "To the extent that McCarthy through his careful analysis of Marshall's record, has contributed to cutting Marshall down to size, he has performed a valuable service."

The effect of this type of attack on Marshall was to inhibit somewhat his dealings with the Congress and the public as secretary of
defense. It did help to reawaken some of the old argument that the
Far East was being sacrificed to Europe's welfare.

Edmund S. Wehrle

Professor Kaplan's comprehensive and judiciously balanced paper
establishes a proper framework for further speculation and analysis
with respect to the impact of the Korean War on America's posture in
world affairs over the last quarter century. His analysis of the development of the military structure of the NATO alliance is fresh, well documented, and should be required reading for students of European and
American affairs. When Kaplan undertakes larger judgments concerning
the overall impact of NATO on Western Europe or the long run impact
of the Korean War on America's foreign policy, his arguments are impressive but not necessarily convincing.

With respect to the general effect of the Korean War on American
policy, Kaplan rejects the assumptions associated with what he calls the
domino theory. He insists that it would be wrong to assert that the
Korean War was the first of the falling dominoes which led inexorably
to the last falling domino in Vietnam. His historical common sense leads
him to reject the view that after Korea American policy was set on an
irreversible course; the Korean War, he suggests, did not lead Americans
to brand all future wars of national liberation as Russian-inspired con-
spiracies. It is difficult to deny his conclusion that "new situations
created new possibilities for statesmen to move in more than one direction." But Kaplan himself balances this by his admission that "American
foreign policy was deeply influenced by the choice to fight in Korea."
Kaplan's preference is to regard the Korean War as simply a "milestone"
or perhaps a "turning point" in the Cold War; but his own recital of the
pivotal impact of the Korean War on European affairs and the build-up
of NATO's military capacity appear to make more of the Korean War
than a mere "milestone." In reviewing NATO's development he finally
refers to the Korean conflict as a "watershed."

These contradictions, if such they be, are the product of a forthright
attempt to gauge accurately the causal imprint of a seminal event.
Kaplan is convincing when he asserts that American statesmen retained
a real freedom of choice in international affairs after Korea. They came
to face new decisions in new circumstances—the image of falling dominoes is too simple and, ultimately, repellent to the historian. Kaplan
rejects this approach even though he is drawn to emphasize the crucial

88

nature of the Korean War in influencing basic decisions in Europe. My own preference, admittedly an escape into a verbal formula, would be to argue that Korea confirmed a pattern of response. American credibility was maintained by means of limited war; henceforth it would be all too easy to resort once again to limited war in order to maintain that necessary credibility. The fact that Washington was said to be seeking "a Korean solution" to the Vietnam War might tend to confirm my suggestion that a pattern of response had been established. There was no lock-step inevitability about it; but what worked once might work again. Indeed, in his own way, Kaplan agrees when he finally suggests that with Korea America accepted the challenge of world leadership. Henceforth it would be difficult to deny that the credibility of the leader must be maintained.

Kaplan rejects the view of those who would see the American response to the outbreak of war in Korea as an example of "cold-blooded imperialistic planning." One's instinct is to agree with Kaplan when he describes President Truman's reaction to the Korean invasion (in the words of David McLellan and John Reuss) as a case of leaders "faced with desperate and compelling choices, forced to act under circumstances of greatest uncertainty, and acting while straining to avoid plunging the world into a new maelstrom." This assessment may be substantially true; but we must not allow this sympathetic judgment to preclude further analysis. Indeed, with respect to the Korean War, John Gittings observed that the fundamental cause of the Korean War remains "an open question." He adds: "We should be honest enough to admit that we simply do not know enough about this period to reach any conclusion."[1]

Clearly, we are dealing in an area of the "greatest uncertainty." Recent scholarship has come to emphasize the indigenous aspects of what Robert Simmons refers to in his study of East Asian international politics as the Korean Civil War.[2] Even though Simmons suggests that Stalin was involved in the preparations for an eventual invasion of the South, he stresses the unsettled political conditions in Korea which paved the way for Soviet involvement. In the hectic postwar and postcolonial periods, hopes for national unity had been thwarted, and agitators, in the North and South, were pressing for the restoration of unity. In short, a reasonable reassessment of the Korean War might look first to Korean politics.

Moving beyond Simmons's thesis, it could well have been the case that the North Korean attack was solely due to the precipitate actions of Moscow's unruly satellite, the Democratic People's Republic of Korea. In any event, Soviet diplomacy moved rapidly during the summer of

1950 in an attempt to negotiate a settlement of the war. The point is that Washington may have overreacted in presuming the Korean War was Moscow-inspired.

Whatever weight be given to this speculation, one cannot easily dismiss the suggestion that Truman, acting under "circumstances of the greatest uncertainty," made the best possible decision in electing to intervene. This must be balanced, however, against the fact that the United States had placed itself in an exposed position in Korea. The unsettled social and economic conditions which prevailed and the artificial division of the peninsula led many observers to conclude that an explosion of one kind or another was inevitable. To the extent that America's credibility in the Cold War depended on the maintenance of a stable South Korea, the United States became subject to forces neither it nor Moscow could fully control. Here was the lesson we did not learn in Korea, since a few years later we allowed ourselves to become victim to a somewhat similar postcolonial upheaval in Vietnam.

If it was assumed in Washington that the Russians inspired the North Korean invasion, it was equally evident that the Soviet Union constituted an immediate threat to the security of Western Europe. In an interesting series of speculative comments, Kaplan raises the basic question as to whether an invasion of Western Europe had ever been part of Russian intentions during the 1950s. Why build a major military machine, he asks, if the Russians had no "plans" to push to the Atlantic or even toward the Mediterranean? If Soviet intentions were misread, the rearmament of Western Europe, especially Germany, was unnecessary; in fact, Kaplan adds, the American build-up of NATO would have worked to prolong the Cold War by inducing the Russians to establish the Warsaw pact to counterbalance NATO.

Such speculative propositions, Kaplan concludes, are based on information that the historian does not possess: the validity of Soviet overtures for a settlement of the German question in 1952 cannot be judged since Russian sources are not available. This is a curious way of putting it. It might be argued with equal validity that the presumed Soviet threat in the early 1950s should have been dismissed as mere bluff since Soviet sources were not available to prove it real. Would it not be preferable to suggest that even though there may have been some doubt concerning the real nature of the Soviet military threat to Western Europe, the problem was seen primarily in military terms? It was presumed that only a military build-up would be understood in the Kremlin, while political negotiation was uncertain of fulfillment and might prove unpopular at home (as had the Yalta agreement). To put it in slightly different terms: why risk the loss of West German economic and military power for the sake of a political settlement which would surely diminish the military and economic power of the West by neutralizing Germany?

Certainly the Korean War had accentuated a tendency among American policymakers to assess problems from the point of view of military power; this was just what happened with respect to the confrontation with Russia in Europe. One can argue that this was realistic; and one can suggest that it succeeded since, in fact, it produced no great war and contributed to the creation of a Western community of nations. But, as the West painstakingly erected a political, economic, and military structure to oppose the Soviet threat, the Cold War became increasingly institutionalized; flexibility of response to political change became more difficult. Perhaps the Cold War—with the substantial danger of nuclear conflict—was prolonged beyond its time; more specifically, the Berlin crises of 1958 and 1961 could have gotten out of hand. From our present perspective, it would appear that discussions involving the future of central Europe might have avoided these confrontations. It may be too much to suggest that the Cold War was prolonged, but clearly, détente was delayed.

On the broader question of NATO's impact on the development of Western Europe, Kaplan argues that NATO provided a framework for creative cooperation and helped foster the impressive economic recovery which followed during the late 1950s. Kaplan appears to be on the verge of suggesting that the cooperative achievements of the Western alliance were of such magnitude that they were worth the price of a slight prolongation in East-West tensions. Truly, we tend to forget that the spirit of cooperation in Western Europe was the product of exhaustive political effort—an effort in which bitter enemies were realigned as allies. Kaplan is certainly correct in noting the American contribution to this new spirit, and also in implying that fear of Russia made cooperation easier. Still, one gleans the impression here that without American prodding, Western European unity would have floundered, and presumably the Common Market would not have emerged in such impressive form during the late 1950s.

In the final analysis, the New Europe with its economic achievements and its approach to European unity through the Common Market was a European achievement. Planning for the European Coal and Steel Community preceded the establishment of NATO; and economic recovery (admittedly aided by the Marshall Plan) was well underway in 1949 and 1950. In the short run, the American-inspired arms build-up that came with the Korean War retarded economic recovery. It is far from self-evident that were it not for the establishment of NATO, Europe

91

would be less unified and less prosperous today. The increase in political and economic cooperation which came with NATO must be balanced against the losses due to the sudden diversion to military production and the overly great dependence on the United States which followed.

Ultimately the vision, noble as it was, of political unification of the Common Market nations was the product of unique and temporary circumstances. In 1958, as the Common Market got underway, Charles de Gaulle returned to power in France, and an alternative goal—that of a Europe of the states—competed with the integrationist ideal of the Common Market proponents. Political unification within the framework of the Common Market proved to be premature, but the spirit of cooperation which arose in the early postwar period, and which was reinforced by the NATO experience, lived on. What is suggested here is that greater weight should be given to those European leaders who saw the need for closer political cooperation and some form of economic integration. With the perspective of the last quarter century, it would seem that the essential ingredient here was European creativity; the Americans played a useful role, but the basic achievement was European.

Almost unavoidably, historians tend to describe the development of events in Europe and Asia along separate tracks. A major exception is Kaplan's integration of the impact of the Korean War with the building of NATO and the end of American isolationism. The linkage of events took place at a crucial time, and Kaplan makes clear its impact on the several issues related to the development of NATO. It is reasonable to go one step further and suggest that the interaction of events in Europe and Asia had become part of a single system. A radical change in one part of the system affected all parts of that system. This sort of interaction was continuous and tended to reinforce tension. Thus, the Korean War influenced the development of NATO; in turn, the development of NATO reinforced the move to draw Japan into an American alliance, and became a rough model for SEATO. But, over the long run, the easing of Cold War tensions in Europe rendered illogical the maintenance of a rigid attitude toward Communist China. The East-West system was capable of conducting the heat of conflict as well as the cooling spirit of détente.

Keeping in mind the interaction between events in Europe and Asia, let us return to Kaplan's interesting discussion of the short-run and long-run effects of the Korean War. Whatever the origins of the war, it led to the adoption of a tough political and military policy of confrontation with the Soviet Union in Europe. Since the East-West system was in operation, the firming-up of NATO encouraged the formation of alliances in East Asia which worked to encircle China. This led to a peculiar

COMMENTS

development. In the short run the Korean War had a greater impact on the political structure of Europe than of Asia; the response in East Asia—in terms of shifting political structures and alliances—developed more slowly, but once established was of longer duration.

From this point of view, the long-run impact of the Korean War was greater in Asia than in Europe. But this was because the institutionalized response to the presumed Soviet threat, which first developed in Europe, was applied more wholeheartedly and with less discrimination in East and Southeast Asia. The cost came in the form of a rigid confrontation with the People's Republic of China. Eventually Moscow came to be regarded as our reasonable adversary and Peking, an irrational foe.

As suggested earlier, Washington's reaction to the Korean War helped establish a pattern of response. The pattern was reinforced by the success of a limited war in Korea and the building of strong institutions to oppose Soviet power in Europe. When a renewed challenge to the treaty system occurred in Vietnam, it was all too easy to rely on the tried-and-true response of limited war which had proven itself in Korea. The response to the presumed Chinese challenge in Vietnam was not the inevitable product of the Korean success. It was, however, necessary to maintain the credibility of the alliance system constructed in Western Europe and Eastern Asia. Only in this complex, interrelated, and ultimately problematical sense was Vietnam the "logical" product of the Korean War.

NOTES

1. John Gittings, "Great Power Triangle and Foreign Policy," *China Quarterly* 39 (July-September 1969): 41–54.
2. Robert Simmons, *The Strained Alliance: Peking, P'yongyang, Moscow and the Politics of the Korean Civil War* (New York: Free Press, 1975); and see Simmons's synopsis of his argument, Chapter 5.

Theodore A. Wilson

Professor Kaplan's paper offers a thoughtful and impressively documented analysis of a difficult subject. It may be, indeed, that the diplomatic repercussions of the Korean War present such a sprawling, multidimensional problem that Kaplan has chosen the only practical method of dealing with it: to focus on one issue, NATO, describing the background and effects of the Korean War on strategy in Europe as a "case study." This approach offers several advantages. It permits Kaplan to treat a manageable—though still frustratingly complex—question:

Korea's impact on Europe and, in particular, on NATO. It also allows him to make use of the special knowledge garnered from his service as a historian with the Department of Defense and two decades of continuing interest in NATO's history. As Kaplan himself admits, however, the pitfalls attending any case study, the risk of distorting and confusing cause-and-effect relationships, are also great.

Much has been written about the relationship between the series of momentous events from 1947 to 1953 and the next two decades of American foreign policy. So much has been said about the existence of a "containment consensus" that we must look, at least briefly, at the question whether a consensual position regarding the global role of the United States was indeed established so strongly in this period that it defined American policy until the early 1970s. Kaplan asserts that the Korean War caused the United States to undertake "relentless combat against a conspiratorial enemy whose power seemed enormous, whose appeal was insidious, and whose control was centered in Moscow," and that the pattern set by Korea endured for two decades. One can argue that the Korean War only provided confirmation of a point of view already espoused and, indeed, generally accepted in the United States— or, certainly, by the important makers of policy within the United States. One may argue that the Truman Doctrine, the Czech crisis, the Berlin blockade, or some other event in the years before the outbreak of the Korean War more appropriately marks the change from a preoccupation with the economic and psychological reconstruction of Europe to the determination to build a global and forthrightly military shield against Soviet aggression. It is possible to argue that NATO and the Military Defense Assistance Program were not the logical successors to the Marshall Plan; neither were they, as some historians have claimed, the inevitable products of its failure, nor the result of a calculated exploitation of the Korean conflict to justify global military adventurism by the United States. The change from economic to military instruments, far advanced before Korea, resulted from defects in the premises undergirding the European Recovery Program and the skill of the advocates of a military response at the game of bureaucratic politics.

In fact, the central problem with Kaplan's argument may not be its inflexibility or the purported rigidity of the containment consensus. Rather, as Forrest Pogue and others have suggested, the difficulty may arise from the essential vagueness of policy one encounters once one gets beyond the generalities of NSC-68. Before, during, and after Korea, one is struck by the vagueness of Western policy with regard to the most critical issues: the nature of the Soviet threat, how Europe was to be defended, and what kinds of arrangements—political as well as military—were needed to guarantee the security of Europe and the United States. These are questions that still cannot be answered fully; but we may be confident that they will receive increasing attention in the future, even though they are, in an important sense, judgmental issues.

I wish to discuss briefly certain important effects of the Korean War on relations between the United States and Europe that are not fully dealt with in Kaplan's paper. One is the galloping inflation that hit Europe, resulting largely from Korea and the frantic American drive for rearmament. Inflation prevented the game plan of the European Recovery Program from being carried out completely, for the resources committed to economic recovery were eaten away by the mushrooming costs of raw materials and their diversion to military purposes. It returned Europe for a time to a position of outright dependence on the United States, with significant political and, perhaps, social consequences. Furthermore, decisions regarding the allocation of scarce raw materials and manufactures during the Korean crisis importantly changed the "special relationship" between the United States and Britain, bringing the two English-speaking nations together at the expense of American–Western European relations and virtually ending efforts to revive East-West trade.

Secondly, there arises the question of the Korean War's effects on Europe's progress toward economic and political cooperation. Clearly, the movement toward economic integration and possibly even a political union, embodied in the activities of the Organization for European Economic Cooperation, was halted, largely because NATO asserted its primacy as the supranational organization guiding the destiny of Western Europe. Given the United States government's transfer of priorities and resources to NATO, one should not be surprised that NATO quickly outstripped the OEEC in prestige and power. Again, Korea only compounded a situation already made difficult by the effort to give substance to NATO. Kaplan argues—and it is a legitimate way to assess this period—that much that later came about and that is "good" in Europe today was built on NATO. But one may observe that much that could have been good might have been built on OEEC. The stresses of adjusting OEEC and its ambitions to the military necessities imposed by NATO produced great confusion and undoubtedly retarded the economic and political integration of Europe.

Reference to the costs of the Korean War—whether or not they were avoidable—leads inevitably to the thorny issue of NATO's credibility. Kaplan demonstrates convincingly how powerful was the alarm over the likelihood of a Soviet thrust west. But did this anxiety make inevitable, as Kaplan implies, the quantum jump from what originally had been a statement of principles intended for psychological reassurance to the military and political realities we now associate with NATO? He is perhaps correct, but one should also note the problems that Korea posed for NATO's development. For example, scarce resources became even scarcer. As a result, conflict arose between the Defense Department's insistence that the war in Korea come first and the views of those who gave attention to the maintenance of NATO's supply pipeline and the early reequipment of NATO forces. Surprisingly, Kaplan ignores almost entirely the role of the American nuclear umbrella during the period of the Korean War.

If we conclude that the Soviet Union had plans to exploit the situation in Korea by launching a military invasion of Western Europe, the shift from economic to military responses (which actually had taken place before Korea but was confirmed in June 1950) was justified and absolutely necessary. If, however, one assumes that there was no Russian threat, that the Soviet Union was following a cautious, conservative policy, and that the U.S.S.R. was too weak to engage in military adventures, then one is led into a recital of lost opportunities, of tragic waste, of the full-blown paranoid interpretation of American diplomacy that has become so popular in the last few years. The latter argument may well be invalid but it sets forth an analysis of the Korean War that cannot now be answered with certainty or finality. In any event, the estimates of Soviet capabilities and intentions which dictated the West's decisions in the aftermath of the Korean attack were founded not on what was "true" but rather on what policymakers believed to be the true situation. American and European leaders perceived a direct military threat; they were convinced that the Kremlin had orchestrated the Korean War, and they acted on that belief. As Kaplan rightly emphasizes, we are still wrestling today with the implications of those actions.

Discussion

PROF. NORMAN A. GRAEBNER (chairman): As I listen to Professor Kaplan's presentation and the comments on it, I come to the conclusion that the Korean War, if it did have an enormous effect on the American outlook, did so because it created a level of fear in this nation which had not existed previously. Indeed, by November and December 1950, the fears that swept this country, at least as expressed by American officials, certainly went far beyond anything that Hitler was ever able to generate. For example, in late November Dean Acheson made this statement relative to the Korean War: "All governments which are now free and all responsible citizens of free societies must face with a sense of urgency the capabilities for conquest and destruction in the hands of the rulers of the Soviet Union." A few days later a White House press release commented that, if the attack in Korea were successful, we could expect it to spread through Asia and Europe and endanger our national security and very survival.

This leads to a number of fundamental questions. First, what was the source of that tremendous fear, on what was it based, and what was the evidence that seemed to suggest that the Soviet Union really was the enemy we were facing in Korea? Furthermore, how could a limited war in Korea protect the United States and the world against such perceived dangers? These are the types of questions that historians are now raising about the Korean War. This has nothing to do with specific military decisions which, I think, historians overwhelmingly accept. It simply means that as historians look back at the record, as they examine, in detail, the documents of that period, they detect other problems. Many of those problems were raised by commentators on Kaplan's essay.

AMBASSADOR ERNEST A. GROSS: In respect to the impact of Korea on America's foreign relations, it seems to me some reference should be made to the United Nations itself. Much could be said about the impact of the Korean War and its aftermath and the difficulties we faced in the U.N. in connection with the peacemaking apparatus, the Good Offices Committee of the U.N. and a cease-fire group, and so forth. Remember that those activities at the U.N., unlike those during the conflict in

Vietnam, were televised and that the American people saw, not so much the battlefield horrors as in Vietnam, but the political hassling, the badgering by the Soviet delegation, the futility and frustration of United Nations diplomacy and politics. That represented to the American people a terribly frustrating contrast: American boys were fighting and dying in Korea and this was going on at the U.N. In the context of American attitudes toward the United Nations, it had to be baffling and worrisome to see the initial enthusiasm with regard to the first collective action in history to meet aggression change into the frustration of that mechanism—even as the bloodshed continued and the difficulties of armistice and peacemaking and political building emerged.

I am referring to the period from June 25 right through 1950, particularly after the Soviet representative came back to the Security Council and during the so-called Malik month—August 1950. Speech after speech of his was fully televised, condemning the United States for aggression in Korea and generally attacking our policies and the United Nations as an instrument of U.S. foreign policy. This is what the American people saw, meeting after meeting, and it accounted for literally hundreds of letters a day received at the U.S. mission, very few of which were friendly; most of them were critical of the alleged abuse by us of the U.N. forum.

PROF. ROBERT DALLEK: What is your impression of the impact on the public that this created?

GROSS: I think that a truth emerged. I think that one of the basic fallacies of the attitude toward the United Nations at the outset of the Korean War was that it was a practical proposition that there could be what was called at that time a "preponderance of power" exercised by the United Nations. It was the concept that an aggressor could be bested with force, despite the inability of the Military Staff Committee to agree between the Russians and ourselves about the kind of forces which the military articles of the U.N. Charter contemplated. There was an awakening, and we saw it more and more as the years unfolded. The unified command during the Korean War was far from a farce, it was a genuine state of mind. But on the other hand, it was American-dominated and American-led; there were a disproportionate number of American forces involved in the war; it was an American show. The unified command is important symbolically but that is about all. So, the U.N. ended its hope to become a potential military arm of the international community. I think this was the lesson that Korea taught.

PROF. LAWRENCE S. KAPLAN: I wonder how far we, as historians, can go at this time in making judgments. I was very much aware, as we

DISCUSSION

all are, of the mutual frustrations of the time. The United States—both the government and the public—were impatient over the reluctance of the United Nations to act as we were acting and to see the urgency we saw. On the other hand, it came through at a time when there was a certain distrust of American leadership in many quarters at the U.N.

The lessons of the Korean War for the U.N. seem to me, at this stage, rather ambiguous. In one sense, you could say that the Acheson "Uniting for Peace" resolution, elevating as it did the role of the General Assembly, and the use of a police force, even though it was an American force primarily, may be signs of enhancement of the U.N. As a consequence of the Korean War, the U.N. was more important in the period from 1950 to 1956 than it had been from 1946 to 1950. But I am troubled by the suspicion that all this also confirmed the fears and apprehensions of much of the U.N. membership that the organization was what the Soviet Union claimed it was—an arm of American foreign policy.

GROSS: In de Tocqueville's famous battery of quotations, one has struck me for many years: there are two things a democracy finds extremely difficult; one is to start a war and the other is to stop it. It does seem to me that the United Nations made it easy for the United States to enter the war, really on an overnight decision, a decision that was proper and sound historically. Its wisdom, I think, becomes clear as the years go by. But the United Nations did not help the United States end the war. When one looks back over the two critical aspects—one, the operation of the cease-fire group, and the other, the dilemma posed by North Korean insistence that the North Korean prisoners of war, held in the South, should be forcibly repatriated—we had the greatest difficulty achieving, and then keeping, a consensus in the United Nations on those issues. The Indians and others who were professing great moral stature seemed to us to be perfectly willing to go along with the proposition that in order to end the hostilities, we should agree to the forcible repatriation of thousands of North Korean prisoners of war who were in South Korea and who, we knew, did not want to go back. Here the United Nations mechanisms made it even more difficult for a democracy to end a war.

GOV. W. AVERELL HARRIMAN: I presume Mr. Gross means not only the North Korean prisoners but also the Chinese prisoners.

GROSS: Yes, both.

HARRIMAN: But the Chinese prisoners were by far the majority, and Rhee opened the gates and let them out . . .

GROSS: He let them loose and that ended the dilemma.

THE KOREAN WAR

GEN. MATTHEW B. RIDGWAY: I recall that in 1949, we sent representatives to Sweden to negotiate new rules of land warfare under the Geneva Convention. My own chief of staff from the Caribbean command was our military delegate on that. I think the United States was a signatory to those revised rules, one of which required the return of all prisoners of war.

GROSS: Against their will, General Ridgway?

RIDGWAY: It didn't say. That is a point that might be verified for historical importance.

May I ask one other thing? Governor Harriman, what was the extent of the Soviet Union's responsibility for the North Korean invasion?

HARRIMAN: I can only say I consider the whole enterprise, as far as touching it off, a Stalin enterprise. He had trained the North Korean armies with his military, which went there. There were, of course, some Chinese units that came over, but there were Korean nationalists who had fought in the Red Army and who were brought back and helped train the North Koreans. If you read Mr. Khrushchev's memoirs, he says that Kim consulted Stalin and that Stalin gave him the nod. In my judgment, based on my own personal experiences and information I received at the time, there isn't any question that Red Army officers trained the North Koreans.

GRAEBNER: I think there is no question, Mr. Harriman, about the nature of the North Korean Army and how it was trained and supplied. I think the real issue is whether or not the actual invasion was ordered or prepared for by a Stalin decision rather than by a decision of the North Koreans.

HARRIMAN: Stalin was far more cautious than most people think. He did not want to get involved. Also, during this period we had a monopoly of the nuclear weapons. Consideration of using nuclear weapons in the Korean War was never discussed; I'm glad that General Collins made that clear and I confirm it. But as far as Stalin was concerned, there is no doubt in my mind that his caution was due, among other reasons, to our monopoly of nuclear weapons.

PROF. EDMUND WEHRLE: Governor Harriman, did this cautiousness which you perceive in Stalin exist in 1950?

HARRIMAN: I do not mean cautious in terms of using subversive actions or trying to develop situations. I am talking about military action which might lead to a confrontation with the United States. That's the area of caution I am talking about.

DISCUSSION

WEHRLE: We have Glenn Paige's book on the Korean War decision—a very rich, detailed description of the conversations among Mr. Truman and his advisers in late June 1950. The question must be asked: Why was there such apprehension that the Korean attack might signal an attack in Europe and against Germany? Why was there this fear that there might be war, or warlike acts, in other places?

HARRIMAN: There was a great deal of evidence of Stalin's aggression. The first shock was the Czech take-over; the second shock—even greater—was the blockade of Berlin. So there was ample evidence of Stalin's desire to expand his influence.

RIDGWAY: I think you might also recall the difference between capabilities and intentions. There is no question of the absolute incapability of the Western European nations to stop a Russian overland advance had one been initiated at that time.

WEHRLE: Governor Harriman, may I pursue a further point on the question of the Russian culpability at the outset of the Korean War. What I am doing is adding speculation on speculation, but I can't resist the temptation. It has been clearly supported that we had to be very careful of our ally, Syngman Rhee; he had sufficient military force himself to go north over the line. He was a difficulty; he was a concern. Well, isn't it a reasonable conjecture that Stalin may have had difficulty with the North Koreans as well? They were, perhaps, equally nationalistic, equally desirous to reunite Korea. I am suggesting here the possibility of politics in North Korea itself as the explosive factor.

HARRIMAN: Of course, the only documented evidence is in Khrushchev's memoirs, in which he says that Kim came to consult Stalin before he did it. Now, if Stalin had said no, he could have withheld spare parts or withheld additional ammunition; and he could have blocked the whole thing if he had wanted to. As far as I am concerned, Stalin used that aggressive vigor which North Koreans have for the unification of their country to his advantage—but he could have stopped it.

Let me tell you that I went to see Tito in 1951, with a military group, in order to find out from him what he needed. He outlined his needs and they seemed to me quite limited. He was developing a force that seemed to be so limited that it would not be able to deal with the Red Army. He said he was preparing for attack by the satellites, particularly Rumania and Bulgaria, and I said: "Well, what will you do when the Red Army comes in, will you go to the mountains?"

He said, "No, we're going to fight on the plains, I'll never go to the mountains again. But I can assure you that Stalin will never send the Red Army outside of the first tier of countries."

So, Tito was not concerned in any way that the Red Army would come in. He was bending every effort to be strong enough to resist attack from the satellites. Tito believed that Stalin would use the satellites but that he would not get Russia itself directly involved. Action on the part of the satellites, however, would be inspired by Russia because, obviously, Bulgaria and Rumania had no aggressive intentions against Yugoslavia.

GRAEBNER: I think this indicates again the problem we have in coming to grips with the Soviet problem. Here is evidence that the Soviet Union was not a direct military threat. Certainly Tito did not regard it as such.

HARRIMAN: No, I do not now think that Russia was a military threat. But the blockade of Berlin was a fairly reckless action, as far as we were concerned, and we could not tell what Stalin intended. I think General Collins or General Ridgway could give you further views on how the Pentagon viewed the situation. But the Russian capabilities, at that time, were so great compared to ours that the implication was quite obvious. That is correct, isn't it, General Ridgway?

RIDGWAY: Yes, sir. I think General Collins would agree that you cannot overstress the importance of distinguishing between capabilities and intentions. What the intentions of the Soviet Union were, nobody could be sure; what their capabilities were, based on early intelligence, we knew pretty well.

HARRIMAN: I am utterly convinced that Stalin decided not to cooperate with the United States and the Western allies in the postwar world—a course of action which was open to him. He told me when I saw him in October 1945 that they had decided to pursue an isolationist policy. I don't have any doubt that one of the reasons was that the hunting looked too good in the West. You had strong Communist parties in Italy and in France, and the conditions in Western Europe were in such a state economically that, had it not been for interim aid first and then the Marshall plan, the Communists would have taken over Italy, possibly France, and the whole of Europe would have been—I used to say "Finlandized" but the Finns don't like that so I don't use it any more.

I am satisfied in my own mind that Stalin felt that the Communist parties in the West were ready to take over—of course, the Communist parties in these countries always exaggerated their strength. This was true of Poland and true of Rumania. I am satisfied that one of the

DISCUSSION

reasons why Stalin was so tough to deal with over Poland was that the Polish Communists told him that the Red Army would be accepted as a liberation force. I think he was awfully hurt when he found out they were seen as a new invading army and that the Communists were not nearly as strong as he had expected. Don't forget that he permitted a vote to be taken in Hungary and the Communist party only got some 17 percent of the vote. I think that in the early days Stalin had much greater expectations of the influence of the Communist parties, certainly in Western Europe. He was relying on that rather than the Red Army to expand his power.

AMBASSADOR JOHN J. MUCCIO: The Scammon Report, later published as "a case history in Communist control," clearly calls attention to the role the North Koreans who were Russian citizens played in setting up the government, the army, and the whole apparatus in North Korea. That has a very important bearing on the culpability of Moscow.

When the Japanese went into Korea, the Koreans who could not live with the Japanese gradually moved into Manchuria. Later, when the Japanese moved into Manchuria, a lot of these Koreans ended up in the Russian Maritime Provinces. Then, in 1947, the Russians picked up all these Koreans living in the Maritime Provinces and took them down to Kazakhstan. Thence came the pilots and the tank crews that later appeared in Korea; the whole government apparatus in North Korea was directed by these Koreans who had become Russianized.

HARRIMAN: And had fought in the Red Army.

MUCCIO: Yes. And that puts the culpability of the organization and the planning in the North mainly in the hands of those Russians of Korean ethnic origin.

HARRIMAN: That was my explanation, too.

AMBASSADOR LUCIUS D. BATTLE: Before we go on with this very interesting discussion of Russian intentions, I would like to return to a theme Professor Graebner advanced and a question he raised, that is, the public attitude in this country—a subject I think has been somewhat neglected in our discussion. I believe that ultimately foreign policy depends on the acceptance of that policy by the people. I think there are some rather interesting aspects of Korea here that have been neglected.

I think the tendency today is to believe that Korea was a very unpopular war. This was not at all true in the beginning. There was support from very diverse points of view in the country: there was the right-wing pressure to do something; the China lobby wanted attention

103

focused on China; those who wanted to see an end to isolationism and were looking for a new era of international involvement put great hope in the U.N. and in the collective security aspects of the Korean intervention. As long as everything went well everyone loved it. It was only when things began to fall apart and after the move to the Yalu that the defections began. Statements made during the early part of the war— say, the week of June 25 to the first of July—and statements made in December were notably different.

John Foster Dulles is one example of this shift I have particularly in mind. I had a talk with him right after he returned to this country, and he said he was speechless in admiration of what had been done. He felt that the administration had made the United Nations a living, vital force in the world, and he strongly applauded the whole aspect of collective security. The week of December 2, when things were going sour, he said that he thought it had been a mistake all along; he never would have put manpower in there; and the most he would have ever given was air cover. Now, he was simply reflecting what seemed to be the mood of the country at the moment. This was typical of many other people who praised at one point and condemned at another. Largely this was because we were, as a society, simply not accustomed to failure.

GRAEBNER: And yet those who did not want to use the ground forces were those who demanded victory in the war.

BATTLE: Precisely, and one of the real conflicts here is that in order to get appropriations, in order to get congressional support, there has to be a threat. But if you build up that threat too far, it inhibits your ability to limit the war. If you take it too far, you increase the pressure for action: let's win and do it quickly.

GEN. J. LAWTON COLLINS: One of the points that I find lacking in our discussion of the effects of the Korean War is what it did to the American people's confidence in the United Nations as a peacekeeping organization. Remember that when we went into NATO it was the first time we had signed an agreement committing the United States, subject to congressional approval, in broad terms to taking action in the event of naked aggression. This was the first time we ever signed any such agreement. Now, in the Korean War, for the first time, we had the support of the United Nations. We appealed to the United Nations; the United Nations condemned the North Korean attack and called on the others to assist in correcting this situation.

As Mr. Battle has said, everybody was enthusiastic about it at the beginning. It was later, after we reached a stalemate, that people began to have their doubts. I would say that one of the things needing investi-

DISCUSSION

gation is: What was the impact of the Korean War on the future of the United Nations as a peacekeeping organization?

GRAEBNER: That was, I believe, a rather unique situation: the United States committed itself to fight and then, having made that decision, asked for support in the U.N. and got it. But had the United States not made the decision, had there not been the Blair House meeting, would the collective security have been forthcoming? It certainly was not in Vietnam. So I have an idea that we are dealing here with something that worked. There certainly was a principle of collective security applied in Korea, but under unique circumstances which have never been repeated.

COLLINS: And never will be again, in my judgment.

MUCCIO: I might suggest that a case study be made of the relative advantages and disadvantages to the United States of that body's being involved in Korea, the lack of such involvement in Indochina, and the way the Congo situation was handled in July 1960. I think this is a study that should be undertaken.

HARRIMAN: The fact that President Truman did not get congressional approval has not been discussed so far. I want to say that when I got back from Paris, among the things I recommended to the president was that he get a Joint Resolution from Congress—an action which would have tied the hands of a great many people. (Of course, I think that I did not know at that time who was against it.) Mr. Truman said he had considered such a move; if he got a Joint Resolution it would tie the hands of a successor. He was always thinking about his responsibility to the presidency and what effects his actions would have on the office. I did not realize until later that Dean Acheson had opposed going to Congress. Dean Acheson did such a brilliant job in getting the United Nations together that I hate to be critical of him, but the effect of this on future presidents is something that, perhaps, you may want to dwell on.

BATTLE: I talked with Dean Acheson about this at the time, and I felt very strongly that it would be very easy to get a Joint Resolution. I argued that we ought to do it and get all the congressional support we could muster. He thought it would be a mistake, and I presume it was he who advised the president that a Joint Resolution would tie the hands of future presidents. I think Acheson also made the point that if Congress debated a Joint Resolution, it might challenge what the president had done without the Joint Resolution. It is interesting to speculate what might have happened on such a Joint Resolution and what later happened on the Tonkin Gulf Resolution.

HARRIMAN: Of course, President Truman would have gotten such overwhelming support that it would have silenced some of those who later were critical.

BATTLE: The Tonkin Gulf Resolution did not silence those who voted for it.

HARRIMAN: But that was a different situation and related to a different subject. In Korea, a Joint Resolution would have been for the specific action in connection with the attack. The Tonkin Gulf Resolution was only in connection with aggressive action on a naval ship off the coast. It was not dealt with as specifically as a Joint Resolution on Korea would have been.

KAPLAN: Governor Harriman, had there been a congressional resolution in June, would it have removed the heat from the debate of January and February 1951 over the assignment of troops to Europe? Could you make that connection?

HARRIMAN: It would be speculation. I don't think I can contribute anything to that.

PROF. RICHARD S. KIRKENDALL: Mr. Harriman and Mr. Battle, would you pin down more precisely just when your conversations took place on the advisability of a Joint Resolution?

HARRIMAN: That took place early in July.

BATTLE: Yes, I would have said it was the latter part of the first week when the subject first came up. There were two or three discussions that I happened to participate in. I would have said one was during the first week and then later, I would think early in July, the possibility came up again and was ruled out. I do not recall that it ever came up after that. Probably later you could not have gotten it anyway.

DALLEK: Can you speculate at all as to why a Joint Resolution was thought unnecessary?

HARRIMAN: President Truman had an extraordinarily deep sense of responsibility for protecting the power and authority of the president of the United States under the Constitution against all comers, including Congress. He said to me, "We cannot do that because if I do it will tie the hands of a successor president."

BATTLE: That really was the main point. There was a collateral point, a relatively minor one: the president had done what he did; why open up the question of whether he should have done it. It had been

DISCUSSION

accepted; everyone had overwhelmingly supported it; therefore, there was no problem—and who knew what was ahead.

HARRIMAN: May I say, I disagreed and I think Battle did. I thought it was a mistake and so did many others at that time. But the president's inclination to protect the office—not to allow anything or anybody to weaken the authority of the president of the United States—that was something to which President Truman paid a great deal of attention.

PROF. ALONZO L. HAMBY: It seems to me that one very important question we have not given much thought to—perhaps the most favorable part of the Korean decision in the long run—was the decision to neutralize the Formosa Straits. I wonder if we might ask some of the distinguished participants what the rationale was for that particular decision. Was it essentially a political or a military decision?

HARRIMAN: I can answer to some extent, and it relates to my mission to General MacArthur. One of the two things the president asked me to do was to make it plain that he wanted MacArthur to leave Chiang Kai-shek alone; he did not want to have Chiang get into a war with mainland China. He did not want to encourage Chiang in any way.

Put yourself back to that period. Chiang was definitely anxious to return; he felt that the regime on the mainland was weak; and he definitely believed he could get ashore. General MacArthur was all for encouraging him to do so and was not concerned with the risks involved. President Truman clearly—and consistently throughout—had no desire to get into a conflict with the Chinese. The Formosa Straits decision was a political act, in my judgment, not a military act.

HAMBY: Then it was mainly to reassure Mao. But a number of historians have suggested it had precisely the opposite effect, that Mao took it as an effort to protect Chiang rather than vice versa. Were there efforts made to convey this intention to the Red Chinese through diplomatic channels of one sort or the other?

HARRIMAN: I have no idea. I don't think so.

COLLINS: I would challenge one of the basic assumptions in Professor Hamby's question: that is, whether this was purely a military decision or purely a political decision. There is no such decision ever made.

HARRIMAN: I think that it started as a political decision to affect the military situation.

COLLINS: I would agree with that. I am sure the Joint Chiefs were

107

Gens. Omar Bradley and J. Lawton Collins arrive for a briefing—December 8, 1950.

consulted but I don't remember that we ever took a position on this. But, second-guessing a little bit now and in retrospect, we certainly did not want to get involved. We were involved up to the limit of our capacity in Korea. We did not want to get involved militarily in expanding our responsibilities with respect to China. Isn't that right, Matt?

DISCUSSION

RIDGWAY: Absolutely right.

COLLINS: We felt that any encouragement of Chiang to go back to the mainland of China, from which he had already been driven, would inevitably have produced a call on us to assist him—and we did not have the capability.

RIDGWAY: We had neither the tactical capability nor the logistical means, all of which we needed for our own uses in Korea.

COLLINS: Furthermore, I was convinced that Chiang and his Kuomintang forces had already been licked once and that they were no better having moved to Taiwan.

HARRIMAN: May I say that the view of the Joint Chiefs, which I as a layman certainly shared, was not shared by General MacArthur.

PROF. ROBERT GRIFFITH: There is a question that I would like to advance: To what extent did what happened in Korea influence what has happened in Vietnam?

GRAEBNER: Let me amplify on that. Whether you run in a straight line from Korea to Vietnam is certainly very doubtful. Each administration had the power to alter if not reverse the trend—if there was one—and none of them chose to do so. But what we do get out of the Korean War is a concept of a global threat that had not really appeared before in American official statements.

Let me give you one statement from John Foster Dulles, this from the spring of 1951. Mr. Dulles observed that the Russians took control of China by building the Communist party in China, and through it they were ruling the country. Then he goes on to say: "By the test of conception, birth, nurture, and obedience the Mao Tse-tung regime is a creature of the Moscow Politburo and it is on behalf of Moscow, not China, that it is destroying the friendship of the Chinese people toward the United States."

Now, that is a very typical statement coming out of the State Department *Bulletin* during 1950 and 1951. This is the kind of statement that is of tremendous concern to historians because it helped lay the intellectual and emotional foundations for an enormous involvement thereafter. It does not necessarily mean a straight-line involvement, but it does mean the foundations were laid during Korea for additional involvements.

I am simply trying to reinforce with this statement the question that has been asked. And I hope that before we end we can obtain some comment from our distinguished guests.

HARRIMAN: I would rather have General Collins answer first. He was in Vietnam and he recommended against action, as I recall it, in 1954.

All I can say is that Stalin agreed in the Stalin-Soong agreement to support Chiang Kai-shek and his government as the government of China; the protocol said "militarily, economically, politically, and morally"—those four words were used. He thought the Chinese Communists were too weak. Several times when I talked to him he said they were not very close to Mao Tse-tung. You remember in the twenties Mao Tse-tung was almost thrown out of the Communist party because he said in China, the Communist party must be based on the peasant and not on the urban masses as was the philosophy of Marxism-Leninism.

Stalin himself, up to and including August 1945, spoke of the very limited access he had to Mao. I asked him why he was supporting Chiang, and he said that Chiang was the only force that could unify China and for at least twenty years the Chinese would need outside help—industrial help—which would have to come from the West, which Russia could not give them.

Every evidence was that Mao Tse-tung was an independent agent as far as Stalin was concerned—that is, while I was in Moscow. Later on the evidence points in other ways, but the assumption that Stalin dominated the moves in China just has no basis. It was true very largely in other parts of the world but not in China.

GRAEBNER: At that same public meeting in New York at which Mr. Dulles made that statement, Dean Rusk, who was then assistant secretary for far eastern affairs, said: "The Peiping regime may be a colonial Russian government—a Slavic Manchukuo on a larger scale. It is not the government of China. It does not pass the first test. It is not Chinese."

HARRIMAN: Dean Rusk was not a Russian expert.

GRAEBNER: I think what is disturbing, Mr. Harriman, is that those statements were made by top officials of the United States government. These men made such statements repeatedly throughout those years, and yet these are views which you and Dean Acheson did not share. One wonders how statements like this could have been made . . .

HARRIMAN: I agree with you that this was the impression created by those who spoke out on the question. Those who disagreed, either their voices did not carry or they did not speak.

GRAEBNER: As a matter of fact, in his defense of American policy in the MacArthur hearings, Dean Acheson said precisely the opposite of all these things. Nevertheless, the contradiction does cause historians to

DISCUSSION

wonder about the policies of an administration which permits its top officials to state views so utterly opposed to one another.

BATTLE: You have to remember the rather odd position John Foster Dulles was in at that period. He was not leashed, shall we say. He was speaking part of the time on behalf of himself and what he thought to be his future, and, on occasion, he was speaking officially, especially with respect to those things he was working on during most of the period—largely, but not exclusively, the Japanese peace treaty. He tried to make this distinction later and claimed he had only been involved in that treaty, but that was not true. He was capable of saying a lot of things with which the top level of the government did not agree.

I think this, in part, answers the question that was raised. Professor Graebner, you say the question of the direct line between Korea and Vietnam is doubtful. But there is a line, in my judgment, between the charge of "losing" China and our entry into Korea and the charge of "losing" China and our entry into Vietnam. I think this is part of the political climate we are talking about. I think that the concern on the domestic political side had a great deal to do with our presence in Vietnam, much greater than in Korea.

4

The Korean War
and American Society

John Edward Wiltz

In the week before the news flashed around the world that Communist regiments had crashed across the 38th Parallel in Korea nothing seemed more remote from the minds of the people of the United States than the prospect that within a fortnight tens of thousands of their youthful countrymen might be committed to bloody combat on a rugged peninsula in East Asia. If brewers were worried about a decline in the consumption of beer, the national economy in the week of June 18–25, 1950, was nearing the end of its most prosperous six-month period since the end of the Second World War. Indeed, consumers were buying so many automobiles and television sets—largely on credit, a source of concern to Edwin G. Nourse, the former chairman of the Council of Economic Advisers—that the food and clothing industries were preparing a campaign to lure people away from auto and TV showrooms by reducing prices. Thomas E. Dewey announced that he would not run for a third term as governor of New York (a decision he would reverse less than three months later); Sen. Joseph R. McCarthy of Wisconsin sought to explain a payment of $10,000 received from a prefabricated housing manufacturer for an article on housing he had written in 1948 while serving as vice chairman of the Joint Congressional Committee on Housing. At the Pentagon, meanwhile, army leaders were fretting that the new "balanced forces" conception would result in a larger navy and air force and that Europeans would be expected to provide most of the ground forces to meet military requirements of the North Atlantic Treaty Organization.

For the thirty-third president of the republic the week before the

Communist onslaught in Korea was most satisfying. Beneath a headline proclaiming, "The Sun Shines on Harry Again," *Newsweek* exuded: "Just in case there was anyone who had forgotten November 1948, Harry S. Truman proved anew last week that it's always too early to count him out. No matter how bad a beating he's taking, he keeps coming back for more, boring in. And he doesn't seem to care how many of the early rounds he loses. In politics it's the last one that counts." Overcoming the conservative coalition of northern Republicans and southern Democrats on Capitol Hill, the president had secured an extension of rent controls and a displaced persons act, making it possible for additional refugees from communism to enter the country, and he seemed on the verge of winning passage of new social security legislation increasing benefits. Equally comforting, a grand jury in New York, expected to assail the administration's handling of the celebrated *Amerasia* case (involving stolen diplomatic documents), cleared the government of charges that it had bungled the investigation.

Elsewhere on the national scene, fifty-one-year-old Gloria Swanson continued to move about the country as an advance agent for her much-publicized "comeback" film, *Sunset Boulevard,* and the Cole Brothers Circus, featuring William Boyd (better known to legions of movie fans as Hopalong Cassidy), was preparing for a five-day appearance at Yankee Stadium. Of larger moment, in the view of many Americans, was a survey released by the *Christian Herald* disclosing that church membership had soared to an all-time high—81,862,328—and that 54 percent of the national populace belonged to churches compared with 20 percent in 1880 and 35 percent in 1900. Finally, *Argosy* magazine reported the results of a poll in which editors of fifty-one of America's largest newspapers were asked to enumerate the types of stories their readers would most like to encounter in their daily papers. News that the Stalinist dictatorship had collapsed and that war had been permanently abolished, so the editors surmised, were the stories that would most gladden Americans. After that, they thought, Americans would like most to read that scientists had found a cure for cancer, that Jesus of Nazareth had returned to earth, and that science had proved the existence of life after death.

"The news hit the United States like lightning out of a clear sky." So went one report of the initial response of Americans when, on Sunday afternoon, June 25, 1950—in much the same way as they had done on a epochal Sunday afternoon eight-and-a-half years before—broadcasters interrupted regular programs to report the first fragmentary dispatches disclosing that the army of Communist North Korea had invaded South Korea. For tens of millions of Americans whose memories reached back over the previous two decades the dispatches brought forth visions of doomsday. Clearly the Soviets, who, in the view of most of the people of the United States (70 percent according to a Gallup poll taken six months before), were conniving to become "the ruling power of the world," were behind the North Korean attack. Just as the Japanese and the Italians and the Germans had begun their play for world conquest during the 1930s by armed aggression in Manchuria and Ethiopia and Czechoslovakia, so the Soviets were making their play in Korea. And just as the failure of America and the Western European democracies to intervene against initial acts of aggression by the Japanese, Italians, and Germans had encouraged further acts which eventually produced World War II, so a failure of the "free world" to intervene against Soviet aggression in Korea would encourage the Kremlin to new aggressive acts, and the outcome, inevitably, would be World War III.

In view of such reasoning most of the citizenry grimly approved when President Truman, enjoying a quiet weekend in Independence, rushed back to Washington and over the next few days committed American air and naval units and then army troops to combat in Korea. The columnists Joseph and Stewart Alsop seemed to catch the popular mood when they wrote: "The whole momentous meaning of President Truman's decision to meet force with force in Korea can only be grasped in the light of what would surely have happened if he had decided otherwise. For there can be no doubt that the aggression in Korea was planned as only the first of a whole series of demonstrations of Russian strength and Western weakness, designed to lead to the crumbling of the Western will to resist." Beneath a headline announcing, "Uncle Sam Takes Role as World Cop"—a headline that in the aftermath of Vietnam has the ring of another century—*Newsweek* proclaimed: "Never before had the United States risked so much in defense of freedom. Never had the American people seemed so firmly united in their approval of an audacious national policy. Never had the nation's prestige risen so high in the part of the world still free to admire courageous knight errantry." About the only discordant notes came from Sen. Robert A. Taft of Ohio, the *Chicago Daily Tribune*, and members and supporters of the American Communist party. Taft complained that Truman had violated the Constitution by sending American forces into combat without consent of Congress; the *Tribune* trumpeted the charge that the Communist aggression in Korea was an inevitable consequence of a decade of woolly-headed and even treasonous appeasement of the Soviets by Democratic leaders in Washington; and at a rally in Madison Square Garden in New York some nine thousand Communist party members and friends demanded "hands off Korea."

THE WAR AND AMERICAN SOCIETY

The broadsides of Taft, the *Tribune*, and domestic Communists stirred hardly a ripple of interest in the United States during those hot days following the commitment of American forces in Korea. The republic was caught up in a crisis variously called a war, a conflict, and a police action; in the view of 57 percent of the national populace, so a Gallup poll revealed, the United States was engaged in the opening round of World War III. In such circumstances a patriotic citizen rallied around the flag—and also looked out for himself.

If they remembered that appeasement of aggressors during the 1930s had begot the Second World War, Americans of 1950 likewise recalled that the United States entry into the global conflict in late 1941 had begot shortages of many food items and manufactured goods and that their favorite machine, the automobile, had become unobtainable. Fearing that a new period of shortages might be at hand, Americans went on a veritable buying orgy in the aftermath of President Truman's decision to intervene. A special object of their attention was sugar, and across the entire republic sales skyrocketed. A New York housewife who had placed two large orders for sugar in a week explained, "I'm trying to get some before the hoarders buy it all," and in Plainfield, New Jersey, shoppers snatched up six tons of sugar from a single grocery store in four hours. Shortening and canned goods, soaps and cleaning agents also disappeared from grocery shelves. Scare buyers meanwhile were zeroing in on furniture, bedding, linens, towels, deep freezes, television sets, refrigerators, tires, nylon hosiery, and razor blades; inevitably, scores of thousands of Americans made their way to automobile dealers. So ravenous was the national appetite for cars, both new and used, that before long there appeared a "gray market" in which dealers agreed to make sales only when customers anted up "bonuses" ranging from $200 to $800. Said a dealer in Chicago, "People need cars. They got the money and we got the cars. What would you do?" Not everyone endorsed the easy materialism of the Chicago auto dealer, and several department stores took out full-page advertisements in newspapers to appeal to customers to refrain from scare buying. Macy's in New York moralized: "Every decent American should look on hoarding with revulsion! It always plays squarely into the hands of our enemies." A short distance away, in Brooklyn, Abraham & Strauss urged: "Don't spend . . . in any way you'd be ashamed to have a GI in Korea hear about." But it was to little avail. Only when fears of an expanded war diminished and hoarders found themselves short of money did the buying binge of 1950 run out of steam.

While scare buyers were making their own special preparations against the possibility that the affair in Korea might escalate into a global crisis, the federal government in Washington was making preparations of a different sort. Foremost, it was setting in motion a dramatic expansion of the national defense establishment.

Over the past two years, prodded by the economy-minded secretary of defense, Louis A. Johnson, Congress had accepted the proposition of reduced expenditures for the armed forces and indeed had voted only $14 billion for national defense for fiscal 1951 (commencing July 1, 1950). As a consequence the army had only 596,000 men at the outbreak of the conflict in Korea, about 20 percent of whom were assigned to housekeeping duties previously performed by civilian employees who had been dismissed as a result of the economy drive. Like the army, the navy and air force had diminished in strength and efficiency. Few people, save military and naval chieftains, had complained about the weakened state of the defense establishment before the commitment of American forces to Korea; but it became apparent in the aftermath of that commitment that the United States was not even remotely prepared to face up to the challenge of combat in East Asia, meet occupation responsibilities in Japan and Germany, and counter the Soviets if hostilities in Korea enlarged into a global confrontation. The outcome was inevitable. Critics on Capitol Hill and in the press attacked Secretary Johnson for his part in shrinking the defense establishment (and after a few weeks, in September 1950, the Truman administration felt compelled to secure his resignation). More important, the White House and Congress, toiling in such harmony that one observer was prompted to write, "Harry never had it so good," set about to gird the republic to meet the crisis in Korea and a larger and infinitely more ominous crisis should that conflict get out of hand.

The first action came in the last days of June 1950, at the same time that American air and naval forces were moving into the Korean combat zone. Because the statutory expiration date (June 14, 1950) of the Selective Service Act had already passed, Congress—unanimously in the Senate and with only four dissenting votes in the House of Representatives—extended selective service for a year. Congress also gave the president something he had not requested: the authority to call to active duty, with or without their consent, units or individuals of the National Guard and other reserve components. Results were almost immediate. Although they had summoned no young men to military service for a year and a half, the 3,700 local draft boards had continued to register men between the ages of eighteen and twenty-five; on July 10, when the Defense Department issued a call for 20,000 men (subsequently raised to 50,000) to be inducted into the army in September, they were ready to act. By September 30 the draft boards had delivered the 50,000 men—

116

with about 930 to spare—and would deliver another 50,000 in October and 70,000 in November. Also receiving orders to report to active duty were reservists and National Guardsmen. In July 1950 the Marine Corps recalled 47,000 officers and men of its organized ground reserve; the navy readied about 9,000 officers and 30,000 enlisted men in its air reserve and several thousand surface reservists; and the army ordered engineering, ordnance, maintenance, and medical units of the National Guard to report to active duty and set about federalizing four infantry divisions of the Guard. From the Defense Department came an announcement of plans to hire 236,978 civilians.

According to a Gallup poll taken in late August 1950, while U.N. forces in Korea still were contained inside the Pusan perimeter, two-thirds of the citizens believed the United States had not erred in projecting itself into the Korean conflict. Few young men, however, felt the slightest enthusiasm for military or naval service. Or as Maj. Gen. Lewis B. Hershey, director of the draft, put it, "Everyone wants out; no one wants in." Reservists and National Guardsmen who received orders to report to active duty and had served in World War II, most of whom now were husbands and fathers, complained it was unfair that they should be summoned in advance of younger men who never had answered a call to the national colors. As for young men who were eligible for the draft, they maneuvered as best they could. Many joined National Guard and army reserve units in the hope that their units would not be ordered into active service; others made sudden decisions to enroll in colleges or universities. Because most draft boards would not take men out of school, they could thus gain security from the draft at least until the following spring, by which time they hoped the police action in Korea would be over.

In July 1950, as the rusty selective service mechanism was beginning to turn anew and reservists were packing duffel bags, President Truman was considering plans for further building up the country's armed forces and accelerating military assistance to America's allies, partially mobilizing the civilian economy, and managing the domestic dislocations that inevitably would result from the sudden shifting of national gears. At length, on the afternoon of July 19, while GI's in Korea were in retreat around the town of Taejon, clerks read his proposals to the House and Senate; that evening in a national radio and television address Truman explained them to the rest of his countrymen. The proposals were breathtaking. The president requested an emergency appropriation of $10 billion for the national defense establishment and removal of the statutory limit of 2,005,882 on the manpower of the armed forces; increased military assistance to the NATO allies and "certain other free nations whose security is vital to our own"; authority to establish priorities and allocations to prevent hoarding and nonessential use of critical materials; review of government programs to eliminate unnecessary use of services and materials needed for defense; curbs on consumer credit for commodity-market speculation; increased taxes to pay the defense bill and restrict inflation; authority to impose price controls and rationing should inflation seem to be getting out of hand; and authority to make federal loans and guarantees when needed to stimulate military production and stockpile strategic materials.

The response to his proposals on Capitol Hill must have startled the man in the Oval Office. Or perhaps they prompted a sly grin. In any event, Republicans as well as Democrats stood and cheered when the clerks completed the reading of his message. In the words of one observer, "Republicans were tripping over Democrats in their eagerness to give President Truman what he thought he needed to win in Korea and prepare for the next Korea, whenever or wherever it might turn out to be." Action, accordingly, came swiftly. Before the sun went down on July 19 the House had voted unanimously—save for the dissenting vote of Vito Marcantonio of New York—to approve a measure passed a short time before by the Senate to grant an additional $1.2 billion in military assistance to America's allies and friends. A few days later came overwhelming approval of legislation suspending the restriction on the manpower of the armed forces; and in early September the president signed the Defense Production Act, a complex law giving the chief executive authority to impose rationing and credit restrictions, make allocations, grant production loans, and establish priorities, and giving him standby authority to control prices and wages. A fortnight later Truman put his signature to the Revenue Act of 1950 which was intended to provide an additional $4.7 billion during the current fiscal year by raising corporate and personal income tax rates and some excise tax rates. Lastly, he signed legislation providing a supplemental appropriation of $11 billion for the armed forces.

The words and directives of the president and acts of Congress triggered a phenomenon which the news media called mobilization. Partial mobilization would have been a more precise term. Semantics aside, the United States was girding itself to meet the challenge in Korea —and a much larger challenge if events came to that. What if the conflict in East Asia should move to an early end? It would make no difference. Or so insisted leaders in Washington. The United States, they emphasized, was committed to a permanent build-up of its armed forces to a level of 3.2 million men and women. Never again would the country drop its guard as it had in the time before Korea. Americans meant business, and the Soviets and their Communist stooges had better understand that point.

That Americans indeed meant business was manifest. As draftees, reservists, and National Guardsmen were beginning to stream to military installations and naval bases, a menacing array of fighter planes, warships, and tanks left over from World War II were emerging from "mothballs" and being outfitted for combat. Hardly a day passed that the daily press did not report another large order for military hardware or supplies placed by the Defense Department: an undisclosed number of 3,500-horsepower engines for B-36 bombers with the Ford Motor Company; $1.14 million of spark plugs with the AC Spark Plug Division of General Motors; shoes and boots for the army worth $1.13 million with the J. F. McIlwain Company. The Pentagon also placed countless orders for such pedestrian items as sandbags, catsup, adhesive tape, garbage cans, repair parts for dishwashers, and kits for seawater distillation. Meanwhile an administrative apparatus for the mobilization program began to take shape. The forty-nine-year-old head of the National Security Resources Board, W. Stuart Symington, became the general overseer of the economic aspects of mobilization. The National Production Authority, under the chairmanship of William H. Harrison of International Telephone and Telegraph, was set up to fix priorities and allocations. To keep a lid on wages and prices, the president issued an executive order establishing the Economic Stabilization Agency and appointed Alan Valentine, former president of the University of Rochester, to be its head. Within the ESA were two subsidiary agencies, the Wage Stabilization Board and the Price Stabilization Board, headed respectively by Cyrus S. Ching, director of the Federal Mediation and Conciliation Service, and (after a protracted search) Michael V. DiSalle, the portly mayor of Toledo. That the national muscle-flexing would at once energize and jar the economy of the United States was inevitable.

Generating the first impulses in the economy in the aftermath of hostilities in Korea was the aforementioned wave of scare buying—not only by anxious housewives and motorists but also by manufacturers and processors who envisioned shortages of the materials required to sustain their operations. The outcome? Inflation. Largely as a consequence of scare buying, prices began to bound upward almost within hours of President Truman's issuance of the orders sending American combat units to Korea. In the first month of the Korean conflict the price of sugar advanced 5 percent; coffee, 9 percent; cocoa, 10 percent; print cloths, 18 percent; tin, 26 percent; and rubber, 27 percent.

As for the president, he was reluctant to impose an elaborate system of controls to restrict inflation. As outlined in his Midyear Economic

Report to Congress in early August 1950 (prepared in the main by the Council of Economic Advisers, headed by the veteran New Dealer, Leon Keyserling), Truman would rely on monetary and credit controls which would curtail consumer credit and loans for housing and commodity speculation. Such measures presumably would slow the demand for goods and services and keep prices in line, while avoiding the aggravations and confusion resulting from price ceilings and rationing. The president also made it clear that he would employ the technique which Americans of subsequent decades would come to know as "jawboning." To no avail. Government officials reported at the end of September that prices of twenty-eight basic commodities had gone up 25 percent since the outbreak of hostilities in Korea, and it was evident that the cost-of-living index soon would surpass the record set in 1948. From the Pentagon, meanwhile, came laments that the rampaging inflation was undercutting the mobilization program—a point driven home when Under Secretary of the Air Force John A. McCone startled a congressional committee by asserting that soaring prices would cost the air force the equivalent of 750 jet fighter planes in the present fiscal year.

The upward spiral of prices during the summer and autumn of 1950 brought few wails from the paneled board rooms of the country's giant corporations. Big business seldom had had it so good. Operating at peak capacity, the steel industry could not keep up with orders. Neither could producers of the chemical benzene, a necessary ingredient in such diverse commodities as synthetic rubber, aviation gasoline, nylon, DDT, dyes, and plastics. Railroads could not provide enough freight cars to meet the demands of anguished shippers. Because of scare buying Kaiser-Frazer set about to increase its daily output of automobiles from 1,200 units to 1,600, while Culligan Zeolite successfully promoted its water-softening equipment as a means of reducing the consumption of such shortage-threatened items as soaps and fats.

The outcome of such frenetic activity? Near-record profits for business. Despite increased taxes, the profits of 500 major corporations in the third quarter of 1950 went up an average of 50 percent over the corresponding period of 1949. Among those registering the most impressive gains were steel manufacturers. When figures for the entire year 1950 were tabulated, they disclosed that United States Steel had realized its largest earnings since 1917; Bethlehem Steel had enjoyed its most profitable year ever. For only one major industry did the economic delirium triggered by the war seem to cause genuine and sustained hardship: construction. Because of credit restrictions imposed by the president and the heavy hand of the National Production Authority in halting construction of such "nonessential" facilities as race tracks, table tennis establishments, and dance halls, the construction industry found itself in a recession of sorts; statistics indicated that new housing starts for 1950 would be some 13 percent below the record level of 1949.

Mirroring the boom conditions prevailing in most of industry was the stock market. After a sharp decline during the first days of the Korean conflict—a result of war jitters, according to analysts—the market recovered its balance, whereupon prices moved steadily upward from July through November 1950; and when the year ended Merrill, Lynch, Pierce, Fenner & Beane, the world's largest brokerage firm (which did about 10 percent of the business on the New York Stock Exchange) reported a record profit in 1950 of $12,544,090.

Notwithstanding the effects of rampaging inflation, wage earners shared in the post–June 25 boom, and many of them indeed must have thought that America had become a sort of economic utopia. The demand for skilled workingmen, particularly die makers, machinists, and aircraft workers, quickly exceeded the supply; unemployment dwindled; and it was estimated that by spring 1951 less than 2 percent of the national labor force would be out of work. In August 1950, to discourage its workers from jumping to more remunerative jobs, the Chrysler Corporation granted substantial pay increases, a move that touched off a wave of similar wage hikes throughout industry. Millions of other working people received cost-of-living raises in accordance with union contracts. Even more fortunate were corporation executives who received large salary increases to offset the effects of higher taxes and to cut down on the pirating of top personnel by competitors. Alas, there was one group of Americans which found its economic circumstances not much improved: the long-suffering farmers. After the outbreak of hostilities in Korea, farm prices moved upward—nearly to the so-called parity level established by the government, which meant that the annual bill for price supports or farm subsidies declined. Unfortunately, increasing costs of production, a consequence of inflation, tended to nullify any gains wrought by higher farm prices.

However caught up in the gyrations of their booming economy, Americans, during the summer and autumn of 1950, never for a moment forgot that they were living in dangerous times and never for a moment faltered in their conviction that the great overbearing threat to world peace and "the American way of life" was being posed by the Communists—those who, in the view of much of the citizenry, were effectively "boring from within" American society as well as those in the Soviet Union, Eastern Europe, and East Asia. It was inevitable that the commitment of Americans to fight and die in the crusade against Communist aggression in Korea would stir anti-Communist passions in America to new levels of intensity. Surprisingly, though, in the first weeks of the Korean conflict the influence of Sen. Joseph R. McCarthy, who had launched his career as a "Red-hunter" only a few months before, seemed in decline. (Said McCarthy to a reporter in July 1950: "My only forum is Page One. I don't have that now, so I'll keep quiet.")

Making their own special contribution to the process of stirring anti-Communist passions in America were the Communists themselves. At the United Nations in August 1950, Soviet Ambassador Jacob Malik infuriated Americans when he assailed the United States as a monstrous power which had planned the war in Korea, was slaughtering Korean civilians in brutal air raids, and was aiming at enslavement of the entire world. The citizenry also reacted to reports of anti-American propaganda in the Soviet Union and the satellite countries of Eastern Europe. Typical of such propaganda was this diatribe against the president: "Mr. Truman, you have no pity for children, for children are not dollars. . . . You are a foul murderer of mothers and children, the personification of a human baseness past and present, a warmonger, a monster among men, an atom murderer, a suppressor of freedom, a user of Colorado beetles and Japanese plague-infested fleas." Far more provocative were news reports, accompanied by grisly photographs, that in their advance southward North Korean soldiers, who sometimes infiltrated American lines disguised in "the baggy, dirty white garb of Korean peasants" and otherwise wore "filthy mustard-colored uniforms," had bound the hands of captive GI's and also scores of South Korean civilians and then put bullets in their heads.

Manifestations of the burgeoning national outrage against Communist words and deeds soon abounded. When officials of the Progressive party demanded the admission of the People's Republic of China to the United Nations and the withdrawal of U.N. forces from Korea, Henry A. Wallace, the Progressive presidential candidate in 1948, resigned from the party. The Congress of Industrial Organizations expelled the International Longshoremen's and Warehousemen's Union and the Cooks and Stewards on the ground that the organizations were tainted by communism. President Harry Bridges of the Longshoremen, in addition to being expelled from the CIO, was jailed in San Francisco on the charge that his activities since the outbreak of the Korean conflict had been "inimical to the security of the United States." When the Cunard liner *Parthia* arrived at New York with ninety-eight tons of Russian crabmeat, members of the International Longshoremen's Association (American Federation of Labor) refused to unload it. A similar fate met a cargo of Russian furs valued at $139,000.

More ominous were rumblings in the nation's capital. In mid-July

1950 the House of Representatives rushed through the so-called Hobbs Bill, which had been languishing in Congress for the past ten years, permitting the detention of alien criminals and subversives pending deportation. Meanwhile Sens. Karl E. Mundt of South Dakota and Homer Ferguson of Michigan and Rep. Richard M. Nixon of California were rounding up support for the three-year-old Mundt-Ferguson-Nixon Bill which would require domestic Communists to register with the attorney general and so-called Communist-front organizations to label their propaganda. Even President Truman, normally suspicious of Communist-control legislation, felt the national urge to do something about domestic Communists; in August 1950 he asked Congress to vote a measure requiring persons who had received instruction in espionage and subversive tactics from foreign governments or political parties to register under the Foreign Agents Registration Act—a request that drew the fire of civil libertarians who charged that such legislation would permit suspension of the constitutional restriction on self-incrimination. But then Sen. Patrick ("Pat") McCarran of Nevada came forward with a sweeping antisubversives bill and, in the end, netted the votes of such champions of civil liberties as Sens. William Langer of North Dakota, Hubert H. Humphrey of Minnesota, and Paul H. Douglas of Illinois. Passed over a presidential veto, the Internal Security Act of 1950 (reviled to the present day by civil libertarians simply as the McCarran Act) directed members of the Communist party and officers of so-called Communist-front groups to register with the attorney general and required front groups to label their propaganda: "Disseminated by a Communist organization." To determine which groups were Communist dominated, the act set up the Subversive Activities Control Board and provided for judicial review of the board's decisions. Under the McCarran Act a member of the Communist party or a front organization could not receive a passport or secure employment with the federal government or in a defense plant. The act authorized the attorney general to apprehend and detain persons thought likely to commit acts of sabotage or espionage; it restricted the entry and activities of aliens; it tightened the espionage laws; and it extended the statute of limitations in spy cases from three years to ten.

As Americans perceived the goings-on in the aftermath of the aggression in Korea, laws to control "Commies" and other subversives were instruments for girding the republic in an epochal struggle with its enemies which presently was reaching a new plateau of danger. Other acts and proposals of the summer and autumn of 1950 had the same purpose. To rebut Communist propaganda the federal government set up the National Psychological Strategy Board. Under supervision of the

State Department, the board would include representatives of the Defense Department, the Joint Chiefs of Staff, and the Central Intelligence Agency. In response to appeals by mayors across the country, the Office of Civil Defense of the National Security Resources Board distributed a 162-page booklet on civil defense procedures, and in early October 1950 two hundred mayors and as many civil defense officers descended on Washington for what was billed as an emergency meeting to discuss the problem of civil defense. Other Americans meanwhile were pressing for legislation to create a system of universal military training (UMT) for all able-bodied young men of the United States. Urged on by the American Legion, Secretary of Defense Johnson in August 1950 rushed a UMT measure to the White House; legislation embodying the UMT principle was introduced in Congress; and in hearings before the Senate Armed Services Committee, UMT received ringing endorsements by Johnson and the chairman of the Joint Chiefs of Staff, General of the Army Omar N. Bradley. The chances of congressional approval appeared bright when a Gallup poll revealed that 78 percent of the national population supported UMT.

Other Americans, however, were not content with merely girding the republic for an enlarged confrontation with the Soviets and their satellites and allies; they wanted to strike at the source of the awful "Red menace" by launching a "preventive war" against the Soviet empire. Because of America's superiority in nuclear weaponry—a superiority that was certain to erode now that the Soviet Union had exploded its own atomic bomb—they were confident that such a holocaust would result in a grand American triumph. As for the man who by law had exclusive authority to press America's atomic button, Harry Truman was aghast when talk of a preventive war began to escalate. Accordingly, he spoke out against the idea of preventive war in a national radio and television address in September 1950, censured Secretary of the Navy Francis P. Matthews when the secretary made a speech in Boston calling for aggressive action on behalf of peace, and suspended Maj. Gen. Orvil A. Anderson of the air force for proclaiming that if ordered to do so he could "break up Russia's five A-bomb nests in a week."

However extensive and frenetic their preparations for a possible showdown with the Soviets and the rest of the world's Communists, Americans were not about to proclaim a moratorium on one of their favorite preoccupations: politics. Inasmuch as voters would be going to the polls in early November 1950 to choose members of the House of Representatives, senators, and numerous other officials, Americans already had begun to feel that special election-year urgency about politics when the Korean conflict broke out.

THE WAR AND AMERICAN SOCIETY

Hardly had President Truman issued orders dispatching American forces to Korea before politicians and analysts began to weigh the political fallout of the Korean conflict and America's involvement in it. An early view was that the Republicans, most of whom had endorsed recent slashes in defense spending and reduced military aid to South Korea, were not in a strong position to exploit the numbing setbacks being endured by the first American troops to move into combat in Korea. That the GOP stood to gain from the inevitable dislocations and tensions resulting from even partial mobilization was, on the other hand, readily conceded. As for the Democrats, the prevailing wisdom was that if American and other U.N. forces could organize an effective counter-offensive in Korea before election day, they would do well at the polls. Conversely, if the war continued to go badly, the outcome in early November would be a Democratic disaster.

Such analyses did not take into account the aggressive mood of the Republicans. After recovering from the initial shock of events in Korea, GOP chieftains made it clear that they would scald the Democrats (who, after all, controlled the White House and had majorities in both houses of Congress) for a range of blunders: budget economies which had resulted in military unpreparedness; alleged bungling since the Yalta and Potsdam conferences of 1945 which had, in the Republican estimate, given the initiative in world affairs to the Soviets and their stooges; and alleged coddling of domestic Communists and subversives.

Republicans fired their opening salvo in late August 1950; four GOP members of the Senate Foreign Relations Committee (Bourke B. Hickenlooper of Iowa, Henry Cabot Lodge, Jr., of Massachusetts, H. Alexander Smith of New Jersey, and Alexander Wiley of Wisconsin) released a manifesto charging that the Democrats had "sold out" Chiang Kai-shek at Yalta and that the resultant collapse of the Nationalist regime in China had opened the way for Communist aggression in Korea. As a first step toward reversing the disastrous course of Democratic foreign policy the senators demanded the dismissal of Secretary of State Dean G. Acheson, the chief architect of that policy according to the GOP. Seriously ill in the Georgetown University Hospital, Sen. Arthur H. Vandenberg of Michigan, hitherto a Truman administration ally in matters of foreign affairs, expressed "general agreement" with the manifesto; the one-time "boy wonder" governor of Minnesota, Harold E. Stassen, registered his assent by declaring that the Truman administration "has sown so many pink seeds that now the American people must reap a red whirl-wind"; and Sen. Kenneth S. Wherry of Nebraska (in an utterance which the president denounced as "comtemptible") declared that "the blood of our boys in Korea" was on the hands of Acheson.

THE KOREAN WAR

As the political campaign gathered steam, however, Democratic prospects in the impending election seemed to brighten. First, in September 1950, came the sudden turn of the military tide in Korea, and after that, in the middle of October, President Truman's dramatic mid-Pacific rendezvous with the U.N. field commander, General of the Army Douglas MacArthur, on Wake Island. (There were some critics who charged that the premier purpose of the meeting was to draw attention to the Democratic administration in the hour of victory in Korea and thus improve the electoral chances of Democrats.) But Republicans did not temper their assault on Democratic foreign policy or their contention that Democrats were to blame for the Communist aggression in Korea and the initial reverses of American troops after their commitment to the conflict. Seeking to unseat Scott W. Lucas, the Democratic leader in the Senate, former Rep. Everett McKinley Dirksen

Corporal P. Romano gets in an early morning shave before leaving for the front lines— July 28, 1950.

of Illinois charged that the Truman administration had invited the Communist attack in Korea by a weak-kneed policy vis-à-vis communism in East Asia. Of the argument of Lucas and other administration stalwarts that the United States—under Democratic leadership—had taken a courageous stand on behalf of liberty in the hills of Korea, Dirksen said: "All the piety of the Administration will not put any life into the bodies of the young men coming back in wooden boxes."

Dirksen's words struck a chord with voters, and on election day the mellifluent orator from Pekin, Illinois, terminated the political career of Scott Lucas. The Senate majority leader was not the only Democratic casualty. Such titans as Francis J. Myers of Pennsylvania, Millard E. Tydings of Maryland, and Elbert D. Thomas of Utah also went down to defeat. In all, the Republicans gained five seats in the Senate and twenty in the House. Of larger consequence, as Alonzo L. Hamby has observed in *Beyond the New Deal: Harry S. Truman and American Liberalism*, the Democrats who lost in November 1950 tended to be of the liberal persuasion (i.e., supporters in varying measure of Truman's Fair Deal program). The result was a substantial diminishing of liberal influence in the national government and a corresponding enlargement of anti–Fair Deal, or conservative, influence.

When President Truman issued the orders sending United States troops to Korea many Americans expected that the GI's would be returning triumphantly within two or three months. But from the first days of the American intervention in Korea there had been a nagging fear that the Soviets might enter the war—or, more probably, that they would press their Chinese allies to throw themselves into the battle on behalf of the North Koreans. Then came the operation at Inchon, and in the flush of victory such fears seemed to evaporate. As the decision to send U.N. troops across the 38th Parallel was shaping up, a reporter caught the popular mood in America when he wrote that the time for intervention by the Soviet Union or China apparently had passed. As for Premier Chou En-lai's promise to plunge "Red" China into the war if the 38th Parallel was violated, Americans construed it as nothing more than a bluff. Events in Korea over the next few weeks appeared to justify such a construction, for U.N. troops pressed forward on all fronts and the Soviets and Chinese seemed to be doing nothing. In truth, a kind of euphoria appeared to settle over the American republic in October 1950, and one can imagine the delight of the citizenry when Lt. Gen. Walton H. Walker, commander of the Eighth Army, called the action in North Korea "a complete rout." Walker, a quail-shooting Texan, exulted, "We have flushed the covey, and we are now kicking up the singles." A short time later *Newsweek* printed a dispatch under the headline "Doug Oversees the End," quoting General MacArthur as saying that "the war very definitely is coming to an end shortly" and reporting that "the possibility of Russian or Chinese intervention . . . has now been completely discounted."

Then, as October was giving way to November, the national euphoria lapsed. Dispatches crackled across the Pacific reporting that Chinese battalions had crossed the Yalu River, made contact with U.N. forces, and blunted the U.N. advance. Americans readily agreed with the newsman who wrote that China's intervention constituted the Korean conflict's "most fateful turn" to date; when George Gallup's pollsters asked a cross section of the populace whether the U.N. should carry the war into China's territory if the Chinese intervention continued, only 39 percent responded affirmatively. But in mid-November, the Chinese broke contact with U.N. troops and virtually disappeared from the battle zone. What were they up to? Nobody seemed to know. Stated one report: "Their strategy in Korea was as inscrutable as the most traditionally inscrutable Oriental. Only here and there did the slowly advancing UN forces meet scattered resistance last week. Otherwise, the Chinese seemed to have vanished into the wintry wasteland—possibly to establish tough border fortifications in the vital passes before the Manchurian border."

And so it was that in late November, as a blizzard accompanied by gale-force winds was battering the northeastern quarter of the United States and floodwaters were inundating large areas of the far West, Americans again began to hope for an early conclusion to the affair in Korea. Or as one reporter put it, "Cold in their bones intensified the sympathy of stay-at-home Americans for their colder and more exposed sons still fighting for a decision by Christmas in the forbidding highlands of North Korea." Hope expanded during the last week of November when newspapers bannered reports that General MacArthur had flown to Korea to announce the opening of a general offensive to end the war and restore peace and unity to the Korean nation. Said the general, "I hope to keep my promise to the GI's and have them home by Christmas." With that, American, South Korean, and British soldiers and marines moved forward into a no-man's land which the Communists had mysteriously evacuated. Then it happened. Against a background of blaring bugles, rolling drums, and clashing cymbals, the Chinese, in the last days of November 1950, lunged forward in massive "human-sea" attacks and almost overnight turned the U.N. offensive (or "reconnaissance-in-force," as MacArthur later would term it) into an agonizing retreat.

THE WAR AND AMERICAN SOCIETY

In the United States the psychological effect of the Chinese attack in the frozen wastelands of northern Korea was devastating. Only a few days before, it had appeared that the nasty little conflict in East Asia was about to end in a glorious victory, that America's soldiers and marines soon would be boarding transports for a triumphal voyage home, and that save for accelerated activity in the realm of military preparedness, American life would revert to the tempo of six months before. But now the dream of an early victory in Korea had turned to ashes. Indeed the question in early December 1950 was whether the United States and its allies, short of unleashing a coordinated air-sea assault against the territory of China—i.e., short of a dramatic escalation of the war (a prospect that sparked only scattered enthusiasm among Americans and none at all among their NATO allies)—could establish a foothold in South Korea or whether they should even try; many people thought the time had come to forget Korea and build American strength in Europe against the real enemy, the Soviet Union.

During those bewildering days of early December 1950 Americans vented their frustration and anger in a variety of ways. Many demanded the immediate removal from office of Secretary of State Acheson, still widely viewed as the symbol of everything that had gone wrong in East Asia in the recent past. Supporting the anti-Acheson mail that poured into Washington was a petition demanding the secretary's ouster that carried (literally) a block-long list of signatures. Other Americans demanded renewed military assistance to Chiang Kai-shek and his Nationalist regime on Formosa and urged coastal raids on China's mainland by the Nationalist forces. In Birmingham the women of the Wake Island Marine Corps League Auxiliary, who had given marines a rousing sendoff to Korea the previous July, appealed to the president to "evacuate our troops immediately." In St. Louis two mothers put an advertisement in the *Post-Dispatch* urging "parents, wives, sweethearts, and friends" to flood the White House and Congress with demands for the rescue of beleaguered American troops; and in Montana a selective service board refused to issue any new draft calls pending use of the atomic bomb against the Communists in Korea.

Even President Truman, described by newsmen as tense and shaken by the dispatches from Korea, let his emotions get the better of him during those agonizing days of December 1950. When the music critic of the *Washington Post*, Paul Hume, wrote an unflattering review of Margaret Truman's singing during a concert in Constitution Hall, the president responded with an angry letter to Hume which the *Washington Daily News* subsequently paraphrased: "I never met you, but if I do you'll need a new nose and plenty of beefsteak and perhaps a supporter below.

Westbrook Pegler, a guttersnipe, is a gentleman compared to you. You can take that as more of an insult than as a reflection on your ancestry. H.S.T." Reacting to the reference to himself in the letter, Pegler, a columnist of dubious journalistic reputation, issued a statement: "It is a great tragedy that in this awful hour the people of the United States must accept in lieu of leadership the nasty malice of a President whom Bernard Baruch, in a similar incident, called a rude, uncouth, ignorant man. Let us pray." (Hume was more understanding. Of Truman he wrote, "I can only say that a man suffering the loss of a close friend [presidential press secretary Charles Ross] and carrying the terrible burden of the present world crisis ought to be indulged in an occasional outburst of temper.")

A trivial affair which perhaps only Westbrook Pegler took seriously, the incident quickly faded as the American public tried to sort out the meaning of the Chinese attack. As they sorted, Americans (81 percent of them, according to a Gallup poll taken in early December) quickly reached one conclusion: the order that sent the Chinese crashing into the combat in Korea had originated in Moscow, not Peking. Clearly, then, the Soviets had not weakened in their resolve, made manifest the previous June when they dispatched North Koreans across the 38th Parallel, to expand the Communist empire by force of arms. That being the case, America and its allies probably were facing a long and violent struggle—and possibly World War III. Wrote one reporter in late December 1950, "Americans fortunate enough to be at home with their families made the most of what could well be their last chance for a long time to celebrate Christmas in a traditional way."

But was it necessary that the United States have a showdown with the Soviets over Korea and other areas of peripheral importance to Americans? Responding to the sweet and enticing call of a siren—isolationism—which many people had thought extinct in the New World's premier republic, a segment of the citizenry thought it not.

A debate (soon to be referred to in the press as a "great debate") over foreign policy had begun; in truth, it got underway a fortnight before the Chinese attack in Korea, when Senator Taft, in the aftermath of his reelection triumph, called for a thorough reexamination of American policy and asked: "Is Europe our first line of defense? Is it defensible at all?" Taft's remarks drew a retort from Secretary Acheson: "We are told . . . that all isolationists are extinct, as dead as the dodo or the saber-toothed tiger. But there is a new species that has come on the horizon, and this new species I call the 're-examinist'." The secretary compared "re-examinists" with the farmer who pulled up his crops in the morning to see how they had done during the night. However witty, Acheson's comments probably touched few of his countrymen who were flirting with a new-style isolationism, the more so after Chinese battalions began their rout of U.N. soldiers and marines in the rugged reaches of northern Korea.

While his countrymen were absorbing news of the disaster in Korea, in early December 1950, a new spokesman entered the "great debate": Joseph P. Kennedy, a pre–Pearl Harbor isolationist and one-time ambassador to Great Britain. Addressing the University of Virginia Law School Forum, Kennedy urged an American withdrawal from overseas areas. "Where are we now?" he asked. "What have we in return for this effort [to shore up the non-Communist world]? Friends? We have far fewer friends than we had in 1945. In Europe they are still asking for our dollars but what kind of friendship have we bought there?" The first step in pursuit of a new policy, Kennedy said, was "to get out of Korea—indeed, to get out of every point in Asia which we do not plan realistically to hold in our own defense." A second step would be to apply the same principle to Europe. Kennedy thought the United States had profited little from the attempt to contain communism, and he shrugged off the Marshall Plan and Berlin airlift. "What have we gained," he asked, "by staying in Berlin?"

The response to such transparent isolationism must have surprised even Kennedy. From his audience in Charlottesville came raucous applause, and from across the republic approving letters poured into newspaper offices. The *Wall Street Journal* printed three columns of letters endorsing Kennedy's views. As for critical letters, the editors explained that they had not received any.

The response to Kennedy's speech was mild, however, in comparison with that accorded a national radio address delivered later that same month by former President Herbert C. Hoover. Following Hoover's speech, New York's senators, Irving Ives and Herbert Lehman, reported their mail was running better than ninety to one in favor of Hoover's views. The former president's secretary said that more than five thousand letters had cascaded into his office, fewer than a hundred of which were critical. In Moscow the official organ of the Communist party, *Pravda*, gleefully printed the entire speech. What had Hoover said to stir such enthusiasm? Most notably, he had propounded the theory that "the foundation of our national policies must be to preserve for the world this Western Hemispheric Gibraltar of Western Civilization." He saw no need for a large army; for with powerful air and naval forces, he thought, the United States could control the Atlantic and Pacific. Regarding Korea, Hoover believed the Communists had won there, hence the United States should leave the East Asian mainland and concentrate its strength in that part of the world on Japan, Formosa, and the Philippines. Regarding Europe, America should not put "another man or another dollar on their shores" until the Europeans "show they have spiritual strength and unity to avail themselves of their own resources." In the European area, Hoover explained, the main line of defense should be the British Isles.

Not all Americans, of course, felt the attraction of the new isolationism. In mid-December 1950 Governor Dewey of New York declared that "unless we are going to shrink within our own borders and wait to be conquered by a Communist world, we must boldly make decisions that will keep friends of our cause both in Europe and Asia." The journalist Ralph McGill wrote in the *Atlanta Constitution* that the program proposed by former President Hoover, if embraced by the United States, would amount to national suicide. Former Secretary of War Robert Patterson called Hoover's words "the counsel of discouragement, despair, and defeat." More effective were the comments of John Foster Dulles, a Republican foreign policy adviser in the State Department. During the last days of 1950 Dulles told the American Association for the United Nations: "It is possible to plan, on paper, and describe in words, what it seems should be an impregnable defense, a China Wall, a Maginot Line, a Rock of Gibraltar, an Atlantic and Pacific Moat. But . . . such a defense carries within itself the seeds of its own collapse. A defense that accepts encirclement quickly decomposes. That has been proved a thousand times." Dulles concluded that "a United States which could be an inactive spectator while the barbarians overran and desecrated the cradle of our Christian civilization [Europe] would not be the kind of United States which could defend itself."

Far weightier were the words of America's foremost nonisolationist, Harry Truman. On the evening of December 15, 1950, his face tightly drawn, the president sat down before a battery of microphones and a television camera in the White House and intoned: "Our homes, our Nation, all the things we believe in, are in great danger. This danger has been created by the rulers of the Soviet Union. . . . They have tried to undermine or overwhelm the free nations one by one. They have used threats and treachery and violence. [By their aggression in Korea] they have shown that they are now willing to push the world to the brink of a general war to get what they want." To "overcome the danger that threatens our country," Truman believed the United States must use force if necessary to uphold the principles of the United Nations, help "other free nations" strengthen their defenses, enlarge America's armed forces, and expand the national economy. Accordingly, the president urged a fivefold increase in aircraft production over the next year, a fourfold increase in the production of combat vehicles, and nearly a five-fold increase in the production of defensive electronic equipment. He requested that the manpower of the armed forces be brought to 3.5 million "as soon as possible," and, to provide central control over mobilization activities, he announced creation of a new agency, the Office of Defense Mobilization. Headed by Charles E. Wilson, president of General Electric, ODM would have unprecedented authority to impose price and wage controls immediately in some areas of production and to establish voluntary standards in others. The following day Truman formally proclaimed a national emergency: "I summon all citizens to make a united effort for the security and well-being of our beloved country and to place its needs foremost in thought and action that the full moral and material strength of the Nation may be readied for the dangers which threaten us."

The response to the clarion call of the president was immediate, notably on Capitol Hill. "Not without holding our noses," according to Rep. Norris Cotton of New Hampshire, Congress rammed through a bill granting $38 million in aid to the Communist regime of Marshal Josip Broz Tito of Yugoslavia whose celebrated quarrel with the Kremlin no longer appeared to Americans as a Communist trick. In event of a general war, the logic in Washington went, Tito's thirty-two divisions would immobilize a like number of Soviet divisions. Over the opposition of only Representative Marcantonio of New York, Congress steamrollered an emergency appropriation of $20 billion for the armed forces, approved an excess-profits bill intended to produce more than $8 billion in revenue over the next two years, and authorized $1.65 billion for "military public works," much of which dealt with construction of secret weapons. Congress also passed a civil defense act, establishing a federal civil defense agency and authorizing $3.1 billion for a federal-state civil defense program, and restored portions of the War Powers Act of 1941 to permit renegotiation of federal contracts (to allow for increasing costs). The army, meanwhile, enlarged its draft call for January 1951 from 40,000 to 80,000 and for February from 50,000 to 80,000, and prepared to receive two additional National Guard divisions which the president had announced he would call into service. From the newly organized Committee on the Present Danger, a private group led by President James B. Conant of Harvard, atomic scientist Vannevar Bush, and former Secretary of the Army Tracy S. Voorhees, came a dramatic appeal to Americans to take revolutionary steps to meet the "aggressive designs of the Soviet Union." The committee sought a program of universal service which would mandate two years of military training for eighteen-year-old males. That training "should embrace radically broadened standards of fitness."

The committee wanted economic controls "more exacting than those now in effect, particularly in the field of credit, government and private," and a drastic reduction in federal spending for nondefense purposes. "The doubt is not whether such a program is too arduous," committee spokesmen said. "The doubt is whether it is arduous enough." They concluded: "The bitter fact is that our country has again been thrust into a struggle in which our free existence is at stake, a struggle for survival. We have no time to lose."

What did the summons to build military strength mean to champions of liberal reform in America, whose influence had already been diminished as a result of the recent election? It meant that their chances of registering important gains for liberalism in the near future were about nil. In the words of Senator Humphrey, "Every liberal movement has been stopped cold at the time of national emergency." Continued Humphrey: "It [the liberal movement] is a casualty now, but not a corpse. Our job is to keep the patient alive." Other Democratic liberals agreed and decided to press for statehood for Hawaii and Alaska, a federal antilynching law, and a presidential order establishing a new Federal Employment Practices Commission under a different name. It did not appear that they would receive much encouragement from the president, absorbed as he was with the national mobilization effort and the conflict in Korea. In his January 1951 State of the Union message, Truman made only passing reference to the Fair Deal program, and a short time later in a press conference, while reiterating support for the Fair Deal, asserted that "first things come first, and our defense program must have top priority." Perhaps the president's only liberal act of any consequence during early 1951—apparently triggered by word that Chairman McCarran of the Senate Judiciary Committee was about to undertake a new investigation of alleged Communists in government— was his appointment of a nine-man Commission on Internal Security and Individual Rights, headed by retired Fleet Adm. Chester W. Nimitz, to study the question of how to guard against subversion while protecting civil liberties. Of larger moment in the view of Truman and most of his countrymen, no doubt, was the draft.

When the president, in his address of December 15, 1950, announced a new manpower goal for the armed forces of 3.5 million—an increase of 700,000 over the target set in the weeks after outbreak of the Korean conflict—it was manifest that draft calls would be accelerated during the months ahead. The repercussions were immediate. To avoid service in the infantry young men of draft age began cascading into recruiting offices of the navy and air force; others set about to wrest deferments. More notable perhaps, college and university presidents in every corner of the republic began to lament the probable consequences of increased draft calls on higher education. How could colleges and universities, particularly the smaller ones which received no appropriations from state legislatures, survive in the face of lost income from tuition fees if legions of young men marched off to training camps? How, they asked, would the country maintain an adequate reservoir of physicians, dentists, engineers, physicists, chemists, and mathematicians if young men were indiscriminately hauled into the army? No less worried were youthful college men. How would a two-year interruption for service in the army affect an individual's educational development? Would it be difficult to pick up the threads of college or university education after a two-year absence from campus?

To resolve some of the concerns of educators and students while Congress was drafting a new selective service law, President Truman, at the end of March 1951, issued an executive order announcing that young men who were eligible for the draft might take an intelligence test to be prepared by the Educational Testing Service of Princeton, New Jersey. If a student scored seventy or better on the examination, local draft boards would have the option of deferring his military service. The order stirred a reaction; critics charged that it would be undemocratic to link deferments with intelligence. Nonetheless, in May and June 1951, at more than nine hundred locations, 400,000 young men (including the author of this essay) sweated through the college deferment test. Between 60 and 65 percent of them passed.

When they began deliberating new selective service legislation in January 1951, members of Congress seemed particularly anxious to revise the physical and mental standards by which the army measured a potential draftee's fitness for military service. That came as no surprise. From the onset of the army's build-up in mid-1950, congressmen had complained that the army was rejecting too many men—upwards of a third of those examined—because of trivial physical defects and failure to pass unduly rigid intelligence tests. Chairman Carl Vinson of the House Armed Services Committee voiced a prevailing sentiment when he said: "We read where some [professional] football player, able to draw $10,000 a season, just hasn't got the strength to carry a rifle. . . . Even if a man can't read Latin or Greek, he can do a little fighting." Other members suggested that a young man whose nearsightedness, for example, might prevent him from becoming a combat infantryman could operate a typewriter at an army post in the United States or Japan. Unmoved by such complaints and suggestions were the army's leaders. They wanted the most qualified men available and thus resisted the idea of lowering physical and mental standards.

Where, then, did the army propose to find the young men to fill out its ranks? Secretary of Defense George C. Marshall had the answer: eighteen-year-olds. (Under existing law a youth did not become eligible for the draft until he turned nineteen.) Eighteen-year-olds, the secretary thought, would make "splendid soldiers." Drafting eighteen-year-olds, moreover, seemed to fit in with another of Marshall's favorite schemes, namely, universal military training, or as he rechristened it, Universal Military and Service Training. But when Marshall and Assistant Secretary of Defense Anna M. Rosenberg spelled out the defense establishment's views before committees of the House and Senate, they provoked a minor eruption. Angry parents bombarded Congress with mail claiming that eighteen was too tender an age to take a young man from the warmth of his family home and expose him to the temptations of barracks life. Educators complained that execution of the defense establishment's ideas would drain colleges and universities of students and thus undermine the educational life of the republic. Particularly concerned about its psychic effects, peace organizations feared that UMST would result in a sort of creeping militarism which, in turn, would subvert the democratic ideal in America.

At length Congress voted, and in June 1951 the president signed, the Universal Military Training and Service Act. Notwithstanding its title—and notwithstanding the results of a recent Gallup poll showing nearly 80 percent of those interviewed favored universal military training —the legislation did not provide for a program of UMT (or Marshall's UMST). The only concession to UMT was a provision establishing a five-man commission to study UMT and report to Congress. (At the end of October 1951, the commission recommended six months of military training for all young men on reaching age eighteen.) Otherwise the new law extended selective service to July 1955; lowered the draft age to eighteen and a half; lengthened the period of service for draftees from twenty-one to twenty-four months and imposed on the men a six-year reserve obligation after their separation from active service; established lower physical and mental standards for induction (in spite of which the army's preinduction rejection rate continued to climb, until by the end of the year it was approaching 50 percent); provided that conscientious objectors must perform twenty-four months of service which contributed to the national interest; and authorized the president to issue regulations for deferring men whose occupations, including study activity, were deemed necessary to the national health and safety and also those whose induction into the army would result in extreme hardship for their families.

If the draft—and, consequently, the prospect that they might have

136

to fight Chinese soldiers in the distant hills and valleys of Korea—was the great overbearing concern of several million young Americans at the end of 1950 and in the first months of 1951, the performance of the national economy was of larger moment in the minds of most of their countrymen. On the eve of the Chinese offensive in Korea, when it appeared that the conflict in East Asia soon would become a hazy memory, leaders in Washington fretted that peace would cause the citizenry to lose interest in the military build-up to which the government had committed itself in the aftermath of the Communist attack across the 38th Parallel. They had reason to worry. Chieftains of business and labor were grumbling about cutbacks in the output of civilian goods and resultant unemployment stemming from the diversion of steel and copper and brass from the manufacture of automobiles and television sets to the production of planes, tanks, and guns. Americans were feeling the pinch of the decision to produce more guns and less butter, and many of them did not like it. (The guns-and-butter theme turned up repeatedly in news columns, editorials, and editorial cartoons during the autumn of 1950.) But then came the disastrous turn of events in Korea, a fresh outbreak of alarm that the United States might be edging toward a global confrontation with the Soviet Union, and President Truman's proclamation of a national emergency, whereupon Americans set about to adjust to the dislocations deriving from a new acceleration of the military build-up.

The process of adjustment, however, did not bring an end to grumbling. On the same day that the president proclaimed a national emergency, the government's economic stabilizer, Alan Valentine, issued an order rolling back retail prices of automobiles to their level on December 1, 1950—an act which negated price increases announced a few days before by the manufacturers. General Motors countered the order by halting sales, "pending examination of the discriminatory order," and the United Automobile Workers lamented the consequences of the resultant cutback in auto production. (Within a week the industry capitulated and accepted the rollback.) Other spokesmen for business and labor complained of the effects on production and employment of shortages of critical materials. A shortage of fabricating metals at the end of December 1950, for example, idled 100,000 workers in Detroit; and in early 1951 a shortage of sulphuric acid impeded the output of steel, petroleum, and fertilizer, while a shortage of benzene upset the chemical industry. The object of the most widespread and vocal complaints, however, was the sharp increase in prices that followed the president's proclamation of a national emergency and the issuance of his annual budget message in mid-January 1951, disclosing that the federal government planned to spend $71.6 billion in fiscal 1952, of which $48.9 billion or 69 percent of that sum would be spent on the armed forces and aid to our allies. (When the figures for fiscal 1951—ending June 30, 1951—subsequently came in, they revealed a total expenditure of $44.633 billion, of which $25.189 billion had gone for the armed forces and foreign aid. And where the president estimated a deficit of more than $8 billion for fiscal 1952, budget receipts for fiscal 1951 actually yielded a surplus of $3.51 billion.)

Almost from the moment of the Chinese attack in Korea, at the end of November 1950, wholesale and retail prices in the United States, which had moved up steadily since the onset of the East Asian conflict, began spiraling to new levels; an eight-city survey by the Bureau of Labor Statistics disclosed a staggering increase in the cost of living of 1.2 percent in the eighteen days between December 15, 1950, and January 2, 1951. One of the casualties of the new round of inflation was the "nickel Coke." Observing that "our industry was born and has grown strong on a 5-cent retailing price for Coca-Cola," the Coca-Cola Bottling Company regretfully announced that because of the mounting cost of bottles, caps, cases, and labor it no longer was possible to hold the line. Of larger moment was the sharp increase in food prices. All items in the food line, from meats and fish to vegetables and dairy products, were marked up, while a renewed wave of scare buying sent the prices of nylons, appliances, and tires bounding upward. Prices in the spring-summer catalogs mailed to customers of Sears, Roebuck and Company and Montgomery Ward in January 1951 were substantially higher than the year before, and prices of such industrial raw materials as cotton, wool, rubber, and scrap steel were soaring—up 58 percent since the outbreak of hostilities in Korea, according to a January 1951 report by the Bureau of Labor Statistics.

There was no uncertainty about what President Truman intended to do to bring inflation under control. Sooner or later he would issue an order imposing a freeze on prices and wages. The reason for delaying such an order, he explained to newsmen in December 1950, was the time required to recruit a staff and establish enforcement procedures. But at length, in the face of inflation in all sectors of the economy, the president, fully supported by mobilization director Wilson, felt compelled to act, despite the fact that the means of enforcement were not in place. Accordingly, at 6:00 P.M. on January 26, 1951, price stabilizer DiSalle and wage stabilizer Ching entered the ornate conference room of the old State Department building; while flash bulbs popped, DiSalle told the hundred or so reporters who had crowded through the doors that "this is 'F-Day'." Prices of most commodities would be frozen at the highest levels reached between December 19, 1950, and January 25, 1951, while wages and salaries would not exceed rates prevailing on the latter date.

Worn and haggard, DiSalle made it clear that the decision to freeze prices and wages had not come easily. The decision, in truth, had emerged only after acrimonious debate at the highest level in the White House—debate so bitter that Alan Valentine, chief of the Economic Stabilization Agency, resigned when the president's decision was known. Valentine was succeeded by the handsome president of the Motion Picture Association of America, Eric Johnston. Another opponent of the freeze was Cyrus Ching, although, for the time being, he remained as head of the Wage Stabilization Board. During the ritual of announcing the freeze Ching was heard to mumble, "If I ever get out of this mess, I'll never love another country."

By most contemporary estimates the attempt to put ceilings on prices and wages was less than a howling success, and for the rotund DiSalle the months following "F-Day" must have been a nightmare. Subsequent modifications of the freezing order permitted adjustments in price-wage ceilings under certain circumstances, embroiling DiSalle in interminable haggling with cotton growers and meat processors and representatives of countless other economic interests who demanded that price ceilings for their products be raised. In the face of such pressure the government usually gave ground, and as a result—inevitably—labor became restive. In March and April 1951, the three labor representatives on the nine-man Wage Stabilization Board, claiming that the government had not enforced the price freeze and that the national mobilization effort had fallen under the domination of big business, boycotted the board and caused leaders in Washington to fear crippling delays in the build-up of the armed forces. Prodded by the president, the recalcitrant labor chieftains grudgingly returned to the WSB, while wage increases sanctioned by the government dampened the protests of labor's rank-and-file. The consequence of these "adjustments" in price-wage ceilings, of course, was predictable: the consumer price index, which advanced less than 1 percent from February to July 1951, moved up 2 percent between August and December. If a comparable rate of inflation would have been cause for rejoicing two decades later, in 1973 and 1974, increasing prices remained a source of concern to Americans through 1951, particularly when the price of sirloin reached a dollar per pound; the outcome was a decline in popular enthusiasm for the price-wage freeze. (In the first week of January of that year, 62 percent of those interviewed in a Gallup poll thought a freeze a good idea.) Congress, accordingly, was able to respond to pressure by assorted economic groups and turn aside President Truman's appeal for more effective means of enforcing price-wage controls; instead, Congress actually weakened his authority to enforce the freeze when, in June 1951, it voted to extend the Defense Production Act for another year.

Notwithstanding inflation, sharp increases in corporate and personal income taxes (as a result of the Revenue Act of October 1951), and a severe slump in the sale of automobiles and television sets in the spring of 1951 (after a government regulation requiring substantial down payments for such items took dramatic effect), the months following China's intervention in the Korean conflict were a time of economic bonanza for most Americans. Fueling the economy, obviously, was lavish spending for national defense: the American Locomotive Company received a contract worth $100 million to build 500 medium tanks; the Coach Division of General Motors received an equivalent contract to build two-and-one-half-ton trucks. The Oldsmobile Division of GM accepted a contract to manufacture ammunition for the army's 3.5-millimeter rocket launchers ("bazookas"); Willys-Overland, a contract valued at $63 million to build quantities of its celebrated "jeeps"; and the Fruehauf Trailer Company, a contract worth $40 million to turn out 35,000 all-steel military trailers. In truth, nearly all of the nation's large manufacturers and many lesser ones were recipients of government contracts.

As the industrial establishment whirred and clanked and hissed, it must have seemed that the citizenry was taking to heart a newspaper campaign undertaken at the end of 1950 by the Advertising Council, urging a dramatic increase in productivity as a defense against communism. (The first ad read: "It's Time We Got *Working* Mad.") Whether Americans needed such urging was doubtful. In any event, all sectors of the economy were booming; as a result, corporate profits remained near the impressive level achieved the year before, disposable personal income reached a new high, and by October 1951 unemployment had declined to 2.5 percent of the civilian labor force, the lowest point since 1944. Even agriculture, plagued by declining returns since 1947–48, felt the effects of rampaging prosperity. In 1951 net farm income surpassed that of 1950 by an eye-popping 18 percent (but still did not reach the 1947–48 level).

As 1950 gave way to 1951 the Chinese remained on the offensive in Korea, and it appeared that the United States and its allies might have to abandon the peninsula to the Communists. For the people of the United States the only cause for rejoicing during those dark days was the news that American marines and soldiers had successfully escaped a Chinese trap and been evacuated by sea via the North Korean port of

THE WAR AND AMERICAN SOCIETY

ACME Newspictures—UPI

Gen. Matthew Ridgway, commander of the U.S. Eighth Army, and staff officers check front line positions north of Anyang-mi—February 16, 1951.

Hungnam. But then, in mid-January 1951, the Chinese attack lost its momentum; the U.N. Eighth Army under the field command of Lt. Gen. Matthew B. Ridgway dug in along a line that stretched across the peninsula from a point some fifty miles below the South Korean capital city of Seoul; and a fortnight later General Ridgway ordered a cautious countermovement. From the Chinese came only token resistance, and in mid-March U.N. troops captured the battered remains of Seoul (the fourth time the city had changed hands in the past nine months) and within a few days were approaching the 38th Parallel.

Should the U.N. forces, as they had the previous autumn, press the attack across the parallel and attempt to expel communism from all of Korea? Back home in the United States, a Gallup poll disclosed that only a minority of the populace thought they should. Of those individuals interviewed by the Gallup organization in early March 1951, only 36 percent registered disapproval of the proposition that the U.N. should allow Korea to be divided at the 38th Parallel, leaving the Communists in control of the northern half of the country. That Americans had little stomach for pressing on with the "police action" should have surprised nobody, for in the aftermath of China's intervention it was manifest that Americans had lost their enthusiasm of the previous summer for the bloody affair in East Asia. A Gallup poll taken in early February 1951 reported that only 39 percent of those interviewed believed America's intervention in the Korean conflict had not been a mistake.

But the prospect of working out a cease-fire which would leave Korea divided did not strike a chord with General MacArthur. Stung that the Chinese had snatched the laurels of victory from his grasp the previous autumn, MacArthur was bent on regaining those laurels. He wanted to expel the Communists from all of Korea and to that end sought to expand the East Asian conflict by sending American bombers against Chinese installations and lines of communication in Manchuria, imposing a naval blockade against China's coast, introducing the Chinese Nationalist troops of Chiang Kai-shek into the combat in Korea, and dispatching other Nationalist forces from their base on Formosa on raids against the Communist-held Chinese mainland. Such a grandiose strategy found no response among MacArthur's superiors in Washington or the leaders of America's European allies. Fearing that an expansion of hostilities in East Asia might trigger World War III, the foreign leaders hoped to terminate the Korean conflict at the 38th Parallel and restore the *status quo ante*. But MacArthur was adamant, and when the president set about to make a peace overture to the Communists in the latter part of March 1951, the five-star general made his own "peace" proposal—a bellicose statement threatening the Chinese with annihilation if they did not come to terms. Contemptuously rejected by the government in Peking, MacArthur's statement undercut the presidential peace overture. (The statement was an apparent violation of a presidential directive, issued the previous December, ordering officials of the government and armed forces to make no public statements on high policy without clearance by the State or Defense Department.) Next came publication of MacArthur's celebrated letter to Rep. Joseph W. Martin, Jr., in which the general castigated the existing (for all practical purposes, American) policy in the Far East. That did it. On April 10, 1951, Truman signed the orders dismissing MacArthur from all of his commands.

Americans who remember 1951 are not apt to forget the popular response to the dismissal orders. From Maine to California came thunderous expressions of outrage that Truman had sacked the imperious architect of the Allied victory in the Southwest Pacific during World War II and the bearer of democracy to conquered Japan. Referring to the president, whose public approval rating recently had slipped to 28

THE WAR AND AMERICAN SOCIETY

percent, Senator McCarthy said, "The son of a bitch ought to be impeached." Many other Americans agreed. *Life* magazine published a picture of a grinning Sen. Richard M. Nixon holding a batch of telegrams urging Truman's impeachment; exuded Nixon, "It's the largest spontaneous reaction I've ever seen." Students in California hung the president in effigy; a woman in Maryland sent a telegram to the White House calling Truman a witling—after Western Union refused to transmit the word *moron*; and in Los Angeles a man told a television reporter that "the country would not be in this shape if Harry Truman were alive." (The same man then told the reporter that he was going out for a "Truman beer." "What kind of beer is that?" the reporter asked. "Just like any other kind," the man replied, "except it hasn't got a head.") When the Gallup organization sought a measure of the public's opinion of the MacArthur dismissal, it found that only 25 percent of those interviewed approved of the president's actions.

Despite the assertion in his memoirs that the events following his sacking of the general "did not upset me," it is hard to imagine that Truman did not experience some unsettling moments during those hectic days of April 1951. When MacArthur, who had not set foot in the United States for nearly fifteen years, prepared to leave Japan he was accorded an emotional farewell by millions of Japanese. After that came tumultuous receptions when the general, his wife, and young son touched down in Honolulu, San Francisco, and Washington. Next came the unforgettable "Old Soldiers Never Die" speech before a joint session of Congress; and there were more mob scenes when the MacArthurs visited New York, Chicago, and Milwaukee. (In New York the police estimated that more than seven million people turned out to greet the general and his family; the sanitation department estimated that the path of their motorcade was strewn with 2,852 tons of paper; and Western Union calculated that they were draped with 1,700 miles of ticker tape.) As for the president, he stayed in the background, although he did emerge from the White House to throw out the first ball of the American League season at Griffith Stadium. Alas, even the baseball park offered no escape from the national preoccupation of the moment: when Truman, a faint smile across his lips, prepared to make the toss, a chorus of boos rolled out from the grandstand, making him the first president since Herbert Hoover to be booed at a ball game. Fans booed again at the start of the eighth inning when the field announcer asked them to remain in their seats until the president and his party had left the stadium.

Whatever the historical estimate of the Truman-MacArthur controversy of 1951, it is not difficult to explain the popular response to the president's dismissal of the general. By the spring of 1951, despite the

Eighth Army's success in stemming the Chinese tide in Korea and in pushing the Communists back to the 38th Parallel, Americans had become disenchanted with the armed conflict which no longer seemed likely to end in a magnificent victory. Furthermore, Americans had become increasingly disenchanted with the president, the more so in recent weeks in light of a succession of disclosures of cheap influence-peddling by high officials in his administration. Whether the citizenry, on the other hand, was as infatuated with MacArthur as it appeared in the spring of 1951 is an open question. In a special survey taken in the weeks after the general's dismissal, the Gallup organization asked a cross section of Americans which of two generals, Eisenhower or MacArthur, they would prefer as president. Fifty-one percent named Eisenhower, only 27 percent MacArthur. The same individuals then were asked whether they thought MacArthur would make a good president. Only 36 percent thought he would. Still, MacArthur was a bona fide national hero. His Olympian demeanor and finely turned phrases contrasted starkly with the cocky manner and peppery oratory of "Give-'em-hell Harry." The dismissal of MacArthur, then, gave Americans a fleeting opportunity to put aside the frustrations occasioned by the failure of their World War II crusade to produce the kind of world envisioned by the Atlantic Charter and the Charter of the United Nations; it provided an occasion for the release of a host of pent-up emotions as Americans shouted their approval of a man who stood forth as a glorious symbol of a bygone era—when America had scorned limited conflicts for limited objectives, accepted the dictum that there is no substitute for victory, and fought its enemies to the finish.

Meanwhile, critics of President Truman and his foreign policies, notably Republicans who, in the "great debate," had espoused the views of Senator Taft and former President Hoover, hit on the idea of a congressional investigation of MacArthur's dismissal and America's Far Eastern policy. The purpose of the Republican critics was transparent: to discredit the Democratic administration and prepare the way for a victory by the Republicans—ideally, a victory for Taft—in the presidential election of 1952. In light of the popular enthusiasm for MacArthur, the Senate could not easily turn aside the demand for an investigation, and on April 25, 1951, it unanimously approved the resolution offered by Richard B. Russell of Georgia providing for a joint inquiry by the Armed Services and Foreign Relations committees. The outcome, beginning on May 3, 1951, was an eight-week grilling of MacArthur, Secretary of Defense Marshall, the Joint Chiefs of Staff, Secretary Acheson, and several lesser individuals who presumably had some expertise on the questions at issue.

144

THE WAR AND AMERICAN SOCIETY

The so-called MacArthur hearings went more or less as expected. Although they were given the most extensive media coverage of any congressional inquiry to date, it is hard to measure the hearings' impact on the thinking of Americans. Citing an alleged incident at a baseball game in New York a few days after his testimony (an incident not mentioned in the *New York Times* report of the event), the historian Eric F. Goldman, in *The Crucial Decade*, opined that popular support for MacArthur and his ideas was declining rapidly. (John Spanier, in *The Truman-MacArthur Controversy*, and Merle Miller, in *Plain Speaking: An Oral Biography of Harry S. Truman*, also cited the same incident as proof of MacArthur's diminishing popular approval.) Still, when Gallup's pollsters sampled popular opinion between May 19 and May 25, 1951, on the question of MacArthur's dismissal, only 29 percent of those interviewed approved of Truman's action—an increase of only four percentage points from the results of a poll taken immediately following the dismissal. Moreover, the president's overall approval rating, based on a sampling of popular opinion in mid-May, had slipped to 24 percent, down four points from the end of March 1951.

Whatever the effect of the hearings on popular views of MacArthur and Truman, the issues which had prompted dismissal of the five-star general seemed passé by the time the Senate's inquiry droned to its end on June 27, 1951. The new reality was the prospect of an armistice in East Asia. During a weekly U.N. radio program on June 23, after U.N. forces had broken up a large-scale Communist offensive in the battle zone, the Soviet ambassador to the U.N. Jacob Malik, appealed for an end to the conflict in Korea. Speaking softly with a heavy Russian accent, he said, "The Soviet peoples believe that as a first step discussions should be started between the belligerents for a cease-fire and an armistice providing for the mutual withdrawal of forces from the thirty-eighth parallel." Despite suspicions that it was some sort of Communist trick, leaders in Washington were very much interested in the Malik overture; and on June 30, General Ridgway sent a message over the Armed Forces Radio network proposing armistice negotiations. The following day a radio message from Peking suggested that such negotiations should take place at Kaesong, just below the 38th Parallel along the western end of the battle line. On July 3 Ridgway radioed approval of the Kaesong location, and on July 10 negotiations began.

The people of the United States were not caught up in euphoria as the discussions at Kaesong got underway; there was no illusion that a termination of hostilities in Korea might signal an end to the global confrontation between the so-called free world and international communism. In the opinion of many Americans, the Communists merely

145

were planning to liquidate the costly adventure in Korea in order to clear the way for action against more tempting and vulnerable targets, such as Yugoslavia, Iran, or Indochina. Thus when Gallup's pollsters, during mid-July 1951, asked a cross section of Americans whether the United States should continue to strengthen its defenses in the event of an early conclusion of the Korean conflict, 82 percent of those interviewed favored continuation.

Still, Americans were ready for a termination of hostilities in East Asia, notwithstanding the certainty that any settlement negotiated under present circumstances would leave the northern half of Korea under Communist rule. A second Gallup poll taken in mid-July 1951 showed that 74 percent of the respondents thought the peace talks in Korea a good idea. Most of the citizenry, moreover, calculated that the talks would succeed—that, to borrow an expression made famous two decades later, peace was at hand in Korea. After all, the war was hopelessly stalemated, and there was no earthly way that the prospect of total victory could justify the staggering losses that either side would have to accept as the price of a breakthrough. Logic, then, dictated an early settlement. Indeed, observers of the national scene began to ponder what the columnist Ernest K. Lindley called "the pitfalls of 'peace'": a slowing down of rearmament and new assaults on foreign aid by the "isolationist-economy bloc" in Congress.

Unfortunately the logic of Americans and that of Communists—to borrow an expression of GI's in Korea—were "no same-same." As negotiations at Kaesong, and later at Panmunjom, dragged on for month after dreary month and endured a five-month "recess" from autumn 1952 to spring 1953, as hope that a settlement was imminent swelled during late 1951 and the spring of 1952 and then collapsed, it became apparent that, in the Communist view, there was no compelling reason for haste in working out a battlefield armistice. The Communists obviously understood that prolonged negotiations offered unique opportunities for scoring points in the game of diplomatic "one-upmanship," as well as a forum for a host of propaganda activities; and it seems not unlikely that they were counting on American weariness with the apparently interminable conflict in East Asia to result in substantial concessions by the U.N.

The Communists surely were correct in assuming that the negotiations would present endless opportunities to embarrass and nettle their adversaries and draw attention to their propaganda broadsides: from the day the cease-fire talks got underway, their attempts to humiliate U.N. negotiators and rally world opinion to their side—for example, by renewing charges that the United States was employing germ warfare in Korea—received maximum publicity. They also were correct in surmising that the prolongation of truce negotiations would increase American weariness with the Korean conflict. A Gallup poll taken in October 1951, less than four months after the beginning of cease-fire talks, found that only 33 percent of Americans disagreed with the proposition that the affair in Korea was "an utterly useless war." A similar poll taken in late February and early March 1952 indicated that only 35 percent of the citizenry believed America's intervention in the Korean conflict had not been a mistake.

The Communists were wrong, on the other hand, if they thought that weariness with the goings-on in Korea would persuade Americans to press their leaders to make whatever concessions might be necessary to extricate the United States from the frustrating and expensive conflict. On the contrary, the petty insults and propaganda diatribes authored by Communist delegates at Kaesong and Panmunjom, and also the bloody rioting in Communist prisoner-of-war camps on the islands of Koje-do and Cheju-do during 1952, seemed to offer dramatic proof of everything that the champions of anticommunism in America had been saying for years—namely, that Communists were conniving, deceitful and cruel; that they were masters of "the big lie"; and that they were willing to fabricate the most outlandish arguments and, as the Koje-do uprisings demonstrated, to brutally sacrifice their own people to achieve their ends. In addition to stirring the Cold War spirit of Americans to new levels of intensity and providing sustenance for the enterprises of Senator McCarthy and other "Red-hunters" in the United States, the insults, diatribes, and riots of the Communists steeled Americans against any suggestion that U.N. negotiators in Korea ought to make peace at almost any price.

In truth, the unfaltering determination of the American people to stay the course in Korea—despite the frustration and expense of the military operation, despite the widely held view that America's intervention had been a mistake—seems almost incredible in retrospect. It is particularly striking when one recalls that by the spring of 1952 the armistice negotiators had nearly resolved all of the major issues save one: whether prisoners of war would be repatriated against their wills, an issue that had arisen when U.N. officials discovered that some fifty thousand POW's whom they held did not want to return to communism. Perhaps it was a testimonial to the depth of Americans' commitment to the proposition that the nation must stand forth as the uncompromising champion of freedom in the world—or perhaps a testimonial to the extent to which Senator McCarthy and other spokesmen of anticommunism had influenced their lines of thought. In any event, Americans overwhelmingly agreed with President Truman, who in May 1952 said, "We will not buy an armistice by turning over human beings for slaughter or slavery." For the sake of fifty thousand enemy POW's, then, the people of the United States (as Walter Hermes has observed in *Truce Tent and Fighting Front*) permitted the Korean conflict to be prolonged for fifteen months—during which time the United Nations Command suffered 125,000 casualties.

Apart from their views about America's role as leader of the "free world" and their perceptions of the Communist menace, what accounted for Americans' steadfastness of purpose regarding Korea during 1952 and 1953? One might offer several explanations. After the fierce struggle for Heartbreak Ridge during the autumn of 1951, the battle line in Korea became stabilized, and for the balance of the conflict, notwithstanding bloody clashes at such quaintly named places as Pork Chop Hill and Old Baldy, combat remained at a comparatively low level. Meanwhile, as Gen. J. Lawton Collins has written in *War in Peacetime*, the United States carefully built up the South Korean army and gradually moved more ROK's into the battle line in place of American GI's. As a result, the weekly figures on Americans killed and wounded in Korea—which never received the publicity casualty reports from Vietnam did, a decade and a half later—declined perceptibly. As casualty lists became shorter, the Korean conflict tended to fade from the public consciousness; events in Korea lost their place on the front page of daily newspapers; and in weekly news magazines, those events sometimes received less than a single column. (Needless to say, the evening television news programs, then in their infancy and only fifteen minutes in length, transmitted in black and white pictures of varying quality, did little to stir viewers' emotions on the subject of the conflict in Korea.) Then there was the policy, inaugurated in mid-1951, of rotating troops back to the United States after a year or eighteen months of service in Korea, depending on the individual's proximity to the battle zone. The knowledge that GI's did not face an indefinite tour of duty in "the land that God forgot" (a GI expression) made acceptance of the danger of service in Korea less difficult for relatives and sweethearts back home.

Another circumstance which made it easier for Americans to keep a stiff upper lip during the frustrating twenty-four months of on-again off-again negotiations at Kaesong and Panmunjom was the continuing hum of the national economy. Occasionally, to be sure, some cogs in the mechanism rattled and squeaked and slipped. During late 1951 and early 1952, because of the voracious appetite for metals in that part of the economy turning out military hardware, the automobile industry was compelled to shut down assembly lines, laying off 120,000 workers in Detroit. During the spring of 1952, amid widespread talk that a recession might be imminent, General Electric and Westinghouse trimmed production and the Continental Oil Company reduced output at its chief refinery. Then, during the spring and summer of 1952, the steel industry underwent nearly four months of turmoil. The trouble in steel came to a head when the industry, after the government had refused to sanction what President Truman called outrageous price increases, turned aside a recommendation by the Wage Stabilization Board that steelworkers be accorded a pay hike of twenty-six cents an hour. The United Steelworkers prepared to strike. The president, in part it seemed to keep the chiefs and braves of organized labor on the Democratic reservation during the impending election campaign, declined to order a ninety-day "cooling off" period, in accordance with the Taft-Hartley Act; instead, Truman seized the steel industry. His action, of course, infuriated business leaders and most Republicans. Nor did it seem to set well with Americans at large: a Gallup poll taken a week or so after the seizure disclosed that only 35 percent of those who had heard of the seizure approved of it. In early June 1952, when the Supreme Court invalidated the seizure of the industry, the steelworkers went streaming out of the mills; they remained out for fifty-three days. Finally, near the end of July, increasingly concerned that the work stoppage in steel was forcing curtailment of production of 105-millimeter artillery shells and F-86 Sabre jets (not to mention automobiles and other civilian goods), Truman summoned Benjamin Fairless of the steel industry and Philip Murray of the USW to the White House and told them to settle their differences "or else." On receiving the presidential ultimatum the two retired to the Cabinet Room; an hour and twenty minutes later they emerged with the outline of an agreement which brought to an end the longest and costliest steel strike then on record.

Despite the squeaks and jolts, the overall performance of the economy during the final two years of the Korean conflict was impressive. To confirm that assessment one need only examine the figures on the gross national product (i.e., the total output of goods and services). During the second quarter of 1951, as armistice negotiations were about to get underway at Kaesong, the gross national product had reached an annual rate of $325 billion. During the second quarter of 1952 it reached $343 billion, and during the second quarter of 1953, on the eve of the signing of the armistice, $372 billion. Other figures provide additional confirmation. Spurred by the line in the president's budget message of 1952 estimating that the government would spend $52.868 billion for defense in fiscal 1953 (compared with an actual outlay of slightly over $41 billion in fiscal 1952), business leaders stepped up investments in new plants and equipment until by the second quarter of 1953 such expenditures had reached a record annual rate of $28 billion. In the aftermath of the steel strike in mid-1952, industrial production literally "took off"; in March 1953 it reached a record plateau. Such output inevitably was reflected in employment figures. By June 1953, a month before the Korean conflict ended, the civilian labor force numbered 64,734,000, an increase of 344,000 over June 1952, while the number of unemployed in June 1953 came to 1,562,000, a decline of 256,000 compared with June 1952. Meanwhile, disposable personal income (i.e., income after taxes) bounded to new highs; by August 1953, the month after the armistice, it had reached an annual rate of $287 billion, an increase of $15.7 billion over the August 1952 figure. Inflation, moreover, remained securely under control from mid-1951 through the end of the Korean conflict, largely because the production of consumer commodities tended to keep pace with the expanding volume of disposable personal income. Even in early 1953, when President Truman's successor terminated price and wage controls, the overall rise in retail prices was negligible. As for corporate profits after taxes, they reached an annual rate of $25.7 billion during the second quarter of 1953, not as high as before enactment of the Revenue Act of 1950 but sufficient to enable corporations to pay $9 billion in dividends during the first two quarters of 1953.

During those months from July 1951 to July 1953, while GI's in Korea were moving out nightly to patrol the no-man's land in front of "Line Minnesota" (the main line of resistance), diving into bunkers and ditches to escape enemy mortar fire, and counting the months and days they had left before becoming eligible for "Big R" (rotation to the states), Americans at home were relishing the fruits of rampaging prosperity. In early 1952, after the Truman administration, no longer so afraid of a new Soviet military adventure and sensitive to the need to keep voters as contented as possible in an election year, had set about to "stretch out" the national rearmament program (i.e., set back schedules for military production and thus make possible substantial increases in the output of civilian goods), Americans bought automobiles, television sets, appliances, and nearly every other kind of consumer item with seemingly reckless abandon. They freely indulged their ravenous appetites for pleasure and recreation and, during the summer of 1952, helped book nearly every transatlantic steamship and airplane to capacity as they descended on Europe in record numbers. Indeed, judging by the output of the popular media, one might have been excused for thinking that the United States had become a veritable utopia or a sort of twentieth-century Garden of Eden.

Nevertheless, during those months of rampant prosperity, Americans remained troubled in spirit, for slithering about in their Garden of Eden (or so millions of them ardently believed and millions of others strongly suspected) was a legion of serpents—Communist subversives—toiling day and night to tempt the citizenry away from the true faith of Americanism. As Richard Rovere, Robert Griffith, and other writers have ably demonstrated, Senator McCarthy and his fellow "Red-hunters" capitalized on that troubled spirit. In truth, in early 1952, instead of fading in the face of his outlandish exaggerations and distortions and the appearance of new issues, as some political figures and newsmen had expected, McCarthy's influence reached a new plateau. As a consequence, the senator's Democratic critics on Capitol Hill backed away from a proposal to investigate his accusations, supporters of Senator Taft's White House ambitions openly embraced McCarthy, and supporters of General Eisenhower's presidential candidacy declined to repudiate McCarthy.

The Truman administration, meanwhile, stepped up its antisubversive activities. During the summer of 1951, after the Supreme Court had upheld the constitutionality of the Alien Registration (Smith) Act of 1940, making it unlawful for any person to advocate the violent overthrow of any government in the United States, Attorney General J. Howard McGrath outlined new plans by the government to move against Communists and so-called fellow travelers. Officers of the Federal Bureau of Investigation began apprehending leaders of the American Communist party for alleged violations of the Smith Act; within a month more than forty party officials were in jail, under arrest, or in flight. The following year, amid considerable publicity, congressional investigators and a grand jury in New York charged that Communist subversives who also were American citizens were in the employ of the secretariat of the United Nations. As a result, President Truman, in one of his last acts as president in January 1953, issued an executive order requiring Americans working for the U.N. to undergo the same loyalty screening to which federal employees were subjected.

Continuing to nourish American anti-Communist impulses during the final two years of the conflict in East Asia were the weekly burials—with full military honors—of young men who had fallen victim of Communist bullets and shrapnel in Korea, the Communist diatribes emanating from the tea house at Kaesong and the tent village at Panmunjom, and the daily news reports and pictures to which the citizenry was subjected. It must have been with sheer disgust, for example, that Americans absorbed accounts of the *Weltjugend Festpiele* in East Berlin in August 1951, during which North Korean spokesmen trumpeted alleged American atrocities in Korea and youthful "Reds" displayed a poster showing half of Harry Truman's face merged with half of Adolf Hitler's and carrying the caption: "Truman der Erbe Hitlers." Americans doubtless seethed in April 1952 when, at a meeting of the U.N. Disarmament Commission in New York, the Soviet delegate, Jacob Malik, proclaimed that American aircraft had rained North Korea with germ-infected crackers, pork, spiders, crows, ants, yellow leaves, crickets, canned food, fleas, flies, and goose feathers. And it is probable that they saw little humor in a Soviet attack on American comic books and the alleged indoctrination of America's youth, published a short time later:

> One of the most "popular" series of "comics" published in the U.S.A. for the "education" of the young generation—this is what Superman is called. The only thing this "superman" does is to beat up and torture everyone he comes across. "Comics" with their scenes of violence and murders replace all other literature for American children. . . . "Boy Scouts," "Cubs," and "Girl Scouts" supplement the militarist indoctrination of the young generation. . . . The children belonging to these organizations are called "troops"; they are trained in military drill. Here also brutal instincts are injected in the children, human feelings are also hounded out.

There was no letup; one can only speculate on Americans' thoughts when they read in February 1952 that a succession of Polish emigrés had paraded before a congressional committee to explain how the Soviets, not the Germans, had perpetrated the infamous massacre of Polish officers in the Katyn Forest in 1943 or what they thought about the headline in *Newsweek* in January 1953 proclaiming, "War on the Red World's Jews—Moscow Sets Stage for Pogrom," introducing an account of the arrest of Jewish physicians in the Soviet Union for allegedly plotting the murder of Soviet leaders. Another *Newsweek* headline which appeared during March 1953, in the aftermath of the death of Joseph Stalin, read, "From Red China to Red Berlin, A Slave State. Can Stalin's Heirs Hold His Empire Together?" Beneath the headline was a two-page map of the sprawling Soviet "empire" (which included China), accompanied by an article comparing the Soviet domain with the Mongol empire of the Kublai Khan—whose warriors, according to the article, cared only for plunder and conquest.

Once in a great while the rhetoric of anticommunism in America took a lighter turn, but even then there was usually an anti-Communist sting, as in the incident of Nam Il and the matches. During the truce negotiations at Kaesong in August 1951 the chief Communist delegate, Lt. Gen. Nam Il, a chain-smoker, tried to light a cigarette with "Red Star" matches and then with a Communist-made lighter. To no avail; the matches and lighter sputtered without effect. In desperation, Nam picked up some American-made matches that were lying on the table, and, of course, they worked every time. On hearing of Nam's predicament, the president of the Diamond Match Local of the United Match

THE WAR AND AMERICAN SOCIETY

Workers in Oswego, New York, cabled the chief American delegate at Kaesong, Vice Adm. C. Turner Joy: "Products made by free men under a competitive economy will always be of high quality and superior to those of regimented slave labor. With the thought that they might demonstrate this point if presented by you to Gen. Nam we are sending you air express a case [2,500 books] of good American matches. . . . Who knows but what they will help the general see the light."

To be sure, more than a dread of communism was troubling Americans during those prosperous months following the opening of armistice negotiations at Kaesong. In early 1952, as that quadrennial spectacle which is unique to America—a presidential election—neared, it seemed clear that in some fashion the Korean conflict would become an issue in the campaign. The cloak rooms on Capitol Hill began to buzz with reports that Republican orators had found that a mention of General MacArthur's name invariably sparked a vigorous audience response. Senator Taft, addressing the Women's National Republican Club in early February 1952, labeled the conflict in Korea "the Truman War"—"an unnecessary war" which would not have come to pass if the United States had not withdrawn its troops from Korea in 1949, had provided adequate armament to the South Koreans, and "if we had given notice that we were going to do exactly what we actually did do in the case of aggression."

Still, as Ronald J. Caridi has written in *The Korean War and American Politics: The Republican Party as a Case Study*, a range of issues, including scandal in the Truman administration, confronted politicians as the electoral mechanism began to shift into high gear during the spring of 1952; and the more cautious political operatives seemed unsure of how the Korean conflict might shake out as a campaign issue. The reason for such uncertainty was not hard to assess: for all of its frustration over the stalemated conflict, the electorate was transmitting no clear signals about Korea. No important national group was seriously urging either peace at any price in East Asia or a dramatic enlargement of the conflict, and one could find support for the view that the Truman administration had done well to restrict combat to the Korean peninsula and salvage the independence of South Korea. Among those who were speaking with notable restraint on Korea, as the national party conventions approached, was the front-runner for the Republican nomination, General Eisenhower. In June 1952 Ike said of the Korean conflict, "I do not have any prescription for bringing the thing to a decisive end." Eisenhower continued his cautious approach even when General MacArthur, in his keynote address to the GOP convention the following month, criticized the Democratic administration for "discarding victory as the military objective" in Korea and when former President Hoover evoked whoops and whistles from delegates after denouncing the Truman administration for appeasing the Communists.

After capturing the nomination, however, Eisenhower put caution aside and set about to make Korea a central issue in his campaign against the Democratic nominee, Gov. Adlai E. Stevenson of Illinois. Encouraging Eisenhower and his strategists in that regard, no doubt, was a Gallup poll taken during mid-August 1952 in which a cross section of the population was asked which candidate could best handle the situation in Korea. Sixty-seven percent of those interviewed named Eisenhower, only 9 percent named Stevenson. Thus, in mid-September the general declared: "We are in [the Korean conflict] because this administration allowed America . . . to become weak . . . because this administration abandoned China to the Communists. . . . Must we go on writing off the Far East at one moment and at almost the next fighting and dying in Korea?" In early October, in what was billed as a major foreign policy address in Cincinnati, the Republican standard-bearer touched off roars from his audience when he proclaimed: "In January of 1950 our Secretary of State declared that America's so-called 'defensive perimeter' excluded areas on the Asiatic mainland such as Korea. . . . Five months later Communist tanks were rolling over the 38th parallel to assault South Korea. Twenty-seven months later the United States had suffered 120,000 casualties in a bloody, continuing conflict." A fortnight later Ike charged that the Truman administration had fallen into a Soviet trap when it agreed, during the summer of 1951, to enter armistice negotiations in Korea. Then, barely a week before voters would troop to the polls, Eisenhower electrified his countrymen, particularly the mothers of GI's in Korea (including the mother of the author of this essay), by announcing that the first task of a new Republican administration would be to bring the conflict in Korea to an early and honorable end. "That job requires a personal trip to Korea. . . . I shall make the trip. . . . I shall go to Korea." Still, Eisenhower never intimated that he would consider a dramatic expansion of the fighting in East Asia if the Communists refused to come to terms. Nor did he indicate the slightest willingness to procure an armistice by making concessions on the thorny issue of repatriating prisoners of war—the last serious obstacle to a truce in Korea.

As for the Democrats, they maneuvered as best they could on the issue. In the platform adopted at their 1952 national convention, they contended that "Korea has proved once and for all that the United Nations will resist aggression," but it was hard to stir voters with the suggestion that the dreary and stalemated conflict in Korea had, in truth, yielded a magnificent victory for the American side. Led by President Truman, who came out punching in the closing rounds of the campaign, the Democrats tried to counter the Republican contention that withdrawal of American troops from the Korean peninsula in 1949 had been a key ingredient in the mix which encouraged the Communists to make their lunge across the 38th Parallel by charging that in 1947, while chief of staff of the army, Eisenhower himself had recommended evacuating the remaining GI's from Korea. The assertion that he somehow was partly responsible for what he considered had been a disastrous train of events in East Asia infuriated Eisenhower, and his bitterness spilled over after the election when Truman offered him use of a presidential plane for his trip to Korea—"if you still want to go."

When the balloting on November 4, 1952, resulted in an Eisenhower landslide, political analysts set about to assess the importance of Korea in the campaign. The Survey Research Center of the University of Michigan concluded that Korea had been a minor factor, that domestic considerations had far outweighed Korea in persuading nearly thirty-four million Americans to vote for Eisenhower. In his book, Ronald Caridi cautions against placing too much emphasis on Korea as a campaign issue. Nevertheless, Caridi observes that the East Asian conflict substantially reinforced Republican arguments on such questions as government spending, taxation, corruption in government, and Communist subversion. Thus he seems to imply that Korea may have been a larger factor in determining the outcome of the 1952 election than the Survey Research Center and other analysts thought at the time.

After Eisenhower's trip to Korea, which seemed to stir the South Koreans more than it did GI's in the combat zone, the Korean conflict again slipped to the inside pages of America's newspapers; the stalemated battleground continued to be a place of long periods of silence punctuated by grim firefights and mortar barrages.

At length, in March 1953, the Communists agreed to an exchange of sick and wounded POW's ("Operation Little Switch"); at the end of April they consented to resume the plenary negotiations at Panmunjom, which had been in recess since the previous autumn. After a month of discussion and deliberation, negotiators worked out a compromise solution to the prickly problem of repatriation of prisoners of war. The attempt by South Korea's president, Syngman Rhee, to undermine the projected truce in the vain hope of keeping the war alive and somehow driving the Communists from North Korea came to naught, and finally on July 27, 1953, news agencies flashed the word around the world that Communist and U.N. delegates at Panmunjom, with a minimum of ceremony, had signed an armistice. The response of Americans?

They did not dance in the streets as they had in 1945 on "V-J Day." Instead they seemed to breathe a collective sigh of relief that the ordeal in Korea was over. Perhaps their sentiments were best expressed in the results of a Gallup poll taken less than a month after the armistice. Reminded that the United States was presently sending war materials to help the French fight communists in Indochina, a cross section of the populace was asked, "Would you approve or disapprove of sending United States soldiers to take part in the fighting there?" Only 8 percent said they would approve, 85 percent said they would disapprove.

In conclusion, one may say that except for those weeks at the end of 1950, when it appeared that the Chinese might kick U.N. forces off the Korean peninsula or, worse, that the combat in East Asia might escalate into World War III, the conflict in Korea from 1950 to 1953 was not a particularly traumatic interlude in the life of the people of the United States. Frustrating, perhaps—notably when weeks and then months dragged by and negotiators at Kaesong and Panmunjom were unable to arrange an armistice—but not unduly traumatic. Barely 33,000 Americans died in battle during the thirty-seven months of fighting in Korea—less than a fourth as many as died on the nation's streets and highways during the same period, about a tenth as many as perished in forty-four months during the Second World War. Thus, the supreme agony of armed conflict directly touched only a fraction of the citizenry. As for the 1.4 million young men who were tapped by their "friends and neighbors" (so stated the "Greetings" that draftees received when ordered to report to active duty) to serve in the armed forces during the Korean conflict, a majority of them never heard a shot fired in anger. Nor were more than a small percentage marked by psychological or physical scars when they returned to civilian life. On the contrary, the great preponderance of men who served in the armed forces from 1950 to 1953, upon separation from the service, slipped with comparative ease back into their former lifestyles. Nearly a fourth of them took advantage of Public Law 550, the Korean GI Bill of Rights enacted in 1952, to attend college or to receive vocational or job training. For those scores of millions of Americans who never had to submit to a diatribe by a drill sergeant or try to avoid frostbite while manning a mortar tube in Korea, such dislocations and inconveniences as did result from the partial mobilization effort from 1950 to 1953 were, in most instances, more than compensated for by the rampaging performance of the economy during the Korean conflict. Perhaps, too, it was comforting to know that the dislocations and inconveniences were nothing compared with those endured less than a decade before in "the big war." Nor were Americans on the home front unsettled, as they would be a decade and a half later during the conflict in Vietnam, by antiwar students' angry demonstrations and raucous charges that the United States was carrying on an inhumane and indefensible military campaign in East Asia. Throughout the affair in Korea the people of the United States remained serene in the conviction that their cause in East Asia, however frustrating, was noble and just. And the students? Their most raucous activity came during the spring of 1952, when on campuses from Maine to California young men invaded women's residence halls in the celebrated "panty raids" and, as coeds urged them on with giggles and shrieks, snatched assorted items of lingerie.

If it was not particularly traumatic for Americans, the Korean conflict nonetheless left its marks on American society. One might think of those marks in terms of pluses and minuses. On the plus side, America's participation in the conflict provided a powerful stimulus to the national economy, and, as a consequence, the level of prosperity in the republic reached a new plateau. Notwithstanding the outpouring of popular support for the general, the MacArthur-Truman controversy of 1951 caused Americans to ponder anew the national tradition, dating from early colonial times, of civilian ascendancy over the military; the outcome, it is clear in retrospect, was a decided reinforcement of that tradition. Likewise, the MacArthur-Truman controversy compelled citizens to reconsider time-honored ideas about total victory in armed conflict. The result, it seems fair to say, was a new sophistication in the United States about the nature and purpose of armed combat. (During the conflict in Vietnam, for example, the most committed "hawks" were reluctant to echo General MacArthur's dictum that there is no substitute for victory.) The Korean conflict also had some notable social consequences. There was the repudiation of the old clichés that black Americans were ineffectual in combat and that black and white troops could not function efficiently in the same units. As Donald R. McCoy and Richard T. Reutten have demonstrated in *Quest and Response: Minority Rights and the Truman Administration*, blacks performed well in Korea—and blacks and whites performed well together. Such performances strengthened the pride and morale of black Americans and prompted many whites, particularly the young who had served alongside blacks in Korea, to question hoary notions about black cowardice and ineptitude. Thus, the conflict in Korea made an important— though perhaps not clearly determinable—contribution to the gradual erosion of the racial caste system in the United States. Finally, the Korean conflict's GI Bill of Rights performed similar educational and training services for new veterans that the earlier GI Bill had performed for veterans of World War II—and provided a similar enrichment of the life of the American republic.

Turning to the minuses, i.e., the unfortunate marks left on American society by the Korean conflict, it would seem that the most notable minus was the dramatic stirring of the Cold War spirit in America from 1950 to 1953. This assertion is not intended to question the propriety of the decision to intervene in the East Asian conflict for the purpose of preserving the Republic of Korea. Nor is it calculated to imply that the Communists did not provide the people of the United States with abundant reason for becoming stirred up in the early years of the 1950s. Still, as President Woodrow Wilson allegedly told newsman Frank Cobb on the evening before he asked Congress to declare war on Germany in April 1917, armed conflict inevitably stirs national passions, and the result sometimes is patterns of behavior and thought that the populace might deplore in a less inflammatory period. In any event, as an outcome of the Korean affair, when Americans became increasingly agitated about the machinations, real and alleged, of international communism, the upshot—in the estimation of this author—was consequences not altogether laudable: the shattering of any lingering chance that important parts of President Truman's Fair Deal program might pass through Congress; the strengthening of the appeal of Senator McCarthy and like-minded purveyors of half-truths and innuendo; a reinforcement of the national determination to scorn and boycott the People's Republic of China and the corresponding national embrace of Chiang Kai-shek and his regime on Formosa; the strengthening of the idea that the United States must be ready and willing to stand firm against international communism at virtually every point on the face of the earth (an idea which helped move the United States into the quagmire of Vietnam); an enhancing of the idea (as Arthur M. Schlesinger, Jr., has observed in *The Imperial Presidency*) that only the executive branch of the federal government has the breadth of vision and capacity to provide effective national leadership in the volatile arena of world affairs.

Do the minuses outweigh the pluses? That is an open question.

Comments

Ronald J. Caridi

Professor John Wiltz's incisive and sometimes poignant synthesis provides a perspective for considering the impact of a particular overseas engagement on the domestic life of the nation. This has been a considerably neglected area since most studies of the war are concerned with political or military aspects of the conflict.[1] By contrast, in the great outpouring of literature about the Indochina struggle, domestic implications have not been overlooked. It is for this reason that Professor Wiltz's survey is particularly welcome.

His essay concludes that "the conflict in Korea from 1950 to 1953 was not a particularly traumatic interlude in the life of the people of the United States. . . . [Nonetheless, it] left its marks on American society." Professor Wiltz believes that America's participation in the conflict was a positive experience because the war:

a. provided a powerful stimulus to the national economy, resulting in new levels of prosperity;
b. reinforced the tradition of civilian ascendancy over the military, despite the early popular support for General MacArthur's position;
c. helped develop a new sophistication in the United States about the nature and purpose of armed conflict;
d. repudiated the clichés that black Americans were not effective in combat and that blacks and whites could not function efficiently in the same units; and
e. enriched the life of the republic through the Korean War GI Bill of Rights.

Again according to Wiltz, the war was a negative experience for Americans because it:

a. intensified the Cold War spirit in the United States;
b. shattered President Truman's last hopes of securing passage of important parts of his Fair Deal legislation;
c. strengthened the appeal of Senator McCarthy and his ilk;

159

    d. reinforced the nation's inclination to reject the People's Republic of China and embrace the regime of Chiang Kai-shek;

    e. strengthened the belief that the United States must be ever-vigilant against the spread of international communism anywhere on the globe; and

    f. encouraged the belief that only the executive branch could provide effective national leadership in international affairs.

Having offered this catalog, the author concludes that it is an "open question" whether the "minuses outweigh the pluses." My own view is that Wiltz underestimates the negative impact of the Korean War on America. I question some of the items he considers "positive" experiences, and I believe that he has failed to identify additional negative aspects of America's involvement in the conflict. The sole item on the list of positive influences with which I am in full agreement relates to the Korean War GI Bill of Rights since it is reasonably clear that many who took advantage of its benefits were given the opportunity to live fuller lives. Nevertheless, the Korean War cannot claim credit for the concept of a GI Bill of Rights as a reward given (or a debt owed) to servicemen.

One must question the proposition that the war "repudiated" the myth about the combat abilities of black Americans "and made an important—though perhaps not clearly determinable—contribution to the erosion of the racial caste system in the United States." Barton Bernstein's important essay, "The Ambiguous Legacy: The Truman Administration and Civil Rights" suggests that the effect of the Korean War on the armed forces was actually quite limited. For example, in September 1948 President Truman had called for the desegregation of the armed forces "in such a way that it is not a publicity stunt."[2] Yet the movement was very slow; so intense was the opposition that the president was forced to promise that quotas on blacks could be restored if the army received blacks in disproportionately high numbers. "Well into the Korean War," Bernstein writes, "the Army retained many segregated units, and integration in Europe did not even begin until April 1952."[3]

In his study of Truman as commander-in-chief, Richard F. Haynes concludes that the desegregation order "had an immeasurable influence upon the domestic civil rights movement in the 1950s and 1960s," but concedes that it was "politically motivated and was not vigorously pursued."[4] I would conclude, therefore, that Wiltz overstates his case about the effect of the war on the position of blacks in the military. Some of the integration during the conflict was token in nature; and twenty-five years after the Korean War, the armed services continue to

COMMENTS

demonstrate that they have not accomplished a harmonious integration of the races.

Professor Wiltz's contention that the Korean War fostered a new sophistication about the nature and purpose of armed conflict should be examined closely since the example he offers is a curious one. Wiltz writes that during the Vietnam conflict even the most committed hawk was reluctant to "echo General MacArthur's dictum that there is no substitute for victory." Can such an observation be the basis for the claim of growing American sophistication? After all, the Indochina war followed Korea. Presumably, sophisticated policies would not have created a nearly inextricable quagmire. Furthermore, as James V. Compton reminds us, during the Korean War the "search for scapegoats was intensified in order to square American omnipotence with the visible growth of hostile ideology and power."[5] Involvement in Korea, with its attendant frustrations, would appear to have made American reactions to Cold War crises more rigid rather than more sophisticated.

What of the much repeated claim that the Korean War, because of the Truman-MacArthur controversy, reinforced the tradition of civilian ascendancy over the military? Does not such a theory also imply that the tradition of civilian authority had been questioned by a segment of the citizenry? Such was not the case. The crisis was a very personal one—for a single military man whose ambition or self-confidence led to a confrontation with the president. Truman recognized this, and in a letter to General Eisenhower, then NATO supreme commander, he was characteristically blunt and firm. "Dear Ike," the president wrote on April 12, "I was sorry to have to reach a parting of the way with the big man in Asia but he asked for it and I had to give it to him."[6] Moreover, as Alonzo Hamby notes in *Beyond the New Deal*, the tug-of-war between the president and the general had very serious negative ramifications.

> Almost all liberals feared that Truman and Acheson were conceding too much to their rightwing critics. The needless U.N. condemnation of Red China and the increasingly harsh anti-Communist stance of the State Department in early 1951 drew criticism from liberals. . . . Paradoxically, the MacArthur dismissal worsened the situation. The State Department seemed more determined than ever to prove to the public that it stood for hard-line anti-Communism. In Congressional testimony, Acheson expressed unalterable opposition to the admission of Communist China to the U.N. and declared that the United States would never permit the transfer of Formosa to the Reds.[7]

Professor Wiltz stresses the positive impact of the war on the national economy while at the same time noting that "the national economy in the week of June 18–25, 1950, was nearing the end of its most prosperous six-month period since the end of the Second World War." I would suggest that given the level of economic activity prior to June 1950, and the economic problems which followed the peace, a more precise assessment of the war's impact might have been offered. Bert G. Hickman's study for the National Bureau of Economic Research, *The Korean War and United States Economic Activity, 1950–52*, provides some insights. Hickman reports that by late 1949 the economy was experiencing a "vigorous recovery" from the relatively mild recession of 1948–49, and prior to the outbreak of hostilities in mid-1950, the "level of economic activity was high and rising. . . . The Korean War and the associated defense mobilization strongly influenced the trend of economic activity in the United States during 1950–52." Hickman continues,

> Gross private domestic investment and gross national product increased more rapidly in percentage terms between the last quarter of 1949 and the second quarter of 1950 than in any subsequent interval during the [1950–1952] period. . . . *The economic forces set in motion by the Korean conflict impinged on an economy that was already operating at a high and expanding level of activity.* The pool of unemployed labor that could be drawn upon to increase the national output was small.[8]

While the Korean War helped guarantee three years of prosperity, by the close of 1953 industrial production, the gross national product, construction contracts, and manufacturers' new orders were down; unemployment took an upward turn. Nine months after the conclusion of the war, industrial production had fallen 10 percent, the gross national product shrank 4 percent, and manufacturing employment was down by 10 percent. Government spending declined by $11 billion between the second quarter of 1953 and the second quarter of 1954. If this was not a "serious decline," it nevertheless was the cause for "great concern."[9] It is, of course, arguable that these dislocations were the result of the economic policies of the Eisenhower administration and that they were not directly related to the Korean effort.

What is perhaps most troublesome about Professor Wiltz's analysis is his failure to confront the argument of Athan Theoharis and other "revisionists" that the Korean War had a profound domestic impact because it was used by the Truman administration to reinforce the alarmist, conspiratorial tendencies of the Congress and the American public.[10] This charge was made by I. F. Stone even before the war came to a close,[11] and it has had considerable currency with "New Left" historians. For example, in *The Limits of Power*, Joyce and Gabriel Kolko indict the administration:

COMMENTS

The war in its perverse way had proved utilitarian to the Truman administration's achievement of its larger goals in Europe and the world. It had helped to mobilize a reticent Congress, and it galvanized an apathetic population. . . . Certainly throughout 1950 Washington had been unwilling to negotiate an end to the war . . . because of its desire to exploit the new crisis to attain yet other, quite unrelated objectives. . . . The Truman administration . . . kept the war alive later for reasons of domestic politics or fear of being politically outflanked with accusations of appeasement . . . [and the] desire to make more credible the vision of America as the masterful military giant.[12]

To identify this omission in the Wiltz critique is not to advocate the revisionist thesis. The argument, however, should have been examined since such an examination would have provided greater insight into the spectrum of opinion on the domestic impact of the war.

One final point. Toward the close of his essay, Professor Wiltz offers the following observation: "Throughout the affair in Korea the people of the United States remained serene in the conviction that their cause in East Asia, however frustrating, was noble and just." I find such a thesis questionable since I had concluded in *The Korean War and American Politics* that the Republican party had callously, if skillfully, manipuated the public's discontent for partisan gains. The use of the word "serene" is troublesome.

There is some support for Wiltz's position in John E. Mueller's close analysis of public opinion polls taken during the Korean War. Mueller reports in *War, Presidents, and Public Opinion* that the Chinese intervention seemed to "shake from the support ranks those who were tenuous and those who felt that they could support a short war, but not a long one." Mueller also found that after November 1950, the war was "left with a relatively hard core of support that remained generally at a constant level for the duration; changes in fortune and climbing casualty figures apparently became less important."[13] Since this "hard core of support," however, never rose above 50 percent between September 1950 and November 1952,[14] one must resist Wiltz's over-generalized characterization of a "serene" public.

NOTES

1. For example, perhaps the best published study of the war—David Rees, *Korea: The Limited War* (New York: St. Martin's, 1964)—slights the domestic aspects of the war.
2. Truman quoted by Barton J. Bernstein, "The Ambiguous Legacy: The Truman Administration and Civil Rights," in *Politics and Policies of the Truman Administration,* ed. Barton J. Bernstein (Chicago: Quadrangle, 1970), p. 297.

3. Ibid., p. 298.
4. Richard F. Haynes, *The Awesome Power: Harry S. Truman as Commander in Chief* (Baton Rouge, La.: Louisiana State University Press, 1973), p. 268.
5. James V. Compton, "Anti-Communism in American Life Since the Second World War," *Forums in History* 5 (St. Charles, Mo.): 7.
6. Haynes, p. 263.
7. Alonzo L. Hamby, *Beyond the New Deal: Harry S. Truman and American Liberalism* (New York: Columbia University Press, 1973), p. 426.
8. Bert G. Hickman, *The Korean War and United States Economic Activity, 1950–52* (New York: National Bureau of Economic Research, Inc., 1955), pp. 5–7 (emphasis added).
9. Ross M. Robertson, *History of the American Economy*, 2nd ed. (New York: Harcourt, Brace & World, 1964), pp. 647–48.
10. See, for example, Athan Theoharis, *Seeds of Repression: Harry S. Truman and the Origins of McCarthyism* (Chicago: Quadrangle, 1971).
11. I. F. Stone, *The Hidden History of the Korean War* (New York and London: Monthly Review Press, 1952), p. 616.
12. Joyce and Gabriel Kolko, *The Limits of Power: The World and United States Foreign Policy, 1945–1954* (New York: Harper & Row, 1972), p. 616.
13. John E. Mueller, *War, Presidents, and Public Opinion* (New York: Wiley, 1973), pp. 51–52.
14. Ibid., pp. 45–50.

Robert Griffith

I shall restrict my comments to the influence of the war on one or two aspects of American domestic politics. Even here, however, we face a problem analogous to the one we encountered in discussing the impact of the Korean War on American foreign policy: how much do we attribute to the broader context, the Cold War, the reaction to the Chinese revolution, and so forth? In discussing American politics during the post–World War II period we also have to deal with a broader context which includes the end of the New Deal, the slow retreat of Democratic liberalism after 1938, the impact of World War II and the emergence of the Cold War, the return—after more than a decade—of relatively high levels of employment, and a general, if somewhat uneven, prosperity. We may want to guard against burdening the Korean War with the responsibility for too much influence as a causative factor in our history. But it is, nevertheless, possible to argue, if not always to measure, that the Korean War did have an important influence on

COMMENTS

American politics and culture—less as a force that produced sharp discontinuities and radical departures than as a force that accelerated and heightened processes already underway.

Both the New Deal and World War II unsettled traditional notions about the size and the character of American government. As a result, during the years following World War II American leaders were involved in negotiating a series of arrangements to reconcile competing claims to the government's enormously expanded resources. Perhaps the most important of these arrangements involved the competing claims of national security and domestic needs—of guns and butter. Each side of this equation, moreover, involved still other sets of competing claims. Within the area of national security politics, for example, there were competing claims among the various branches as well as among groups pursuing different strategic concepts. Within the domestic arena there was conflict between those who would continue and expand New Deal social welfare programs and those who would lower taxes. Even more importantly, there was sharp competition over the distribution of federal benefits among competing programs—agricultural subsidies versus public housing versus aid to small businesses, and so on. The arrangements made during these years also involved nonmaterial interests. For example, the impact of World War II and especially the Cold War produced a reordering of the prewar balance between the power of the state and the rights of the people, between the values of national security, on the one hand, and freedom and democracy, on the other. The Korean War, I would suggest, influenced the way in which balances were struck in all of these areas and at all levels of government. Let me briefly sketch two examples which may help to illustrate this process.

The first of these involves the expansion of the postwar American military establishment and the way in which the Korean War heightened the already substantial ascendancy of national security values and priorities. During the late 1940s there was a growing belief on the part of State Department and military planners that America's military capacities were not commensurate with the sweeping foreign policy of global containment being set forth by the president and other U.S. leaders. As Secretary of State George C. Marshall put it in early 1948, "We are playing with fire while we have nothing with which to put it out." This belief in the inadequacy of America's military might was reinforced by the detonation of a Soviet A-bomb, by the Communists' victory in China, and by the increase in international tension which accompanied the Berlin blockade. This, in turn, led in early 1950 to the preparation by State and Defense Department planners of NSC-68, a National Security Council paper which called for a drastic expansion of the American military establishment, boosting the annual military budget from its 1949 level of approximately $14 billion to an estimated $35 to $50 billion. Even though NSC-68 clearly represented the desires of key administration leaders, the obstacles to such a massive and costly expansion were many, especially in Congress where proponents of economy in defense spending continued to gain influence.

The Korean War swept aside these and other obstacles and made it possible for the administration to win passage of its military program without opposition and virtually without debate. The resulting expansion of the military, designed to meet not only the needs of the Korean emergency but also to satisfy the dictates of America's expansive new diplomacy of containment, would produce, by the end of the Truman administration, a defense budget of nearly $50 billion, constituting 13.5 percent of the gross national product and accounting for nearly 70 percent of all federal expenditures. Though there would be some

ACME Newspictures—UPI

U.S. soldiers man a machine gun emplacement overlooking a damaged bridge— August 8, 1950.

modest reductions following the end of the war in Korea, American military spending would generally remain extremely high from this point on.

The other side of the coin, of course, was that much less money remained to be distributed on nonmilitary and non-foreign policy objectives. Thus, the Korean War decisively and dramatically affected the way in which American leaders struck the balance between guns and butter, a balance (or perhaps we should call it an imbalance) which would continue to shape American politics and society for decades to come.

The second example I would use to illustrate my point involves the Internal Security Act of 1950, the so-called McCarran Act. As Professor Wiltz has pointed out, the Korean War indeed increased the repressive climate of the Cold War years. Here once again, however, we are dealing with processes and trends which were already well underway before the outbreak of fighting in Korea. Since 1947 the Truman administration had been emphasizing the menace of Soviet communism in an attempt to win public support for its foreign policies. The administration also instituted a tough loyalty-security program, initiated the prosecution of American Communists, and, in general, wrapped itself in the banner of staunch anticommunism. Conservative critics of the administration took an even more beligerent position, condemning the Democrats for their "softness" on communism both at home and abroad. This conservative attack intensified following the explosion of the Soviet A-bomb, the Communist victory in China, and the arrest of men and women accused of spying for the Soviet Union. By early 1950 the targets of such charges included even fervent anti-Communists such as Secretary of State Dean Acheson; Senator Joe McCarthy, the politician who best symbolized the growing climate of political repression, was already a figure of national prominence.

It was in this context that the McCarran Act had its origins. The beginnings were in a bill first introduced in 1947 by Sen. Karl E. Mundt (R., S.D.) and Rep. Richard M. Nixon (R., Calif.). The bill would have required groups labeled as "Communist political organizations" to register the names of their officers and members with the attorney general. If the organization's leaders failed to do so, it then would become incumbent on individual members to register. The bill passed the House in 1948, but was bottled up in the Senate.

Following the outbreak of war in Korea, however, Republicans renewed their drive to get the bill enacted, to prove that they were opposed to communism and to suggest, inferentially, that Truman and the Democrats were not. The response—and I believe this provides some gauge of the reaction within Congress to the Korean War—of Democratic liberals in the Senate was to introduce an alternative bill, a substitute for the Mundt-Nixon bill, authorizing the president to declare a national security emergency which would then allow the attorney general and the FBI to round up and imprison potential subversives and saboteurs. So drastic was the liberals' bill that one White House aide characterized it as a "concentration camp" measure. The final result was a combination including both the "registration" measure introduced by Mundt and Nixon and the "detention" measure sponsored by Paul H. Douglas, Hubert Humphrey, and other Democratic liberals. This bill passed both the House and the Senate by large margins, was vetoed by President Truman, and was then passed over his veto. The passage of this measure thus offers dramatic evidence of the way in which the Korean War heightened the ascendancy of national security values and contributed to the erosion of dissent and political freedom in Cold War America.

Finally, and more generally, the war slowed—if it did not halt entirely—domestic reform on the part of the Truman administration, while further strengthening the power and influence of conservative forces in American society. Truman was forced to abandon the remnants of the Fair Deal and to depend more and more on conservatives, both within Congress, where he was now forced to seek accommodation with the Southern Democrats, and even within his own administration, where the balance seemed to shift toward more conservative advisers. The failure of the Brannan plan, the emasculation of the housing program authorized by the Housing Act of 1949, the shelving of programs for health care and civil rights, all bore witness to the impact of the Korean War. President Truman's reform agenda would not reappear until the 1960s under Presidents Kennedy and Johnson. By then, it seemed, Democratic liberals, like Alice, were running faster and faster in order to only stand still.

Alonzo L. Hamby

Professor Wiltz has provided a fluent, readable account of American life and politics during the Korean War years. The layman or student seeking a brief guide to this topic could hardly do better. The specialist, however, will find that for the most part the paper tells him what he already knows. The chronological organization inhibits any systematic analysis of the war's major themes, and there is little critical discussion of what historians have done or need to do with the domestic side of the conflict.

Few would argue with Professor Wiltz's contention that the Korean

COMMENTS

War did not have a major impact on American society akin to that of World War II. The limited nature of the Korean conflict contrasts sharply with the pervasive mobilization, wide sense of sacrifice, and feeling of national unity that the "big war" called forth. Korea hardly touched the lives of many Americans and does not seem to have left in its wake basic social changes. Yet a close examination of the Korean experience may yield important insights into the nature of American society. Drawn-out, limited wars may not have the massive effects of world wars, but they can impose severe strains on the American system.

Any war waged by a democratic society is dependent upon popular support. A study of the domestic impact of Korea in the absence of major social changes must necessarily examine the way in which the war was received by the nation's political culture. Such an approach can be especially informative if Korea is systematically compared to the other major limited war of American history—Vietnam. Both the contrasts and the similarities can tell us much about the course of history in post–World War II America.

The basic source for such a study is, of course, public opinion polls. They are neither self-explanatory nor utterly reliable, but if intelligently managed and interpreted the polls can give us insights into popular attitudes available to students of few other historical periods. The basic published results are readily available in the contemporary newspaper and periodical press; moreover, Gallup polls covering the years 1935 to 1971 are conveniently available in a recently published three-volume compilation. The ambitious scholar can even obtain the original raw survey data, gathered by most major polling organizations from the Roper Public Opinion Research Center, and subject them to his own modes of analysis. Professor Wiltz's use of the polls is frequently informative but one wishes that he had engaged in a more thorough exploration.

If, for example, one examines Gallup polls designed to measure basic approval and disapproval of the Korean and Vietnam ventures over the first two years of large-scale American involvement in each case, the results are rather surprising. (See poll results, p. 170.)

American involvement in both wars began with about the same high level of support, but the approval level for Korea fell off much more quickly and sharply than for Vietnam. As late as May 1970, Gallup still found 36 percent approval, a figure comparable to that for Korea throughout 1951. Conversely, the rate of disapproval shot up much more rapidly for Korea, peaking after about fifteen months, then declining perceptibly; the rate of disapproval for Vietnam increased fairly steadily, but it took nearly five years (until May 1970) to reach

THE KOREAN WAR

Subject	Interview Date	Approval (%)	Disapproval (%)	No Opinion (%)
Korea	Aug. 20–25, 1950	65	20	15
Vietnam	Oct. 29–Nov. 2, 1965	64	21	15
Korea	Feb. 4–9, 1951	39	50	11
Vietnam	May 5–10, 1966	49	36	15
Korea	Oct. 14–19, 1951	33	56	11
Vietnam	Sept. 8–13, 1966	49	35	16
Korea	Feb. 28–Mar. 5, 1952	35	51	14
Vietnam	Feb. 16–21, 1967	52	32	16
Korea	Oct. 9–14, 1952	37	43	20
Vietnam	Oct. 6–11, 1967	44	46	10

Korea's high point of 56 percent. The statistics, certainly at the least roughly correct, confound one's impressionistic view that opposition to Vietnam was much larger. The question of support becomes all the more perplexing when one considers that Korea is generally regarded as the more justifiable and more intelligently managed of the two wars. Part of the answer, no doubt, is that polls usually provide only one-dimensional frequency distributions; they seldom gauge the intensity of opinions. Beyond this truism, however, a study of the differing popular reactions to Korea and Vietnam reveals that, in significant respects, the America of the early fifties possessed a far different political culture than the America of the middle and late sixties.

The contrasts in the nature of the disapproval of the two wars are enormous and provide a point of departure for an analysis that wishes to emphasize change. Protest against Korea was spearheaded by a political Right outraged by what it considered administration bungling and a no-win policy. Fifteen years later, protest against Vietnam found its center of gravity in a political Left outraged by the alleged moral depravity of American foreign policy. Korean War protesters waved the American flag; Vietnam protesters frequently burned it. Disapproval of Korea was encased in a lifestyle characterized by patriotism and conventional moral behavior; disapproval of Vietnam was inextricably tied to a counter-cultural revolution that defiantly challenged traditional morality. The contrasts seem overwhelming and leave one startled at the velocity with which history has moved in the middle third of the twentieth century.

In June 1950, the Cold War was at its peak. The Czech coup was less than two and a half years in the past; it had been hardly more than a year since the termination of the Berlin blockade; the last twelve months had witnessed the ratification of the North Atlantic Treaty, the fall of mainland China, detonation of the first Soviet atomic bomb, and the American decision to build a hydrogen bomb. The character of the dialogue between the United States and the Soviet Union can only be described as vituperative. Most Americans believed that the grim Stalinist dictatorship was at the head of a worldwide, expansionist totalitarian movement.

Partly as a consequence, the radical Left was in decline. Opponents of the Cold War had failed to present compelling alternatives to the Truman administration's policies. Extending beyond the Communist party and the various groups of Soviet sympathizers, the collapse of the Left included almost every independent radical movement—the various pacifist organizations, the Socialist party, Wisconsin Progressives, Minnesota Farmer-Laborites, and others not necessarily sympathetic toward communism but prone to oppose foreign military involvements. The energetic, militant, talented "movement" of the sixties had no counterpart during the Korean era. The dominant left-of-center force was a "vital center" liberalism willing to accept Soviet-American competition as an unhappy fact of life.

The widespread willingness to engage in such a competition reflected the immediacy of the World War II experience. As a result of that war, Americans were willing to accept the notion that their country must play a major role in world affairs. For many, that idea was made all the more attractive by American dominance of the United Nations, the major surviving symbol of the idealism that had spurred the United States effort during World War II. The memory of the disastrous consequences of appeasement was especially vivid; few observers questioned the Munich analogy. Resistance to Soviet expansion appeared to be the only prudent and honorable way to stave off a larger conflict. The main theme of protest against the Korean involvement was a demand for more vigorous resistance, not for nonresistance.

A crusade against Communist aggression seemed all the more necessary and desirable because of the relatively ideological nature of American politics during the Truman years. American politics was not then and never has been ideological in the European sense, but during the Roosevelt and Truman years the political scene was polarized to an unusual extent around the issues and symbols of the New and Fair Deals. The dynamic force in this process was an angry, resurgent Republican Right that for years had been throwing accusations of authoritarianism, socialism, and communism at Democratic liberals. Even before the Korean War, GOP conservatives had found it natural, as well as

171

politically effective, to carry these charges into the realm of internal security and foreign policy. Once Americans were engaged in combat on the Korean peninsula, it was but an easy step to decry the limitations imposed on that combat and to reinforce the traditional national impulse to seek total victory over an alien threat to American institutions and ideals.

By the mid-sixties, the political environment of the Korean War appeared to have been turned inside out. The process of détente with the Soviet Union was already underway, most notably with the atomic test ban treaty. Munich, and World War II in general, was a dim memory. A New Left was in the process of establishing itself as a vigorous force on the fringes of the American political scene and close to the mainstream of the nation's intellectual life. One of its major themes was a revolt against any world role that smacked of a *Pax Americana*. By contrast, the militant Right had been in decline since Eisenhower had established a bland moderation as the dominant tone of Republicanism. McCarthyism was a bad memory, and charges of "socialism" against liberal Democrats had been relegated to the realm of political comedy. The Goldwater fiasco of 1964, the last hurrah of traditional right-wing Republicanism, amply confirmed the trend. The differences between the political culture of the Korean era and that of the Vietnam era were at least as great as the differences between the two wars.

Yet for all these contrasts, Korea and Vietnam display one essential similarity—each war severely damaged and virtually forced out of office an incumbent president. Each war not only stirred voter resentment itself but magnified other sources of discontent that otherwise might well have been overlooked. A Gallup survey taken a month after the 1952 election illustrates this point. Voters who had cast their ballots for Eisenhower were asked to name the issue that had been most important to them in making their decision:

Issue	All Voters	Normally Republican	Normally Democratic	Independent
Corruption	42%	45%	35%	40%
Korea	24	21	32	23

Each voter category lists corruption first and Korea second, but one may doubt that the relatively minor scandals of the Truman administration would have loomed so large in the absence of the Korean conflict. One may also doubt that the flaws in Lyndon Johnson's personality would have seemed so glaring without Vietnam.

Moreover, one theme united both the right-wing protest against

Korea and the left-wing protest against Vietnam. That theme was a tendency to conceive of foreign and military issues in terms of a dualistic moralism—a struggle of absolute good against absolute evil. The result was the reduction of complex questions to the level of a hysterical morality play for the most vocal and visible of protesters during each era. To those who set the tone of the feeling against the Korean involvement, international communism was an absolute peril that had to be stamped out without compromise. To the left-wing protesters of the 1960s, America had become the world's oppressor, and guerrilla insurgent movements were the hope of humanity. Neither protest movement could leave one with much confidence in the ability of the American political system to sustain a rational foreign policy under stress.

We have all heard Clausewitz's dictum that war is an extension of politics by other means. If we accept that thesis, we must realize that political persuasion of the masses is essential to the success of any war effort by any nation. In a democratic society, a war can be prosecuted only if its assumptions and methods can be sold to the majority. In the short run, this is usually possible, but it becomes increasingly difficult with the passage of time. A totalitarian state has a grip on the media, and its absolute power can control and shape the thoughts of its population. A democracy with widespread civil liberties and a political opposition finds such a situation much more difficult to manage. If the war's objectives are ambiguous and victory is elusive, the task of persuasion becomes nearly impossible.

Intellectuals may argue that limited wars are inevitable in a nuclear world but, whatever the merits of this viewpoint, they must cope with the fact that wars waged by a democratic society require voluntary popular support. It is difficult to argue with the impulse to keep a conflict as small as possible, particularly when one considers the low caliber of the opposition to that decision in the case of Korea. Still, it remains undeniable that the political consequences of both of this century's "little wars" have been poisonous. In the American political system, global strategy and tactics are ultimately only as strong as their domestic political base. Experience seems to show us that this political base will erode rather quickly if a military commitment seems either interminable or unjustifiable.

The examples of Korea and Vietnam, their contrasts notwithstanding, appear to demonstrate that the American people are unlikely to support extended limited wars that carry the promise of neither a decisive victory nor a quick end. A president who leads them into such a war is likely to serve the interests of neither himself nor his party nor, ultimately, his country.

THE KOREAN WAR

Leon H. Keyserling*

Professor Wiltz's long paper on the Korean conflict and American society is interesting, illuminating, and admirable in many respects. But I find that, like most other articles and even full-length books on the Truman period, it pays insufficient attention to basic economic policies and their results. To be sure, it makes some references to the inflation spurt right after the start of the war, refers briefly to the new economic measures at that time, implies criticism of the slowness in applying direct controls, makes references to profiteering and rampant inflation, and refers to some of the troubles with price and wage controls. Nonetheless, these fleeting references occupy a very small portion of the paper as a whole. It also exhibits the tendency to treat inflationary manifestations as the predominant economic problem; there are many other economic problems of even greater significance, the successful handling of which is vital to the effective restraint of inflation itself.

The general tendency among writers to slight the economic aspects of the Truman performance is most unfortunate. The Korean War could not have been conducted even as successfully as it was, and popular support for it could not have been obtained even to the degree that it was, if the wartime economic program, dealing mainly with maintenance of very high levels of employment and production, had not been so successful. Granted the existence of many other factors, one of the reasons why the conduct of American foreign policy over the most recent years has been subject to such public discontent and ambivalent support has been the concurrent existence of very unsatisfactory and dislocating economic conditions at home. Regardless of the merits or demerits of our foreign policy at any given time—which I need not debate here—a strong and reasonably contented domestic economy is the first requirement for the conduct of effective and successful foreign policy. This is manifest today in the breach.

Second, regardless of foreign policy, a successful and popularly accepted domestic performance is always of great importance for its own sake and always has a most important impact on American society. Adequate treatment of that impact cannot be neglected in any full appraisal.

And third, we recently have experienced extraordinarily serious difficulties on the economic front, manifested by intolerably high levels of unemployment, enormous deficiencies in total production measured

* Mr. Keyserling is president of the Conference on Economic Progress and was chairman of the Council of Economic Advisers under President Truman. Last-minute scheduling conflicts prevented Mr. Keyserling from attending the conference.

174

against our capabilities, grievous neglect of the top priorities of our human and social needs, and unparalleled inflation. These would have been avoided, or at least greatly reduced, if the national economic policymakers during these recent years had learned as much as they should have from careful study of the Truman performance, especially during the Korean War. There is amazingly little evidence that the benefits of such study have thus far been forthcoming.

Among economists and others, the easy and prevalent answer to this legitimate complaint on my part is that present conditions and those of recent years differ from the Truman years so profoundly that there is not much of a lesson to be learned from those earlier times. This position is superficial in the extreme; no two eras are exactly alike. The Truman administration, if we view it as a whole, faced intrinsic economic problems greater than any we have faced since. The problem of an orderly transition from World War II to peace, before the advent of the Cold War, has not been equaled since; this included the inflationary pressures generated by the postwar release of savings accumulated during the war. The Korean War was larger, relative to the size of the economy, than the Vietnam War and thus carried the seeds of greater economic dislocation and inflationary stress. At the start of the Korean War, there were shortages quite as acute and serious as those which have occurred during the most recent years. The controlling differences between the Truman era and more recent times are to be found not in the size and severity of the problems, but rather in the courage, decisiveness, and powers of discernment and analysis among those who forged the policies and programs to deal with the respective situations—most of all, President Truman himself.

Before describing these differences in policies and programs, I prefer to commence with an empirical approach in terms of the performance records. Although I hope some day to write a long book dealing with an evaluation of the whole U.S. economic experience since World War II, I must confine myself here to a short, and in some respects preemptory, treatment.

With respect to the Truman years, I deem it appropriate and more revealing to deal with the period from 1947 to 1953 as a whole rather than with the Korean War period alone. The years from 1945 to 1947 are not included, because the immediate problems of conversion from World War II to peace were unique and nonrecurrent. To allow for the momentum effects of policies, the first year of any one administration is also treated as the last year of the preceding administration. Thus, the year 1953 is allocated both to the Truman administration and to the Eisenhower administration.

175

During the Truman years from 1947 to 1953, the average annual rate of real economic growth was 4.9 percent. Average annual unemployment was 4.0 percent. The trend over the period is even more significant in some ways than the average for the period as a whole; unemployment during the last year was only 2.9 percent. Average annual inflation, as measured by the Consumer Price Index, was 3.0 percent and during the last year was only 0.8 percent. The average annual surplus in the federal budget (fiscal years) was $2.4 billion.

During the Eisenhower years, 1953 to 1961, the average annual rate of real economic growth was only 2.4 percent. Average annual unemployment was 5.1 percent and rose to 6.7 percent during the last year. Average annual inflation was 1.4 percent and was 1.2 percent during the last year. The annual average deficit in the federal budget was $2.3 billion.

Taking all factors and trends into account, it is clear that the record during the Eisenhower period was vastly inferior to the record during the Truman period. The immensely higher rate of unemployment and immensely lower rate of real economic growth were far too great a price to pay for the low average rate of inflation, even if one assumes a connection between the two. And this is quite apart from the fact that the last year of the Truman period registered notably less inflation than the last year of the Eisenhower period.

During the Kennedy-Johnson years, 1961 to 1969, the average annual rate of real economic growth was 4.8 percent. Unemployment averaged 4.7 percent and was 3.5 percent during the last year. Inflation averaged 2.6 percent but was 5.4 percent during the last year. The average annual deficit in the federal budget was $6.4 billion. Again, taking all factors and trends into account, the Kennedy-Johnson record did not come up to the Truman record.

During the Nixon-Ford years from 1969 to 1974, the average annual rate of real economic growth was only 2.5 percent. Average unemployment was 5.1 percent and rose to 5.6 percent during the last year (and reached 8.9 percent by April 1975). The average annual rate of inflation was 6.1 percent and rose to 12.2 percent during the last year. The average annual federal deficit was $10.7 billion. This record, on balance, was worse than during the Eisenhower years and tremendously worse than during the Kennedy-Johnson or Truman years.

There are a number of important differences between Truman's economic policies and those of subsequent administrations. First and foremost, the president's *Economic Reports* under Truman, in accordance with the purposes of the Employment Act of 1946, always set quantitative goals for employment and production during the ensuing year and adjusted policies and programs to achieve these goals. This degree of purposefulness is essential, but it has not consistently been used during later years. Instead, mere forecasts have frequently been substituted for goals, and these forecasts have usually represented supine resignation to the results of unfavorable "automatic" forces at work. For example, neither the Ford administration nor the new budget committees of the Senate and the House have set specific goals for the reduction of unemployment or the expansion of production to tolerable levels within the shortest feasible time. To the contrary, they are forecasting 7–8 percent unemployment rates at the end of 1976 and implying 5–6 percent unemployment rates as late as 1980. The economic, social, and civil strains which such developments would impose are almost incalculable. We are drifting instead of planning.

A second dissimilarity between the Truman policies and those later on is that since the Truman period, and particularly during the most recent years, national policymakers have adhered to the "trade-off" theory that more unemployment and less production should deliberately be contrived in the name of fighting inflation. Even if this theory was correct in a limited sense, it would be unconscionable to impose the hardship and anxiety of unemployment on 10.5 million breadwinners (the true level of unemployment at this writing), and indirectly on the 30 or so million people in their families, on the hypothesis—whether correct or not—that this might enable the employed and even the affluent to buy a second car or some other niceties of life at a somewhat lower price than if the unemployed had jobs. More important, especially as indicated so poignantly during the most recent years, a fully used American economy generates far less price inflation than a sick economy. President Truman always put the full use of our resources first; he understood its prime significance, and this is the very reason why he was so successful in the restraint of inflation.

This is best illustrated in connection with the Korean War. At its start, President Truman received two conflicting sets of advice from two competing groups. The first group urged that inflation was "a greater danger to us than the dictators." They urged that to avoid excessive inflation, we should seek to fight the war mainly out of the existing product, place major reliance on direct controls for this purpose, and avoid vigorous expansion of the production base and of production generally. They also warned that resorting to a vigorous expansionary program would result in very high unemployment and economic collapse when the war was over—forgetting, among other things, the smooth transition from World War II to peace.

The second approach urged upon President Truman was to the effect that expansion of the industrial base and great enlargement of total production would be preferable for a variety of reasons and would even be the best long-range approach to the restraint of inflation. I was a leading spokesman for this group. We urged also that the public would not support a limited and distant war of unknown duration if it involved severe curtailment of civilian supplies for many years. President Truman unhesitatingly favored and put into effect this second approach, the results of which I have already set forth.

This approach did not oppose the imposition of the direct controls; it correctly insisted that the first step was to set in motion a complete system of goals, programming, and priorities and then to implement these through many policies, including controls. In view of the real alternatives then open, it now appears clear that the criticism directed against the delay in imposing controls was mistaken and that the reduction of inflation to 0.8 percent during 1953 was due more to the other steps taken than to the direct controls. Over the most recent years, controls have failed to restrain inflation just because the control of inflation was made an obsessionary preoccupation instead of being developed in the context of serving even larger considerations.

A third difference is that President Truman strongly favored a balanced budget. He did not hesitate to raise taxes at the very outset of the Korean War, instead of following the more recent practice of failing to increase taxes when needed or of reducing taxes for the wrong people. But Truman never sought to balance the budget at the expense of the national economy, recognizing that the blood of federal revenues could not be squeezed from the turnip of a depressed and stunted economy. He ran budget surpluses by attending to the nation's economic health. Most unfortunately, the current national administration, and even the two new budget committees of the Senate and the House, have not set adequate goals for production, employment, and priorities and then shaped the budget to attain these goals. Instead, they have followed the upside-down practice of arbitrarily deciding the allowable size of the budget and of the immediate deficit and then accepting the intolerable employment, production, and priority results which they themselves admit will follow. Ironically, the consequence will be huge federal deficits for as far ahead as we can see.

Fourth, President Truman was dedicated to the maintenance of ample credit at low interest rates. He succeeded in this policy until 1952, with the beneficial overall results already detailed, and then the policy was changed despite his objection. In sharp contrast, we have since then been committed to tight money and excessively high interest rates. This policy has regressively transferred more than $800 billion from borrowers to lenders. It largely explains the lamentably poor economic performance which in itself has spawned inflation. And excessively high interest rates are inflationary per se.

Fifth, and well exemplified by his hostility to tight money and excessively high interest rates, President Truman indicated his fundamental dedication to watering the economic tree at the bottom rather than at the top, to progressive rather than regressive national economic policies, and to considering first and always the problems and needs of the average citizen. This did not rob Peter to pay Paul; it accrued to the benefit of all in a healthy and advancing economy.

Commentators in increasing numbers are beginning to note that President Truman, despite a war which led to popular divisiveness toward the end, presided in the main over a confident and aspiring people. The major cause of this, I believe, was the degree of domestic tranquility which proceeds from successful attention to the general welfare and from a feeling among the people that there was equity in what the government did.

It would be well for historians and especially economists today to ponder and profit by the example of this doughty president. It would be still more valuable for the president today to do likewise.

Richard H. Rovere

The Wiltz paper seems to me an admirable appraisal of the impact of the war in Korea on American society. My differences with Wiltz are marginal, and I will try to make a few of them clear.

Most of what Professor Wiltz has described here, it seems to me, are the consequences of any modern war—inflation, a general rise in employment and some unemployment caused by shortages, a steady progression from enthusiasm and popular support to weariness and dissent, and a spreading disenchantment with the administration held responsible for the war. In these respects, the Korean experience was not unique but more or less typical. In Vietnam, of course, everything was heightened, but the economic and political consequences were quite similar.

Though he offers much evidence, Wiltz does not spell out what seems to me the single most important effect of the war—the militarization of American foreign policy. Our national leaders regarded Korea as a kind of proof of the contention that political problems could be solved by military means. Despite what opponents of the war—ranging from Right to Left—said, it appeared that we had accomplished in Korea what we set out to do—repel armed aggression and demonstrate the efficacy of collective security. In terms of Truman's war aims, a victory of sorts was won in Korea (regardless of General MacArthur's call for total victory), and most American diplomats and military leaders saw it this way. From Korea they concluded that what had been done once could be done twice, perhaps as often as the attempt was made. Korea led to a reliance on arms that later proved disastrous. Without Korea, there would probably have been no Vietnam. Had we failed in Korea, there would almost certainly have been no Vietnam. The connection between the two wars is direct, a fact which leads me—once a supporter of the 1950 intervention—to answer Wiltz's concluding question very much in the affirmative.

I think Wiltz gives Korea a bit too much importance in encouraging anticommunism as a doctrine and McCarthyism as a phenomenon. It helped, of course, but there were McCarthys before McCarthy; the fall of Nationalist China in 1949 had, I think, more bearing on developing anticommunism than Korea did. I have enough respect for McCarthy's gifts as a mischief-maker to believe that he could have gone as far as he did without Korea—he was off to quite a start before the war began—and, as Wiltz points out, McCarthy did go into a temporary eclipse in late 1950.

Every war affects those who fight it, but alongside Vietnam, Korea's impact was relatively slight. Vietnam, I believe, altered the American character. It changed the traditional concept of the presidency. One can hardly think of an institution that, in the aftermath of the Vietnam War, remains the same. And the importance of Korea is that it made Vietnam possible.

Discussion

Prof. Richard E. Neustadt (chairman): Professor Wiltz began by saying that, so far as he could find, it would not be correct to characterize the Korean War as traumatic in the life of the United States. Those of us who went through it may well recall moments of trauma but anyone who has brought up the subject of Korea in a college classroom knows that, as an event of history, it is not recalled with much realization of its meaning. That meaning, as Professors Kaplan and Wiltz and the several commentators on their papers all note, is to be found in the marks the conflict left—marks on legislative programs, on politics and the results of political contests, on the minds of activists, on office-holders and would-be officeholders, on balances of policies and budgets.

Among the marks left on the minds of people were readings that— each in a different way—President Kennedy and President Johnson took to heart from their experiences in Congress during the Korean War period. Certainly in Mr. Johnson's case, one can make direct connections with things he said and did as president—his estimate of the strength of the political Right, his concern for the political Right, his worries about his freedom of action in conducting another war, in engaging in negotiations, and in reversing position. The troubles of Mr. Truman during '51 and '52 must have been lessons learned by a number of politicians then on the Hill. Four of them were to become president of the United States. To the many connections, the many traces worth noting, I would add only that one.

Prof. Richard S. Kirkendall: I find that one event of the Korean War is very much a part of the knowledge of today's college students and the college students of the past few years: the Truman-MacArthur controversy. Students ask more questions about that controversy than about any other aspect of the Truman period—with the exception of the use of the atomic bomb. It seems to me that that part of the war is a very dramatic and important event to them.

Prof. John E. Wiltz: Do you find any pro-MacArthur sentiment among students who show all this interest?

KIRKENDALL: I found a great deal of it a decade ago, not nearly as much today.

WILTZ: I have had the same experience. I find almost contempt for MacArthur and the MacArthur position on this issue. That may have led me into the statement that has drawn some flak here about the support of the notion (or the reinforcement of the idea) of civilian supremacy over the military.

PROF. ROBERT GRIFFITH: Well, it is not just MacArthur. It is the whole presence of the right wing which, for those who can remember or who have studied the Korean period, was such a major factor. I always have to start out by reminding my students that, while during the last four or five years the major debates going on in this country seem to be between the center and the Left, back then the major lines of debate were between the center and the Right. But I do not find much appreciation of that, either as a reality or on an emotional level.

GEN. J. LAWTON COLLINS: Let me tell you about the effect of this controversy between MacArthur and Mr. Truman on the military people of America. I do not know of anybody other than General MacArthur— we have had one or two aberrations who might challenge the basic concept in America of the supremacy of civilians over military matters— but I do not know of anybody in a responsible position in the army other than General MacArthur who ever actually challenged this concept. Certainly none of us who were on active duty at that time ever supported MacArthur's approach. We fully supported the president throughout this particular controversy.

GOV. W. AVERELL HARRIMAN: May I just endorse what General Collins was saying. The tradition at West Point is respect for civilian control. The idea that MacArthur was an outcropping of American militarism in this country is absolutely false.

WILTZ: I have heard it said by people who had some contact with General MacArthur in his later years that he rather regretted the controversy with President Truman. And, of course, in his last great speech— the "duty-honor-country" speech at West Point in 1962—he was very emphatic that the responsibility of soldiers is to obey their civilian superiors. I am not quite sure of the exact wording, but it almost seemed to be a repudiation of what he had said and done in 1951.

AMBASSADOR ERNEST A. GROSS: In connection with the attitude of the students, is there any intense interest in any other events between 1945 and 1955?

DISCUSSION

RICHARD H. ROVERE: The fact that something is forgotten or is not in the forefront of young people's consciousness should not really surprise us. I imagine the same thing will be true of Vietnam in twenty-five years.

NEUSTADT: The issue that I intended to illustrate was whether Korea had been really a traumatic social event. The Great Depression was; Korea was clearly not of that character at all.

WILTZ: When I was preparing my paper I tried to keep my eyes open for evidence of some effects in the pop-culture area. I did not have time to check on comic books but I was watching for movies. I cannot recall the titles, but the first movies on the Korean War appeared sometime in 1952. I believe there were only two that actually appeared during the war. If you want to explore this subject, compare popular music, for example, during the Korean War and World War II: the Korean War did not inspire stirring patriotic songs like "Praise the Lord and Pass the Ammunition."

NEUSTADT: We have suggested that a lot of developments were stopped or started by Korea in governmental terms. Korea left a lot of impressions in governmental and political minds, impressions which carried a lot of weight for the future. There are a couple of things, though, that I have always been puzzled about—legacies that do not seem to have lasted. I would have guessed in, say, 1954 or '55 that the "never again" club—against any land war in Asia—would have had more than ten or fifteen years of life. I am still struck by that and puzzled by it historically. I am also struck that the shift of war aims from the initial aim of restoring the border to the aim of reunifying the country—with what turned out to be disastrous effects—was another lesson which, in the middle '50s, I would have said surely would leave its trace in men's minds. But you cannot find any of it in 1965.

It would help to have some notion of how important or how evanescent the Korean War was in its impact on governmental performance and behavior. Can any of you who were participants, then and after, add a bit of explanation on why those two, apparently strong, lessons had such a limited effect on future policy? One of the reasons I ask is that we talk now as though the effects of the Vietnam War on governmental estimations and on social beliefs are such that certain things will not happen in the future; I am dubious about that assumption, in part because of our experience after Korea.

GEN. MATTHEW B. RIDGWAY: I am afraid I get a little bit wound up on this question, but I do want to touch on several points.

THE KOREAN WAR

First, I would go to the mission assigned to the military. (I want to stick to the military side because Governor Harriman is here as are others who are fully qualified to discuss the political side.) The mission of the military was clear. My mission, as ground commander under Mac-Arthur and later as supreme commander, was to expel the aggressor and to restore peace in the area. That we did. Parenthetically, you come to the question of victory. I do not know just what the word victory means anymore. My definition would be: to accomplish what you set out to do—which we did in Korea.

The suggestion has been made of similarities between Korea and Vietnam. I do not see how the two could be more different. Geographically, Korea was a little sliver off that great landmass of Asia. It was a dagger pointed at the heart of Japan. Japan was, unquestionably, of vital interest to us. As a peninsula we could dominate the air spaces over Korea—which we did—and of the seas around it.

South Korean President Syngman Rhee meets in Pusan with U.S. officials (*L-R*: Commander of Navy Forces in Korea, Assistant to President Rhee, Ambassador John Muccio, President Rhee, Secretary of the Army Frank Pace, Gen. Matthew B. Ridgway)—April 12, 1951.

DISCUSSION

We did not have to go any farther than the 38th Parallel to accomplish our mission. For a time, euphoria took hold and you know the circumstances; they have been discussed in detail so it is unnecessary to repeat them here. We had a very strong president in South Korea who was death on communism. Anything I, as the ground commander, asked him for, I got without question and very promptly. Only when the aggressor had been driven back north of the parallel did Rhee become a hairshirt to us. Then the cry of "On to the Yalu" became more and more insistent: "I'll go it alone, if necessary" and "We have a vast pool of manpower here, why don't you arm them?" I said to Rhee, "Mr. President, your divisions have abandoned all their weapons on more than one occasion; until we can get the spirit into them so they'll stand and fight, you'll get no more weapons as far as my recommendations are concerned." We got to the point where we could pull an ROK division out of the line, but only after the last major Chinese offensive in May 1951. We pulled it apart, started with the squads, and trained them right through, using live ammunition under the kind of intensive training program we used in the United States. They have continued these training policies and, as a result, have steadily improved. In Vietnam, two divisions from the Republic of Korea were pronounced by all observers to be the equal of any other troops there.

Back to the geography for a minute. You did not have to go any farther than the 38th Parallel. Even if you went to the Yalu you were still operating over Korea and the seas around it, keeping your main base in Japan. Vietnam was totally different. You ask why would we engage in another land war on the Asian mainland. Really, we didn't fight on the Asian mainland in Korea. We were based in Japan, and Korea is in many ways closer to Japan than to the main body of Asia.

Now, if you go into Indochina, how far do you penetrate? What is your objective in Vietnam? I have heard at least a dozen statements from high officials and civilian authorities in Washington. None made any sense to me. But if you did go in, the hands of the military were tied. Suppose you invaded North Vietnam and destroyed Hanoi. Do you think for a minute you would have eliminated the Communist menace? Do you think that bullets and bombs can kill an idea? Then you cross the Laotian border, as Mr. Kennedy almost threatened to do at one time. Well, next is Burma, then Thailand, then India. How far are you going in this great Asian landmass? What I am trying to do is to point out the fundamental differences in every respect—political, military, and geographic—between the situation in Korea and the situation in Vietnam.

185

THE KOREAN WAR

NEUSTADT: What you are saying is that "no land war in Asia" was a separate issue from Korea, that there was really nothing to do "never again."

RIDGWAY: At the end of World War II, I doubt if you could have found any prominent man in or out of uniform who would have countenanced this commitment of ground forces on the Asian landmass, not one. MacArthur did advocate the destruction of China's war-making potential. As he said, in his own words: "For a generation, I can think of nothing more adverse to our interest than not to have done that." On the other hand there was a tremendous counter-pressure of Soviet military ambitions. But there was also a very genuine fear on the part of Soviet leaders of China's capabilities and potentials.

ROVERE: General Ridgway has said that Korea and Vietnam are different in every way. Of course, there are some differences, but, it seems to me, there are also great similarities. First, both are peninsulas; and there are some people, notably the late Walter Lippmann, who regarded both areas as part of the mainland. Florida is part of the mainland of the United States and it is a peninsula. Second, you say you cannot knock out the idea of communism by military means. Well, in part, that was what a lot of people thought we were doing in Korea—and if it was invalid in one place it would be invalid in another. Third, the divisions along parallels were quite similar except that in Vietnam, as I understand it, there was a logical and historical division as well as one of military convenience. There was still, I believe, a fortress wall built about the dividing line.

RIDGWAY: But you did not try to knock out communism. In Korea, that wasn't the objective at all. It was to repel the aggression—which was done.

ROVERE: But it was in MacArthur's mind and . . .

RIDGWAY: Yes, but he was repudiated.

ROVERE: Well, I know. But there was, for example, Senator Knowland, who was Republican majority leader . . .

RIDGWAY: I don't want to get into political discussions.

HARRIMAN: General Ridgway, what you are trying to say is that there was no Ho Chi Minh trail in Korea. The Ho Chi Minh trail could go as far west as the jungle extended. What was undertaken in Korea was militarily "do-able"; what was taken on in Vietnam was not militarily "do-able."

DISCUSSION

RIDGWAY: Well, you can hardly geographically compare the Korean peninsula with the Indochinese peninsula. Just look at it on the map.

WILTZ: Well, you had an MLR [main line of resistance] in Korea and you never had that in Vietnam.

COLLINS: One of the points that came up earlier in this conference has to do with why the 38th Parallel was chosen as a dividing line. In writing my book and in outlining Dean Rusk's role and that of "Tip" Bonesteel in the somewhat accidental selection of the dividing line in Korea, I found that although Bonesteel and Rusk did not know it at the time, they had hit on the same parallel that had been proposed to the Russians by the Japanese general, Yamagata, in 1896 to divide the Japanese and Russian spheres of influence, with Japan getting the southern half. The Russian negotiator, Alexis Lobanov-Rostovskii, refused because, as a Russian authority put it, "Korea's destiny as a component part of the Russian Empire has been ordained for us to fill." I think that statement answers the question someone raised about a historical background for why Russia should have supported the training of the North Koreans. In my personal judgment, had we not stopped the naked aggression of the North Koreans supported by the Russians, after the North Koreans had taken over South Korea, the Russians would have taken over the whole country from the North Koreans.

HARRIMAN: Your question, Mr. Chairman, really was why people did not learn from the Korean experience not to get involved on the mainland. I think one has to remember that John Foster Dulles appeared with some quite different ideas. If you have any doubts about what those were, I recommend you read *The Devil and John Foster Dulles* by Townsend Hoopes. You will find that the whole attitude was completely changed from the Truman period to the Dulles period. Dulles started to encircle the Communist world with CENTO and SEATO and brought in "brinkmanship" and all that. Dulles not only changed the political atmosphere, he practically erased what Truman and those who supported him had been trying to achieve.

Of course, the whole moral issue in Korea was perfectly clear. We had the United Nations with us; we had nobody with us in Vietnam. I agree with those who say that the differences between Korea and Vietnam are far greater than any of the similarities.

AMBASSADOR LUCIUS D. BATTLE: I am moving to a slightly different track. I have been rather troubled by the fact that we all have concluded that Korea had not been a traumatic experience for the American people.

187

Thinking over the whole problem, it seems to me that Korea should be considered in the perspective of other contemporary events. What you get is a series of rather fantastic efforts by the United States, under superb and creative leadership, to cope with its problems. NATO, the Marshall plan—all of this is out of one package: our effort to provide leadership and our effort to cope with complex situations. I had a letter, for example, from Dean Acheson during the middle of the Dulles era in which he said Dulles was following the containment policy too slavishly. He said there was room for change, for new directions, new movements, new motion, and we were not getting any. We were getting an overextension of the effort to contain . . .

HARRIMAN: I would go much further than that: Dulles's policy was an entirely different concept.

BATTLE: I think it is tragic that the effort we made to cope in a really creative period under Truman's leadership has never been equaled. Now it is all a resort to: "We can't cope, we can't lead, we can't face." If you lump everything, what is happening to our society is, I think, the retrenchment of our role in the world.

PROF. WARREN COHEN: I want to say that I think Ambassador Battle yielded too much to Governor Harriman on this particular point. I think that we have dumped off much too much on the Eisenhower administration and on John Foster Dulles (for whom I do not want to apologize). What we have is precisely the point made a moment ago: a continuation of the creative policies of the Truman administration. But during the years that followed, these creative policies included some things we are not very proud of. The attitude toward the People's Republic of China, which we see in Dulles's policy during the Eisenhower administration, is very clearly foreshadowed, I think, in all of the statements by the assistant secretary for far eastern affairs [Dean Rusk] from 1951 through 1952.

The point Acheson makes is, of course, very valid: that at a time when Acheson and others might have shifted policies, recognizing that they were no longer applicable, we had in office a man who didn't have that kind of flexibility. But then, I think, we have to ask: What happens when some of these people from the Truman administration come back into office in 1961? Do we not have that straight line from Korea to Vietnam?

BATTLE: I am sorry I mentioned the Acheson letter because we have gotten slightly off the track. I thing that what Dean was saying—and this was early in the Dulles administration—was that there ought to be

DISCUSSION

an exploration with the Soviet Union of what we now call détente. (That was in the letter I got from him much later.) So he was looking for other directions. Now in my judgment, SEATO and CENTO and other attitudes were not an extension of NATO at all, or of the philosophy that created NATO. What Dulles ended up doing during that period was arming the world against enemies *we* saw. Various countries accepted arms against enemies *they* saw, which were not the same enemies we saw. We put arms into Pakistan, assuming they were part of this great effort to stop communism and the Chinese or the Russians or whatever, and what they were doing was getting ready to have a whack at India. We armed Greece and Turkey because they were both in NATO and solidly anti-Communist, and they wound up using the weapons we gave them against each other. NATO, I think, had a clear, unified objective and one single enemy. But the formula was overextended to situations where it could not and did not work.

HARRIMAN: I completely divorce the Eisenhower philosophy from the Dulles philosophy. Eisenhower, after Dulles died, was quite a different man in international affairs. He started détente, and had it not been for the U-2 incident, we would have had détente in 1960. But that is an aside.

As I remember it, the first thing Dulles got Eisenhower to do was to "unleash" Chiang, a complete reversal of the Truman position. This was what MacArthur and Knowland and the China lobby wanted, and it was the first thing that was done by the new administration. Up to that time we had the United Nations approval, we had NATO approval; that was the first time we began to deviate from world opinion. Of course, the most extreme case was what we did in Vietnam where nobody was with us.

GRIFFITH: Mr. Battle, in the context of Secretary Acheson's position in this letter, how do you account for the vehemence with which he responded to Ambassador Kennan's suggestion for disengagement in Europe?

BATTLE: As I remember it, I happened to have talked with him at the time and found he was very unhappy about what he had said to George. But he saw this as the complete reversal of direction. He thought that what Kennan was doing was simply saying, "Let's pull back and then the whole thing will be over." If I remember it correctly—and I don't like to attribute words and thoughts without going back and rereading the letters—what I think Acheson was saying to me in those letters was that he thought we ought to test the possibility of there

189

ultimately being some sort of détente. But I think he felt that Kennan had thrown in the towel completely and had said, "Let's pull away from it all and it will settle itself."

GRIFFITH: Earlier you quoted Acheson to the effect that the Korean War overcame the inertia of people's thinking. If we want to follow that metaphor a little bit further, we can remember that in the laws of physics an object set in motion tends to continue in motion unless it meets a countervailing force. I submit that maybe this is what has been happening over the last twenty years.

HARRIMAN: The idea that Chiang Kai-shek could go back on the continent was something nobody in the world saw as possible, and that is what began the questioning in people's minds as to the judgment of the United States—and that is a real turning point.

RIDGWAY: I want to underscore what Governor Harriman has just said and add one small point that I am sure is on no other record. I was sitting next to Mr. Dulles at a dinner at the American Embassy in Paris just after I had taken over the NATO command [in 1952]. He drew on the table cloth—I hope the ambassador's wife didn't know it because he was using a ball point pen—a three-pronged attack on the China mainland: through Korea, through Chekiang from Taiwan, and through Hainan Island on the south. That represented Dulles's thinking at that time.

GROSS: Just to complete the discussion: we are talking about the impact of Korea on American society. Obviously American society is not insulated; the international context is important enough to justify at least passing reference. I think that the most characteristic feature of the Korean War was the spontaneity of its inception. In Vietnam we stumbled into it, and nobody knew when or how or why the involvement developed as it did. The spontaneity of Korea is an extremely significant factor because it reflects an international society's reaction to an aggression which was perceived as such immediately.

Just to give one example, again in the U.N. context. When we had the job at the U.S. mission of literally waking up delegates the night of June 24 to get ready for the Security Council meeting that Sunday afternoon, the spontaneous reaction of each was remarkably similar. There was no question about the significance they attached to this invasion. At the meeting the next day, at least two delegations, India and Egypt, voted for our resolution without having had the opportunity to get instructions from their government—an almost unheard-of step which no diplomat likes to take.

DISCUSSION

Can one conceive of any similar action being taken in regard to Vietnam—at any stage? I think the contrast is remarkable. And I think that the reaction in America to the aggression in Korea paralleled the reaction in Britain, France, and every civilized part of the world, including India. To talk about Korea in the same terms as Vietnam is simply to misread history and ignore the state of mind of every civilized society throughout the world. We were alone in Vietnam for all practical purposes.

MRS. ANNE EATON: Have you any thoughts on the American people's reaction to the fact that the Korean War was a U.N. operation? I did not understand that this entered into the impact on or the reaction of Americans.

PROF. RONALD J. CARIDI: Are you asking whether American public opinion was more inclined to support the war because it viewed it as an international effort?

MRS. EATON: I think it is possible, in view of some of the complaints about the United States participating in the U.N., that it might have been just the opposite. My question is, did it really matter one way or the other?

CARIDI: I can tell you what my impression is, although I cannot now back it up with any specific study. My impression is that it was easier to sell the war originally because it was perceived to be part of an international effort. Then the war lost ground in terms of public support, partly because of the frustrations that came from cooperating in that kind of an international effort. So I think it began as a positive factor in terms of public opinion and wound up as quite a negative factor.

WILTZ: The war lost support, too, because the people of the United States felt that the other U.N. partners were not making an adequate contribution. During the MacArthur inquiry, conservative Republican senators were continually asking, "Why can't we get more support from our U.N. allies?" I think a lot of national frustration was the result of that sentiment.

NEUSTADT: Mr. Hamby was recounting the Fair Deal measures that were at least on the legislative agenda, but then failed to succeed. It is, of course, very hard to know what was sacrificed by the diversion of the war; but, if there is any single measure in the realm of social policy that may have had a chance for enactment and, if enacted, would have had considerable effect on American social development, it is the Brannan Plan. That was the last serious effort to avoid the collectivization of

American agriculture, and enormous social consequences over the last two decades have followed its nonenactment. Would any member of the panel or of the audience wish to say anything about this aspect of the impact of the Korean War on American society?

WILTZ: Professor Hamby, do you feel that if the Korean War had not intervened, there was any chance that any important Fair Deal measures might have passed?

PROF. ALONZO L. HAMBY: Well, the administration hoped so, of course, and in early 1950 some rather careful plans were prepared for a strong fall campaign, not only to maintain the administration's strength in Congress but to elect those few more congressmen who might have been needed to pass some of the more controversial items on the Fair Deal agenda. None of us can say whether the administration would have been successful or not. What we can say, as far as the 1950 campaign is concerned, is that the war, first of all, took Truman himself off the campaign trail, thereby depriving the party of its strongest national campaigner. In addition, during the fall of 1950 serious inflation was making itself felt. Finally, about a week or ten days before the election there were the first indications of the Chinese intervention, and it is very hard for anyone to say how much of an impact this had on the campaign.

A few weeks ago in Washington I was talking to a distinguished congressman who remembered 1950 rather vividly, and, as he put it to me in almost these words, he had very high hopes until the news of Chinese intervention began to appear in the papers; then everything seemed to be sliding out from under the party. I do not know whether that perception would be generally shared by other people whose memories go back that far. Certainly this was also something that could not have helped the campaign.

As it was, the Democrats did not lose badly, but they did lose some seats. More importantly, those who did find themselves forced to retire from Congress were, by and large, supporters of the Fair Deal. Then, of course, after the MacArthur dismissal, it was pretty clear that Truman had to form a sort of reconciliation with the Southern Democrats in order to protect his foreign policy, and this put the final damper on the hopes of the Fair Deal.

PROF. LAWRENCE GELFAND: In view of the rather decisive leadership of the Truman era with respect to restraining Communist advances in Korea, the establishment of NATO, the Marshall Plan, etc., I was wondering if members of the panel might be willing to comment on

DISCUSSION

why, by 1952, critics of the Truman administration were able to make a rather persuasive case before the American public that the Truman leadership was weak on communism.

ROVERE: I think that was just political nonsense.

HAMBY: Well, why did people believe it? That is a good question, and I do not know if any of us can answer it very well. I think it might be fair to say that in general—and perhaps this is a matter of the style— the Truman administration was rather weak on public relations. A good many people who served in the administration can remember remarks about the weakness and mediocrity of the White House staff. Yet by any reasonable standards it was an extremely competent staff and a very strong one. I have never quite understood why this stereotype was generally accepted. I just put it down to the administration's maybe not having a good advertising man in the White House. It is my impression also that the press tended to be more partisan during the '40s and early '50s than it is today.

GRIFFITH: It seems to me that you had, well before the Korean War, a legacy of strong partisan-motivated attacks on the Truman administration (and before that on the Roosevelt administration), rooted originally in conservative resistance to the social welfare programs of the New Deal. In 1936 Robert Taft was on the campaign trail depicting Roosevelt as the leader of a Menshevik phase of a coming American revolution. What happened after 1945, it seems to me, is that the Cold War created the climate and the environment in which this kind of political attack could be transferred from the realm of social welfare to the realm of national security. There, given the climate of the Cold War, it seemed to have more credibility.

ROVERE: I am reminded of how often this charge of being soft on communism was documented by what people said in other connections. For example, Dean Acheson saying, "I will not turn my back on Alger Hiss"; Truman calling the Hiss case a red herring. Of course, he was completely misunderstood: he did not mean that it was trivial; he was using the phrase in its literal sense—something put up as a blinder to stop his program. I think that sort of thing got great currency.

WILTZ: Nevertheless, whatever the Truman administration did in Korea and in Europe, one simply could not escape the fact that a quarter of the earth's population had fallen under communism while Truman was president. I think that a great many people simply could not get beyond that fact. Look at what the Republicans were talking about in 1952: "Roll back the Iron Curtain" and that sort of thing. And, of course, Truman had been willing to stop at the 38th Parallel in Korea. One might have said that compared with what the Republicans were saying, the Democrats appeared less tough on communism.

CARIDI: And the catch phrases "containment" and "liberation" carried an emotional wallop.

NEUSTADT: Speaking as one of the mediocrities then in the White House, I would say that it is my impression that Dewey's defeat in 1948 snapped a certain amount of restraint in the minds of a lot of hitherto and otherwise respectable people on Capitol Hill. These people had

U.S. Navy

Richard Neustadt, special assistant to President Truman, greets Charles Murphy, special counsel to the president, in Key West before a meeting at the Little White House—March 10, 1951.

been a part of a consensus of sorts and had held criticism down for the sake of bipartisanship. Add to this the frustrations of a war that was going on and on. Lastly—although I would not like to bring Mr. Agnew's complaints into this gathering—to the Eastern establishment press, Mr.

DISCUSSION

Truman simply did not matter. The support for the administration's foreign policy did not carry with it much concern about political protection for the president on the part of an awful lot of those who wrote and edited the major organs of mass communication.

AMBASSADOR JOHN J. MUCCIO: When we were talking about the reasons for the world-wide support for activities in Korea, I think we failed to note the influence of the United Nations mission that was in Korea continuously from the end of 1947 until 1974. The U.N. mission in Korea decided that since most of the issues they faced were military, they would call on their respective governments for military advisers. When the fighting broke out, three of those advisers had already arrived. The U.N. mission was able to wire United Nations headquarters that they had spent the preceding week along the 38th Parallel and had seen no signs of any preparations for aggressive action by the South. I think that that one message had more credence among the neutral elements in the United Nations than all the material we had sent in from the embassy.

ROVERE: General Ridgway and Governor Harriman have spoken about the multinational support in Korea, and it certainly was true, formally, that it was a multinational effort. But it seems to me worth noting that the level of enthusiasm for our position was very low. I was all over Western Europe at the height of the war, and I met no one—in government or anywhere else—who had much zeal for it. I think it was largely a matter of our being supported by client states and allies who found something obligatory about it, who were more satisfied with our general foreign policy than they are now. But I can hardly subscribe to the view that the civilized world rallied to our support. I am not impressed by one hospital unit from India: if India had thought Korea was vital to its defense, it would certainly have done more than send a few medics.

NEUSTADT: Dick, I have to argue with you in one case which I know well, that of the British. The British Foreign Office read vividly into the Korean outbreak all the lessons of the Soviet inimical character; and they did see a danger to Europe. During the first part of the hostilities the British were pushing us on. They became sensitive and cautious when we moved north of the parallel. Then they started a whole bombardment of cables to try to get us to stop at the neck. But their support for our policy of rearmament was very strong—they were then considerably more than clients.

WILTZ: And the French were pretty heavily involved themselves in Indochina at that time.

HARRIMAN: Going back to this question of '52, I think one ought to recognize that one cannot analyze that election on any logical issue basis. Eisenhower was an extraordinarily popular individual who overshadowed everything else and no one else would do. The other thing was—I go back to Roosevelt—F.D.R. thought that the swing to Republicanism would start after his last term, in '48. The Democrats had been in power for sixteen years and Roosevelt did not think that any Democrat could win in '48. Well, Truman did win in '48, but the country was swinging away from some of the Roosevelt policies. So there was a swing against Truman, but he won the '48 election by running against Congress. He got more out of the 80th Congress than any president has ever gotten out of any Congress in international affairs, and then he won his election by running against a "do-nothing" Congress—on domestic issues. It was a superb political job, the best any president has ever done. By '52 all of that had worn off. Eisenhower's personality was something no one could beat.

5

The Communist Side:
An Exploratory Sketch

Robert R. Simmons

The literature of the Korean crisis of the summer of 1950 customarily has described it as occurring in the context of a tight, bipolar world. The predominant view of the causes of the war has been that the Soviet Union completely controlled the North Korean invasion of June 25. This hypothesis, however, is insufficient to explain satisfactorily the events of the summer of 1950 and their consequences.

Most observers of this period have seen the North Korean regime as a satellite of the Soviet Union and Kim Il-song as a mere hireling of the Russians. Stalin, so this version runs, pulled the trigger that started the war. Such a metaphor, of course, neglects the "gun" itself: the government in P'yongyang. Because the origins of the war have been placed in Moscow, research on its Korean paternity has been largely neglected. In a previous publication, I briefly examined the factional divisions within the P'yongyang government, which had an immediate bearing upon the initiation of the war, and concluded that the Kim Il-song regime of 1950 was neither a completely passive "gun" for an itchy Soviet trigger finger nor a monolithic system totally subservient to Moscow.[1] Hence, analysis of its own internal factional components is necessary in order to explain the origins of the war.

War's Context

This short essay presents a fleeting glance of some of the salient factors essential to an understanding of the Communist political context of the war. Although the Russians certainly armed the North Koreans and did expect a war, the timing of the war can best be understood in terms of indigenous conditions on the Korean peninsula.

THE KOREAN WAR

All Koreans were united in their urgent desire for an early reunification. The specific timing of the June 25 invasion, however, was caused by intense rivalry within the Korean Workers' party in the North, combined with appeals from South Korea–based guerrillas. These pressures may have forced Kim Il-song into war before the date on which his Soviet mentors and he had probably agreed. This hypothesis, based on a fresh reconstruction of the available evidence, leads to conclusions which more satisfactorily account for previously unresolved enigmas: the nature of the triangular bonds between Peking, P'yongyang, and Moscow; the reactions of China and the Soviet Union to the North Korean attack; and the effect of the Korean civil war on the Sino-Soviet relationship.

Korea, traditionally within China's sphere of influence, was harshly exploited by the Soviet Union after 1945. This caused ill feelings by both North Korea and China toward Moscow. Furthermore, the Soviet Union consciously froze China out of the United Nations in January 1950 by walking out at the moment when it seemed that China was to be admitted by a majority vote of the Security Council. Moscow probably did this in order to forestall China's contacts with non-Communist states. Both the British representative to the Security Council and U.N. Secretary-General Lie later expressed this belief. The Chinese representative recalled that "Lie once exerted great efforts on the Chinese representation issue and he did not seem too bad then." Again, Russia's behavior alienated China.

Total command of the invasion date by Russia is questionable. Neither sufficient supplies nor command forces were in Korea before July, and the Soviet Union did not reenter the Security Council until August 1. These facts, combined with the sluggish reaction of Russian propaganda to the war's initiation, indicates that Moscow did not expect a war on June 25—but perhaps did in early August.

The Taiwan Straits "interdiction" announced on June 27 was, in its first few months, partially a mirage. Even if Washington wanted the Seventh Fleet in the Straits, the combination of a weak navy (thanks to a budget-minded Congress) and the need to use the fleet to shuttle supplies between Japan and Korea meant, at most, the possibility of only a skeleton force in the Straits. China, abiding by the largely verbal interdiction, hoped for an early end to the war, which would then result in China taking Taiwan. (Of course, this verbal announcement could have alerted Peking to the possibility of an air attack.)

Then came a major landmark date in the war. An agreement between Peking and Moscow about the possible entrance of the P.R.C. (People's Republic of China)—however unwillingly—into the war, if necessary, had previously been implied in the Soviet news media. The decisive incident that was, in effect, to put the signature irrevocably to this agreement was now to come. On October 8, the day after American troops crossed the 38th Parallel, two American fighter planes of the Shooting Star F-80 type attacked a Soviet aerodrome sixty-two miles north of the Soviet-Korean border and eighteen miles southwest of Vladivostok. The attack took place at 4 p.m., in daylight, while the aerodrome building's markings were clearly visible. The Russians claimed that the two fighters approached the aerodrome in a "hedge-hopping flight" and then "fired at the aerodrome from machine guns." The United States staunchly denied this incident until October 19; on that day in the United Nations the U.S. apologized and offered monetary restitution.

Regardless of the genesis of this provocative armed incursion into Russian territory, whether it occurred by design or by accident, it could have served only to solidify in the cautious mind of Stalin the firm resolve not to become involved in a shooting confrontation with the United States. Additional irritant incidents confirmed this decision. Shortly before the aerodrome incident, "Far East Air Force planes 'bombed' eighteen principal North Korean cities with copies of General MacArthur's demand for surrender. . . . Planes equipped with loud speakers and recordings of these declarations soon will begin to fly over the Soviet Union." On October 12, 1950, "the biggest Allied fleet ever assembled off the Korean east coast since the start of the war . . . blasted and burned a 105-mile stretch of the North Korean coast just south of the Soviet border."

The P.R.C. now became the key member of the Communist triangle. On October 9, the Korean Workers' party daily organ, *Rodong Sinmum* (Labor News), published an article commemorating (three days late) the first anniversary of diplomatic relations between the People's Republic of China and the Democratic People's Republic of Korea. In this article the Korean media used for the first time the unequivocal term "aid" in reference to China; previously only the term "support" had figured in P'yongyang's statements on the P.R.C. On October 11, P'yongyang Radio for the first time expressed its thanks to the P.R.C. without, as had been the practice, coupling it with gratitude to the Soviet Union, save for a slight acknowledgment.

A further indication that the days between October 8 and 10 represented the threshold period when Peking fully realized that its Soviet ally had unequivocally passed the torch is the October 10 statement by the Chinese Foreign Ministry, which "proceeded to alert the country for mobilization." *Shieh-chieh Chih-shih* (World Culture) and *Hsueh Hsi*

(Study) echoed this alert; their articles were probably written on October 9 and 10.[2]

Alliance Strains

The potential for strain between the three allies becomes even more pronounced when the type of arms which the Soviet Union was selling to North Korea and China is examined. Much of the heaviest Soviet military materiel, such as the 152mm M1943 howitzer, the 152mm M1937 gun-howitzer, the Joseph Stalin series of heavy tanks, and very heavy artillery, was not turned over during the war to the Communist forces fighting in Korea. The North Korean army possessed no field artillery heavier than the 122mm M1938 and no tank of later vintage than the T-34/85, dating from World War II. Most of these arms came from Soviet surplus stocks and were obsolete. Interestingly, although production was recent (from 1948 to 1950), the models were outmoded, their fire power was that of a decade-old weapon. Overall, each Communist tank was small match for American antiarmor weapons. While the heaviest Soviet tanks were not used in Korea, the best Soviet antitank weapons—e.g., the 85mm and the 100mm M1944—were also not imported; what was supplied was generally incapable of stopping U.N. armored equipment. In sum, the conventional weapons supplied by the Soviet Union to its allies during the war were inferior to the American weapons which they faced. The awareness of weak Soviet support during the war deeply distressed China and undoubtedly was a contributing factor to the Sino-Soviet split which was shortly to follow.

Moscow proposed the Panmunjom truce talks in the summer of 1951, apparently without a thorough discussion with its two allies. This is suggested by the propaganda originating in both of the countries involved in the fighting, each of which sought goals in addition to those set by the Soviet Union. This was followed by the only occasion when Moscow offered North Korea a sizeable gift—50,000 tons of flour.

Meanwhile, there were further grounds for North Korean dissatisfaction with the direction and support supplied by the Soviet Union. It was reported in early May 1952 that P'yongyang wanted to launch an offensive prior to the South Korean election; the Soviet Union and China vetoed this proposal. This had been preceded shortly before by a private speech made by North Korea's minister of national defense, Ch'oe Yong-gon. Although perhaps not an exact quotation (because of its U.S. Army intelligence source), the statement does seem to reflect accurately the feelings of North Korea toward Russia at the time.

THE COMMUNIST SIDE

The Soviets are now attempting to start a general war in which all Asiatics will eventually engage the U.S. alone. The Chinese Communists are unable to understand why the Soviets do not support more strongly the North Korean and Chinese settlement are P'anmumjom. True Korean and Chinese nationalists are becoming suspicious of the Soviet's real intentions, for the Soviets have openly shown that they are more interested in seducing Japan than in peaceful reconstruction of territories which have been liberated by the People's Republics. Unless the USSR makes a definite promise to intervene in the Korean War, the only alternative is for North Koreans and Chinese to come to terms with the U.N. An armistice will permit the communization of South Korea from within; however, the recently revealed Soviet policy clearly shows the Soviet desire to provoke the Chinese into making rash decisions designed to widen the war in Asia. The Soviets plan to keep Asians fighting Americans while the Soviets sit back and talk about Soviet peace. They do not care about the unification of Korea; they merely invested material and professional aid in order to pin down U.N. forces and weaken U.S. strength.

It appeared during the early summer of 1952 that both China and North Korea were eager to break the impasse of the Panmunjom negotiations over the question of the return of the POW's. At that point the U.S. carried out some of the heaviest bombings of the war which brought an abrupt halt to hopes for an early peace. Speeches by Chou En-lai and Liu Shao-ch'i, and radio broadcasts and exchanges of telegrams by each of the three Communist states, suggest an intensifying concern by all three in concluding the conflict.

By this time, North Korea's media had reversed their previous claims; instead of calling for expulsion of the American invaders from Korea, or even declaring that the U.N. forces had been defeated, P'yongyang now stated that the war had been won.

The enemy is subbornly trying to take the offensive, but we are defending our positions and our defensive lines are strong. If the enemy launches any offensive we can foil his attempt and smash him. We have won, but we cannot boast of our exploits and we must improve our war tactics.

Interestingly, about this time the Russians also changed their stand on the origins, and therefore the purpose, of the war. Previously, they had maintained that the war had been initiated by the Americans as a prelude to invading China and then the Soviet Union itself. For this reason, ran their argument, it was the duty of the Communist world to support North Korea. On November 24, 1952, however, Moscow Radio in a Korean-language broadcast declared that the United States "started the criminal war in Korea in order to maintain their highest profits and head off hard times and the economic depression America is facing." The implications of this new Soviet position would appear to have been two:

first, that the Korean civil war was not as intimately tied to the territorial defense of the Soviet Union as had been previously stated in Russian propaganda; and second, that if the war helped the American economy, perhaps it would be in Russia's interests to bring the war to an end.

Meanwhile, China also appeared anxious to reach some sort of accord in Korea. The Peace Conference of the Asian and Pacific Region, held in Peking from October 1 to 12, 1952, was attended by delegates and observers from thirty-seven countries. As compared with the Trade Union Conference held in the same city in 1949, the Chinese rhetoric was markedly less militant; the stress was now on "peaceful coexistence." The speeches contained more mentions of a fear of Japanese resurgence than of the Korean civil war itself.

A further indication that important decisions had been reached on ending the Korean civil war was contained in the year-end review of world events published in *Pravda* on December 31, 1952. This editorial contained only one reference to the war, and even this was coupled to developments in Europe.

The aggressive, adventurous policy is manifested in all the activities of the aggressive North Atlantic bloc. The intervention against the Korean people, the splitting of Germany, and the militarization of West Germany and Japan were the results of this policy, which is aimed at the suppression of the last vestige of bourgeois democratic freedom, the liquidation of the national sovereignty of nations, and the unleashing of a third world war.

Clearly, the war now seemed less important to Soviet policymakers.

Stalin's concluding remarks to the 19th Party Congress on October 15, 1952, underlined this cautious attitude toward foreign adventures. His speech contained only one rather vague reference to the Korean civil war: "Now, when new shock brigades have appeared in the vanguard of people's democracies from China and Korea to Czechoslovakia and Hungary . . ."

In December 1952, Stalin offered to meet with President-elect Eisenhower. Perhaps to indicate his concern with the static and harsh nature of Russia's relations with the United States, and to demonstrate the importance of improving those relations, Stalin appointed a new ambassador to Peking, filling a six-month vacancy. Significantly, A. S. Panyushkin, who arrived in China on December 9, previously had been the Russian ambassador to Washington.

On January 16, 1953, the New China News Agency (NCNA) published an interesting attack on the United States that had not been made before. It claimed that Eisenhower now wished "Asians to fight Asians." This, NCNA claimed, "is a white supremacist tactic to reduce the 'human cost' of the war of aggression in Korea." Considering what we now know about the tensions between Moscow and Peking and the underlying racial hostility between the two peoples, this first use of the term "white supremacist," in reference to the enemy, perhaps sym-

ACME Newspictures—UPI

A Korean civilian carries his daughter and their belongings across a swollen river near Wonju—March 4, 1951.

bolized the reaching of an agreement between China and the Soviet Union. Peking no longer was hesitant about using an epithet which might previously have been misconstrued by Moscow as a veiled criticism of Soviet chauvinism.

On March 5, 1953, Stalin died; the process of Soviet disengagement from the Korean civil war, which had begun half a year before, now accelerated drastically as Stalin's successors concentrated on factional infighting at home. None of the *Pravda* editorials on the death of the leader, for example, mentioned the Korean war. At the Peking memorial meeting for Stalin on March 9, Ambassador Panyushkin hardly mentioned the war that had held the world's attention for the previous two and three-quarter years. His sole inference read: "As a result [of Stalin's genius], the laboring people of Poland, Hungary, Rumania, Czechoslovakia, Korea, Bulgaria, and Albania have established people's democratic rule in their own countries and carried out social reforms. . . ."

On March 10, a new Soviet ambassador, V. Kuznetsov, was appointed to China; the same day *Pravda* published the famous cropped photograph showing Malenkov, Stalin, and Mao alone in a war pose. (This print obliterated four other men present for the original photo, taken February 14, 1950, on the occasion of the signing of the Sino-Soviet Treaty.) The *Pravda* editorial of the following day continued to deemphasize the Korean civil war, mentioning it only in reference to the fighting in Vietnam: "In a stubborn struggle against the American aggressors, the heroic people of Korea are fighting for the independence of their country. The people of Vietnam are fighting courageously against their imperialist enslavers, for freedom and national independence."

The War's End

In early June 1953, as the armistice negotiations approached a successful conclusion, the South Korean government of Syngman Rhee began to threaten to release unilaterally the Communist POW's held in camps guarded by South Korean soldiers. Apparently, the release of these prisoners on June 18 did not come as a complete surprise to either the U.S. or China. Peking was aware that the truce negotiations were endangered by Rhee and called for an early agreement before Seoul could abort an armistice.

> The Syngman Rhee clique evidently intends to detain POW's by force. It must, therefore, be recognized that true settlement of the POW repatriation question now still depends on whether the American side is able to carry out swiftly the provisions of the agreement and avert the danger of possible detention of the POW's.

Peking was charging that Rhee, by releasing the POW's, would actually be "detaining" them away from the U.N. camps as a means of stalemating the armistice negotiations.

The actual release of the POW's by Rhee caused different reactions in the three Communist countries. Peking understood that the action was probably taken independently by South Korea. The NCNA on June 19 quoted approvingly from a UP dispatch from Tokyo which said: "The U.N. command and the U.S. Government are powerless to prevent Rhee from taking any of these [provocative] courses. . . . The immediate vital question of whether Rhee's action today would destroy chances of a truce could not be answered by Tokyo." On June 26, General Teng Hua, deputy commander of the Chinese People's Volunteers, was quoted by NCNA as saying, "The only way of settling international disputes, as shown by the development of the armistice talks, is by peaceful negotiation." On June 28, NCNA commented that "the Syngman Rhee 'tail', or vice versa, is up to Washington to decide and answer." Clearly, Peking was willing to ignore Rhee's sensational action and get on with the signing of the armistice. Implicitly, this meant that China was willing to entrust the Americans with restraining Rhee's aggressive impulses.

P'yongyang, sensitive to the fact that any future South Korean aggression would be aimed at North Korea, reacted furiously to Rhee's precipitous action. On June 27, for example, P'yongyang Radio noted that "all provocative acts and all illegal actions by the traitor Syngman Rhee are scheduled with the connivance and guidance of his master, which is admitted by the world." On July 2 P'yongyang Radio broadcast another comment, which contrasted with the earlier Chinese questioning of which was the "tail": "America can take Syngman Rhee any place and fasten him by the collar; you cannot look upon America as a master incapable of controlling the dog he has raised." *Minju Chosen* (Democratic Korea), in an editorial published on July 1 in honor of the thirty-second anniversary of the Chinese Communist party, observed that China had now "completely mopped up and driven out the forces of foreign imperialists and their lackeys from the soil of their country. . . ." In neglecting to mention the problem of Taiwan, P'yongyang might have been alluding to the possibility of adhering, at least in the short run, to the forthcoming Korean armistice. Alternatively, the remark could have been meant as a pointed reminder to China that it too had an interest in opposing American imperialism, which was occupying Taiwan. In fact, both messages could well have been directed from a nervous P'yongyang toward its past—and possibly future—protector.

At that moment when the armistice negotiations were endangered by Syngman Rhee's release of the POW's, Moscow was more worried about the Berlin riots of June 16 and 17. Most of Moscow Radio's commentaries on foreign affairs were concerned with this European crisis rather than with Korea. *Pravda's* main editorial of June 23, for example, entitled "The Failure of the Foreign Hireling's Adventure in Berlin," contrasted the two situations in a manner which clearly indicated Russia's priorities.

> There is no doubt that these two events, which took place on different continents of the globe, are closely connected. The question here is of the criminal intrigues of the enemies of peace, the intrigue of those reactionary circles who are afraid of peace, who do not want it, and who are doing everything to prevent the easing of international tensions.

The editorial, blaming problems on the vague "enemies of peace," then went on to say that the POW's were released "on Syngman Rhee's orders," while in Berlin, "provocations took place under the direct leadership of the U.S. military authorities." Apparently, Moscow considered Rhee the villain in Korea, while the U.S. was cast in this role in Germany. America, in Moscow's eyes, was not to blame for Rhee's actions.

P'yongyang, meanwhile, was not as tranquil about the release of the POW's nor as charitable about the role of the U.S. as either of its two allies. On June 22, for example, P'yongyang Radio charged that "the vicious American imperialist aggressors and the Syngman Rhee traitor gang are carrying out the outrageous acts of driving the POW's out of their camps by using tank guns against empty-handed POW's." Unlike Peking and Moscow, which were willing to affix the blame for endangering a Korean armistice upon Seoul, P'yongyang suspected Washington's machinations in purposefully prolonging the war.

On July 8, NCNA declared that the U.S. was obliged to agree that "your side must shoulder the absolute responsibility for ensuring that no such incidents occur again." In short, Peking would not allow Rhee's action to hinder the concluding of an agreement on Korea if Washington would bind Seoul to that agreement.

On July 9, P'yongyang Radio, in a sudden and dramatic softening of its position, began to state that it was indeed Syngman Rhee who was the prime villain in the scenario, rather than Washington.

> If President Eisenhower had not encouraged Syngman Rhee, the vicious disturber of peace, with a Republic of Korea–United States defense pact, if Clark's headquarters had been more active and decisive in retrieving the situation caused by the provocations of Syngman Rhee, and if Robertson, the U.S. envoy to Rhee, had avoided the dirty show of trying to find a way of compromising with Syngman Rhee, the open enemy of peace, the situation would not have developed the way it has, and would not be that way

in the future. If Clark's headquarters really want an early armistice in Korea and the realization of peace, the bestial, indiscriminate bombing of inhabited areas in the rear, which has been intensified viciously since the provocative act of Syngman Rhee, would have been unnecessary. The American government and military authorities, however, have not acted that way. Instead, they have become an *unintentional* inspiration for Syngman Rhee. [Emphasis added.]

The reason for this new North Korean expression of conciliation became evident on the night of July 13–14, when the Chinese People's Volunteers attacked and heavily damaged South Korea's elite Capital Division, while largely avoiding contact with nearby American forces in this last offensive of the war. The NCNA on July 20, 1953, referred to this attack as a lesson "against the Syngman Rhee puppet army, which has been obstructing the Korean armistice and provoking the People's forces." China apparently had offered North Korea assurances that she would guarantee P'yongyang's interests; the attack on the Capital Division was meant as a demonstration of her intention to make good on these pledges.

The war ended only a few miles north of where it began; the 1945 population of North Korea, nine million, had been reduced by one-ninth. The end of the war found the three (unequal) Communist partners eagerly expressing their desire for peace. This was perhaps best suggested by the telegram Kim Il-song sent to Malenkov on July 29, thanking the Soviet Union for its aid during the war:

It is believed to be a trustworthy assurance of successful fulfillment of such an important task raised before the Korean people after the armistice as an attainment of unification of the Fatherland and quick rehabilitation of the people's economy, which has been destroyed by the war.

In its home service of July 30, Moscow Radio broadcast the telegram with but one addition: Kim's "unification" had now become the more quiescent "peaceful unification."

The major (although *not* the single) cause for the war's initiation was the thrust of Korean nationalism. The conflict was fought with less than full Soviet assistance, while the war's end came from pressures mostly outside of the peninsula. The war demonstrated to China the doubtful reliability of Russia in crises and underlined for North Korea the strains inherent in its relationship with the Soviet Union. In both cases, interstate experiences between 1950 and 1953 formed the basis for tensions to come.

NOTES

1. Robert R. Simmons, *The Strained Alliance: Peking, P'yongyang, Moscow and the Politics of the Korean Civil War* (New York: Free

Press, 1975). For detailed documentation of the material presented in this essay, the reader is referred to this volume.

2. Allen S. Whiting, *China Crosses the Yalu: The Decision to Enter the Korean War* (New York: Macmillan, 1960), p. 115.

6

The Korean War:
The Historian's Task

Richard W. Leopold

When I accepted the invitation to assess for this conference the scholarly work that has been done on the Korean conflict and identify some of the things that remain to be done, I thought first of a paper that I read before the American Historical Association in 1949 on the problem of American intervention in 1917. With the surrender on the deck of the *Missouri* only four years back and curiosity about the events leading to Pearl Harbor intense, I dared to suggest that before historians became too absorbed in the origins and course of the Second World War, they consider the unfinished business with respect to United States involvement in the First.[1] In preparing this paper I asked myself whether a parallel could be drawn between the situation in 1949 and today's preoccupation with Vietnam that might cause a neglect of some unanswered questions about the Korean War. I concluded, however, that the events from 1950 to 1953 will not be ignored in the coming years, any more than those from 1914 to 1917 were during the 1950s. On the contrary, with archival materials and personal manuscripts soon to be available, I think we shall shortly witness a boom in historical writing in which the rich resources of the Harry S. Truman Library will play a central role.

In planning this paper I also wondered whether I should offer today, as I did in 1949, a chronological survey of the secondary literature to see whether there has developed any discernible pattern in writing and clearly defined schools of interpretation. In my judgment, there has not been such a pattern for the Korean conflict. Nor did I feel that my assignment obliged me to engage in the sometimes useful but often sterile debate on the origins and course of the Cold War, especially since, with a few exceptions, the self-styled revisionists (a rather meaningless label) have barely begun to focus their attention on the events of 1950. Finally, I decided not to undertake the formidable task of evaluating the single most important recent book dealing with the Korean era—*The Limits of Power: The World and United States Foreign Policy, 1945–1954*, by Joyce and Gabriel Kolko, published in 1972. Many of you, perhaps most of you, are familiar with the exchanges in the *Pacific Historical Review* for November 1973 between those authors and William Stueck, pivoting largely on the use of evidence.[2] That kind of exercise, I feel, is more suited to the printed page than to the lecture platform.

My endeavor will be, rather, one of stocktaking. I hope that an inventory of materials currently available—primary and secondary, printed and unpublished—will indicate what has been done thus far and what can be done in the future. Such an approach will, of course, reveal my own interests and biases. It may entail judgments that are not fully explained; it may, in places, border on the counsel of perfection. Hence, it is only fair that I make clear my own qualifications, or lack of them, to pontificate on these topics.

I am not an expert on the Truman era in general or on the Korean War in particular. My research in this period has been confined to printed sources; I have not tapped directly the holdings of the Truman Library. I stand before you as a specialist in United States foreign policy, particularly for the years after 1889, who is also interested in executive-legislative relations and the role of the armed forces in government and society. I can claim some expertise in the historical programs of the federal government. Unlike the distinguished individuals who participated in the opening round-table discussion of this conference, in July 1950 I stood no closer to the seat of authority or the arena of decision than a very hot bedroom in the University Club on Sixteenth Street where, after a day's research in the Library of Congress, I stared out of my window at the adjacent building wondering what deviltry was afoot behind the drawn blinds of the Russian Embassy.

Let me begin this inventory by noting the plentitude of memoirs or volumes that resemble memoirs by decisionmakers and their advisers. These include books by Presidents Truman (1956) and Eisenhower (1963), Secretary of State Dean Acheson (1969), Army Chief of Staff J. Lawton Collins (1969), United Nations Commander Douglas MacArthur (1964) and his two successors, Matthew B. Ridgway (1967) and Mark W. Clark (1954), Eighth Army Commander Maxwell D. Taylor (1974), Twenty-fourth Division Commander William F. Dean (1954), State Department Counsellors George F. Kennan (1967, 1972) and

Charles E. Bohlen (1973), Assistant Secretary for Far Eastern Affairs John M. Allison (1973), Political Adviser to the Supreme Commander Allied Powers William Sebald (1965), and Chargé d'Affaires to the Republic of China Karl L. Rankin (1964).[3] Announced for publication in March 1975, but not yet arrived at my library, is the edited version of a 1952 work by the first secretary of the Seoul Embassy, Harold Joyce Noble.[4] Surely this is a substantial number of first-hand accounts, probably unmatched for any previous war. Those by Truman, Acheson, Collins, Ridgway, Kennan, and Allison are indispensable. Only a perfectionist would complain that Harry S. Truman did not, like James K. Polk, keep a diary or that Dean Acheson did not follow in the footsteps of Hamilton Fish on that score.

Continuing with printed primary sources, legislative materials are very rich. Besides the debates published in the *Congressional Record*, we have the 1951 hearings, conducted jointly by the Senate Armed Services Committee and the Senate Foreign Relations Committee, occasioned by the recall of MacArthur. The five volumes of testimony and documents, deleted where necessary for security, fill 3,691 pages. MacArthur was on the stand for three days, George C. Marshall for seven, Omar N. Bradley for six, the three service chiefs for two days each, Acheson for eight, Albert C. Wedemeyer for three, Louis Johnson and Patrick J. Hurley for two days each, and Adm. Oscar S. Badger, Gen. David G. Barr, and Gen. Emmett O'Donnell for one day each. I will say more later about this treasure-trove.[5]

Under printed legislative records there is the new *Historical Series* of the Senate Foreign Relations Committee which, since January 1973, has been printing hearings, held in executive session, on the major policies of the Truman administration. Two merit mention here. *Economic Assistance to China and Korea: 1949–50* (1974) throws new light on the confused period from March 1949 to January 1950. Of extraordinary value is *Reviews of the World Situation, 1949–1950* (1974) which contains the proceedings of fifteen briefing sessions held between May 1949 and December 1950.[6] I have barely sampled the twelve lively exchanges between Acheson and the committee—before and after June 1950—on Korea, Japan, China, and Formosa. So far as I have determined, Acheson did not use these materials when he wrote *Present at the Creation*; they are must reading for all historians.

Other printed sources would include the State Department's *Foreign Relations* series, which is only now reaching 1950. But two volumes, released late in 1974, suggest the riches that lie ahead. Volume 6 for 1948 contains a six-page conversation on March 21 between MacArthur, Kennan, and the under-secretary of the army which Kennan does not mention in his *Memoirs*—a conversation in which MacArthur drew the same defensive perimeter that he did a year later in the oft-cited interview with the British journalist, G. Ward Price. That line excluded Korea and Formosa. Volume 9 for 1949 includes almost two hundred pages of documents dealing with Formosa and the course to be pursued if and when the Communists triumphed on the mainland.[7] These pages underscore the importance that MacArthur, the Joint Chiefs, and the State Department attached to Okinawa, but they also indicate a divergence, at the end of 1949, between the JCS and the National Security Council on the question of Formosa. These differences come out clearly in the *Historical Series* volume, mentioned above, when Secretary Johnson and General Bradley testified in executive session on January 26, 1950. As to Indochina, pending the publication of the *Foreign Relations* volumes for 1949 and later years, historians can find documents considered by the National Security Council in the so-called Pentagon Papers, especially in the Government Printing Office edition.[8]

Let us now turn from printed primary sources to secondary works. It is not surprising that the books and articles dealing with United States policy and the American scene are much more satisfying than those that focus on the Soviet Union, the two Koreas, the two Chinas, the United Kingdom, the Third World, or even the United Nations. As a consequence, certain key questions regarding the events between 1950 and 1953 cannot now be answered with certainty.

I shall arbitrarily confine myself to five books and two essays, published between 1972 and 1975, that I found most useful in making this inventory. As an introduction to many major issues, I would recommend to novices and specialists alike Chapter 3, "The Test of Korea," in Bernard Brodie's *War and Politics* (1973). Gaddis Smith's *Dean Acheson* (1972), a volume in the *American Secretaries of State* series edited by Robert H. Ferrell, analyzes dispassionately the work of the man whom Walter LaFeber has called "the most creative and successful American foreign policymaker during the 1900–1970 era"; and, in the process, Smith places Acheson's Korean decisions in a global setting. James F. Schnabel's *Policy and Direction: The First Year* (1972), the latest installment in the official army history, supersedes all earlier accounts of planning and execution in Washington, in Tokyo, and in the battle zone. Walter LaFeber's "Crossing the 38th: The Cold War in Microcosm," a lecture given in 1971 but published only in 1974, properly emphasizes the importance and meaning of the fateful decisions taken in the National Security Council and the United Nations General Assembly between mid-September and October 7, 1950. Robert R. Simmons's *The Strained Alliance: Peking, P'yongyang, Moscow and the Politics of the Korean*

Civil War (1975), while resting on fewer unused materials than the author claims, is full of challenging hypotheses; and although they cannot be proven today, all historians in the future must come to grips with the points he makes. Alonzo Hamby's *Beyond the New Deal: Harry S. Truman and American Liberalism* (1973) is only tangentially concerned with the Korean War, but it sheds much new light on sectors of the domestic scene ignored by previous writers.[9]

Last but not least—indeed the most important of all—is the massive *The Limits of Power: The World and United States Foreign Policy, 1945–1954* (1972) by Joyce and Gabriel Kolko. Like Hamby, the Kolkos devote only part of their study to the Korean conflict. Less than 100 of the text's 716 pages deal directly with that struggle; but to that portion, which even critical reviewers call the most successful part of the work and which has already become the bible of incipient revisionists, all authors must address themselves. The Kolkos deserve high marks for their global perspective, for their linking internal and external forces, for their tapping unused sources, for their probing the murky antecedents of the attack of June 25, and for their candid admission that several links in the chain of their argument cannot be documented. But this last virture is also a major defect. Too many of the Kolkos' assaults on what they call "conventional wisdom" tend to be speculative, hedged in with such words as "probably," "perhaps," and "a matter of conjecture." In the space of fifteen lines on page 572, which advances a major point, the reader finds such phrases as "we shall probably never know," and "is still open to question," and "permits no definitive judgment," and "remains an enigma." Further, their contention that Rhee and MacArthur conspired to provoke a North Korean invasion, that their troops retreated needlessly during June and July in order to insure a massive commitment by the United States, and that Truman and Acheson did everything possible to keep the crisis alive—so as to push through Congress rearmament measures for Europe—lacks proof and, in places, defies logic. Like other writers, the Kolkos treat too cursorily the period after MacArthur's recall.[10]

Among the most important of the older secondary works are the official histories prepared by the armed forces. Their authors gained access to records which, in most cases, are still closed to private researchers. Because of the nature of the war, the army series is the most useful. I have already mentioned Schnabel's *Policy and Direction.* Since its publication in 1961, Roy E. Appleman's *South to the Naktong, North to the Yalu (June-November 1950)* has remained the standard account; the Kolkos' footnotes reveal how much they are indebted to it. Walter G. Hermes's *Truce Tent and Fighting Front* (1966) deals with the neglected period from July 1951 to July 1953. James A. Field's *History of the United States Naval Operations: Korea* (1962) is especially good on the historical setting, the deployment of forces after June 1950, and the impact of the war on weaponry. Robert Frank Futrell's *The United States Air Force in Korea, 1950–1953* (1961) is helpful on the problem of bombing the Yalu bridges, but a fuller description of the planes and their capabilities would have enhanced the book's value.[11] The five volumes entitled *U.S. Marine Operations in Korea, 1950–1953* (1954– 1972) are designed for future fighting men. The second volume in the history of the Atomic Energy Commission, *Atomic Shield, 1947/1952* (1969) by Richard G. Hewlett and Francis Duncan, though tantalizingly brief on the problem, is the best available account of nuclear developments during the Korean conflict.[12]

Continuing with the older secondary works, we find all scholars rely heavily on Glenn D. Paige's *The Korean Decision, June 24–30, 1950* (1968), a splendid day-by-day reconstruction of the first week. It rests on printed works, newspapers, and interviews—conducted between 1955 and 1958—with eleven key participants. Similar treatments would be welcome for critical periods later in the war: the last week of September 1950, the first week of December 1950, or the days before MacArthur's relief. After eleven years, David Rees's *Korea: The Limited War* (1964) remains the best one-volume analysis.[13] For decisionmaking, the older works by John W. Spanier (1959), Trumbull Higgins (1960), and Martin Lichterman (1963) can still be consulted with profit, but they suffer from not having had access to personal papers. An excellent 1968 article, though restricted to published materials, is David McLellan's "Dean Acheson and the Korean War," which argues that Acheson failed to alert Truman fully to the dangers stemming from MacArthur's disregarding his instructions after crossing the 38th Parallel in October 1950.[14]

Studies of Congress are few and generally unsatisfactory. Most writers note the initial reactions in June 1950; a few touch upon the Senate hearings in May and June 1951. Ronald J. Caridi's *The Korean War and American Politics: The Republican Party as a Case Study* (1968) is useful for some GOP senators, but it delivers less than the title promises and does not draw upon manuscript collections now available. James T. Patterson's *Mr. Republican: A Biography of Robert A. Taft* (1972) is a superior performance, but the war was only one of many issues to attract the attention of the Ohioan. A very helpful article on the constitutional dilemma posed by Truman's refusal to seek a declaration of war or some other legislative statement is Charles A. Lofgren's "Mr. Truman's War: A Debate and Its Aftermath" (1968).[15]

Equally unsatisfactory are scholarly studies on the policies of the major foreign powers during the Korean conflict. It is not surprising that we must still speculate about many decisions reached in Moscow, Peking, P'yongyang, and Seoul, but the picture is not much clearer when we turn to other capitals. We can catch the flavor, though not the substance, of the United Kingdom's course in the memoirs of Clement Attlee (1962), Anthony Eden (1960), Harold Macmillan (1969), and Gladwyn Jebb (1972)—the last being good on the behind-the-scenes action at the Security Council during the summer and autumn of 1950—but there are no detailed biographies or monographs.[16] Important exceptions to this generalization, however, should be noted. We do know a good deal about the situation in Ottawa thanks to the second volume of *Mike: The Memoirs of the Right Honourable Lester B. Pearson* (1973) and Denis Stairs's *The Diplomacy of Constraint: Canada, the Korean War and the United States* (1974), as well as two volumes of the official history of the Canadian army and navy in Korea.[17] As to the Communist side, in addition to the new book by Robert R. Simmons, mentioned above, there are Allen S. Whiting's *China Crosses the Yalu: The Decision to Enter the Korean War* (1960) and Adam B. Ulam's *The Rivals: America and Russia since World War II* (1971). After fifteen years, Whiting's study for the Rand Corporation has remained an indispensable treatment, though Simmons now challenges some of his theses.[18]

So much for a very selective and subjective inventory of printed primary sources and secondary works. What new unpublished materials can be exploited, now or in the near future? Is it possible—I am not sure—that transcripts of hearings in executive session before the Senate Foreign Relations Committee may be used in the National Archives before they appear in print as part of the *Historical Series*? The State Department's records for 1950 should be open in another three years, but at the recent rate of progress, it will be at least 1980 until State's archives through 1953 can be investigated. By 1980, under the thirty-year rule, the British Foreign Office files should also be open. Declassification of the navy's operational records makes it possible for historians to deal with the deployment of the fleet from 1945 to 1950 and perhaps beyond. The files of the army and air force seem to be being declassified so as to keep up with the opening of the State Department's archives.

With regard to personal papers still closed or in private hands, I shall refrain from naming all individuals whose correspondence scholars would like to see, for those papers may not exist or may be disappointing. Still, a few things can be said. The papers of President Truman dealing with diplomatic and defense matters, long withheld from the editors of *Foreign Relations*, are presumably among the President's Secretary's

Files released to the Truman Library by the Jackson County Probate Court in accordance with Mr. Truman's will. I cannot tell you what riches may be found in that group, whose history Philip D. Lagerquist has traced in the Spring 1975 issue of *Whistle Stop*; but if nothing else, these files should enable scholars to check on the fullness and accuracy of the two volumes of the *Memoirs*, something heretofore impossible.[19] Much may also be anticipated as the MacArthur Papers in Norfolk are opened. Progress has been made in the last few years in itemizing the various record groups.[20] The Kolkos were the first to use, so far as I can tell, the five letters from Syngman Rhee to MacArthur written between October 1949 and August 1950, which can be found in Record Group 7, the United Nations Commander's files. In his exchange with the Kolkos, Stueck cited one more Rhee letter from Record Group 7 and two from MacArthur, dated December 19, 1949, and January 24, 1950. He also cited from Record Group 10, the general's private correspondence, one letter from Gen. Claire Chennault of November 12, 1949.

Meanwhile the papers of Air Force Chief of Staff Hoyt S. Vandenberg are available in the Library of Congress, as are those of his predecessor, Carl Spaatz. Apparently there are no private papers of the chief of naval operations, Forrest P. Sherman, who died suddenly in July 1951, although the Center of Naval History in Washington has his official files; they are scheduled for review during the current phase of declassification. Likewise unavailable at present are the papers of Omar N. Bradley, chairman of the Joint Chiefs of Staff; the most important of these are at West Point, not in the Bradley Museum at Carlisle Barracks. J. Lawton Collins is placing his papers in the Eisenhower Library; Matthew B. Ridgway, his in the U.S. Army Military History Research Collection at Carlisle; Mark W. Clark, his in the Citadel. One caution is in order. Scholars should not expect too much in the way of personal papers of military men; while on active duty and moving about, they find it difficult to organize their files. Correspondence during retirement may prove more fruitful, for after 1953 many uniformed leaders expressed themselves frankly about the Korean conflict.

Although historians may not receive a cornucopia of manuscript collections over the next few years, they should take better advantage of the oral history interviews with key actors, living and dead. Each presidential library periodically issues a catalog of its historical materials, and these list oral history interviews. The *Oral History Collection of Columbia* (1973) is a 460-page compilation that includes interviews that originated under other auspices and transcriptions that can be consulted in other places. The Marine Corps, which has been very active in this field, issued in 1975 a catalog of its collection that runs to 42 pages of fine print.[21] There are also available—a little dated in some cases—lists of oral transcripts for the George C. Marshall and John Foster Dulles libraries and for the U.S. Naval Institute at Annapolis. Students of the Korean War should be eager to see the interviews with Vice Adm. Herbert D. Riley, aide to Defense Secretary Louis Johnson; with Adm. Robert L. Dennison, aide to President Truman; with Kenneth C. Royall, secretary of the army to April 1949; with Adm. William M. Fechteler, who succeeded Sherman as chief of naval operations; with Gen. Clifton D. Cates and Gen. Lemuel C. Shepherd, commandants of the Marine Corps from January 1949 to December 1955; or with Ernest A. Gross, who played so large a role at the United States mission to the United Nations. I have yet to see a publication on the Korean War that has drawn on these interviews.

I come finally to some subjects that I deem worthy of further investigation. I could extend this list ad infinitum, as well as ad nauseam, but I will try to make it illustrative, not comprehensive, and reasonable within the bounds of materials now available. I shall also avoid the perennial problems about which we can never know enough—the invasion of June 25, 1950, the president's difficulties with MacArthur, China's intervention, and the absence of a declaration of war.

First, scholars would benefit from an administrative history of the Truman presidency. It would help to know precisely how the White House staff functioned—who served as counsel and special assistants at specific times and how their duties were defined.* This approach might throw light on the influence of the military aides and those responsible for the work of the National Security Council. We seem to know fairly well how Truman worked with the secretaries of state and defense and with the chairman of the Joint Chiefs of Staff. We know less about his dealings with the individual service heads, the director of the Central Intelligence Agency, and those responsible for congressional liaison. These administrative matters are always the least well documented, for the participants take for granted their knowledge of how business is transacted. The gap is not peculiar to the Truman presidency, but many of Truman's aides are still available to help us—Clark M. Clifford, W. Averell Harriman, Charles S. Murphy, and George M. Elsey, among others.

A second need is to describe the strength of all the armed forces in the western Pacific before June 1950. We have heard a good deal about Acheson's and MacArthur's exclusion of Korea from the nation's defensive

---

* This topic is to be the subject of a conference in May 1977, also sponsored by the Harry S. Truman Library Institute.—*Ed.*

perimeter. Much has been written about the army's withdrawal from South Korea in June 1949, though it now seems that both MacArthur and Bradley had second thoughts soon thereafter on the wisdom of that step. The weakness of the occupation troops in Japan has also been stressed, but little attention has been given to the navy, the air force, and the marines. Were ships, planes, and men shifted from Asia to Europe in accordance with the Europe-first strategy symbolized by the North Atlantic Treaty of April 4, 1949, and the Mutual Defense Assistance Act of October 6? Did the bitter interservice dispute over the merits of the B-36 bomber and a new class of aircraft carriers, the agonizing decision to develop a thermonuclear bomb, the partisan debate over defending Formosa, and the intensive discussions that produced NSC-68 leave uncertain our defensive posture in East Asia and perhaps mislead the enemy into believing that an invasion would not be resisted? We badly need a comprehensive analysis of the capability and contingency plans of American armed forces in the western Pacific during the period before June 1950.

A third area for further exploration is the dual decision that accompanied Truman's orders of June 27 that United States air and sea forces give South Korean troops cover and support. One was the instructions to the Seventh Fleet to prevent a Communist attack on Formosa and to see that Nationalist planes and ships cease operations against the mainland. The second was a directive to accelerate giving weapons and aid to the forces of France and the Associated States of Indochina and the dispatch of a military mission to provide close working relations. The second decision may have stemmed logically from Acheson's statement of May 8, 1950, that Soviet imperialism endangered nationalism and democracy in Southeast Asia, but no one has spelled out clearly why Indochina was included in the June 27 announcement. Adam B. Ulam thinks that the Formosa decision drastically changed American policy in Asia. "No reason or logic or policy," he argues, could justify the orders to the Seventh Fleet "as being in any sense connected with the need to save South Korea."[22] Obviously, it was linked to domestic pressures, but I believe there is an instructive story to be found in the debates among the Joint Chiefs of Staff and within the National Security Council during the preceding eighteen months.

A fourth episode calling for additional research is the vote in the United Nations on October 7, 1950, creating a Commission for the Unification and Rehabilitation of Korea. This commission was, among other things, to establish a unified, independent, and democratic government for all Korea after MacArthur's command had pursued the defeated North Koreans above the 38th Parallel. We know fairly well the United States side of the story—at the White House, the State and Defense departments, the Joint Chiefs of Staff, even MacArthur's headquarters. But the proceedings in New York, both in the General Assembly and in the missions of the sponsoring countries (Australia, Brazil, Cuba, Norway, the Netherlands, Pakistan, the Philippines, and the United Kingdom) are not clear. In view of the hints emanating from Peking about possible intervention and the subsequent distrust of MacArthur manifested by the European and Asian delegations, this neglect is surprising. Since Marshall, in 1951, called the U.N. authorization oblique and Acheson, in 1969, termed it ambivalent, one wonders why the "considerable misgivings" among the U.N. membership which, according to Ruth B. Russell, had been "privately expressed" did not come out into the open more forcefully.[23]

A fifth fruitful subject for study is the hearings in May and June 1951 before the combined Senate Committees on the Armed Services and on Foreign Relations. Entitled *An Inquiry into the Military Situation in the Far East and the Facts Surrounding the Relief of General of the Army Douglas MacArthur from His Assignments in That Area*, the hearings have long been a major source for many of the issues discussed in this paper. But no one has described fully the inquest or evaluated critically, in light of what we know today, the testimony given by the witnesses or the questions asked by the senators. No one has compared the printed version of what transpired behind closed doors with the day-to-day accounts published in the newspapers. No one has determined what was deleted from the official record or even has shown that it is possible so to determine.* Furthermore, too much attention has been given to the Republican participants in the inquiry. In view of the role they played in American foreign and defense policy after 1951, it would be enlightening to scrutinize the questions of Lyndon B. Johnson, Richard B. Russell, J. William Fulbright, Walter F. George, John C. Stennis, John J. Sparkman, and—although then a Republican—Wayne Morse.

A sixth topic that might be profitably restudied is the alleged disagreement in June 1951 between Gen. James A. Van Fleet, the Eighth Army commander, and his superiors—General Ridgway in Tokyo and the Joint Chiefs of Staff in Washington—over the wisdom of pursuing in

---

* Since these words were written, John E. Wiltz has published a valuable essay that does many of the things suggested here and provides citations to the deleted testimony; see "The MacArthur Hearings of 1951: The Secret Testimony," *Military Affairs* 39 (1975): 167–73. See also his "The MacArthur Inquiry, 1951," in *Congress Investigates 1792–1974*, ed. Arthur M. Schlesinger, Jr., and Roger Bruns (New York: Chelsea House, 1975), pp. 383–430.

full strength the defeated and presumably demoralized Chinese–North Korean armies before and during the armistice talks that the Soviet Union had proposed. This controversy is barely mentioned by Acheson and is ignored by Truman and by the Kolkos. Both Collins and Ridgway have asserted that Van Fleet's later charges—that he was prevented from taking steps which would have won a decisive victory—are at variance with contemporary records. I would gladly let their testimony prevail if Brodie had not recently reopened the issue, siding strongly with Van Fleet. Brodie argues that the Joint Chiefs in Washington could not appreciate the disarray of the enemy and that Ridgway did not understand what Van Fleet was suggesting.[24] Without wandering into that minefield and pontificating on matters with which I am ill equipped to deal, I would urge historians to take another look at the problem, keeping in mind some of Van Fleet's other charges after he retired in 1952 about an ammunition shortage and the assurances given the People's Republic that intervention would not lead to bombing Chinese soil. Unlike Collins, Ridgway, and Taylor, Van Fleet has never written his memoirs, but I am told by Forrest Pogue that there are oral history interviews at the Military History Research Collection at Carlisle.

One more suggestion and I shall desist. In light of our experience in Vietnam, it is surprising that so little has been written on the problems of recruitment, training, and morale for the period from 1950 to 1953. There is probably little more to say about the prisoner-of-war issue, the literature of which was well summarized in H. H. Wubben's 1970 essay in the *American Quarterly*. And a start has been made in Richard M. Dalfiume's *Desegregation of the U.S. Armed Forces: Fighting on Two Fronts, 1939–1953* (1969) to measure the impact of the president's executive order of July 1948.[25] But much remains to be done in studying the operation of the selective service law, the recall of reservists, the requests for conscientious objector status, and the rate of desertions. It would be interesting to weigh the influence, if any, of the Uniform Code of Military Justice enacted in May 1950.

What, then, can we conclude regarding the historian's task on this twenty-fifth anniversary of the beginning of the first major war fought by the United States for limited aims with limited means? The conflict continues to attract scholarly attention, and this concern will increase during the coming years with the opening of archival materials and personal papers. It is belaboring the obvious to remind this audience that historians have yet to see many of the key documents of the era. We can also anticipate three major biographical contributions—by Forrest C. Pogue on George C. Marshall, by D. Clayton James on Douglas MacArthur, and by Martin Blumenson on Mark W. Clark. Somewhere down the pike is Billy C. Mossman's volume in the army series, *Ebb and Flow*, covering the months from November 1950, where Appleman stops, to July 1951, where Hermes begins. Even more distant is Martin Blumenson's volume in *The Macmillan Wars of the United States*, edited by Louis Morton. And without wishing to sound ghoulish, I must voice the hope that the distinguished survivors of that exciting period, some of whom have done so much to enrich this conference, have placed in order their private papers, have provided properly for their bequest, and have refrained from placing too many restrictions on their early use.

NOTES

Author's Note: Since this paper was delivered in May 1975, additional works have appeared dealing with the Korean War. I would like to call particular attention to: *Executive Sessions of the Senate Foreign Relations Committee* (Historical Series), vol. 3, pt. 1 (82nd Cong., 1st sess., 1951), published in 1976; *Selected Executive Session Hearings of the* [House] *Committee* [on Foreign Affairs], *1943–50* (Historical Series), vol. 8 (81st Cong., 1949–1950), published in 1976; and David S. McLellan, *Dean Acheson: The State Department Years* (New York: Dodd, Mead, 1976).

1. Richard W. Leopold, "The Problem of American Intervention, 1917: An Historical Retrospect," *World Politics* 2 (April 1950): 405–25.
2. See William Stueck, "Cold War Revisionism and the Origins of the Korean Conflict: The Kolko Thesis"; Joyce and Gabriel Kolko, " 'To Root Out Those among Them'—A Response"; and rejoinders by both sides, *Pacific Historical Review* 42 (November 1973): 537–75. See also, Robert R. Simmons, "The Korean Civil War," in *Without Parallel: The American-Korean Relationship since 1945*, ed. Frank Baldwin (New York: Pantheon, 1974), pp. 143–78.
3. Harry S. Truman, *Memoirs*, vol. 2, *Years of Trial and Hope* (Garden City, N.Y.: Doubleday, 1956); Dwight D. Eisenhower, *The White House Years: Mandate for Change, 1953–1956* (Garden City, N.Y.: Doubleday, 1963); Dean Acheson, *Present at the Creation: My Years in the State Department* (New York: W. W. Norton, 1969); J. Lawton Collins, *War in Peacetime: The History and Lessons of Korea* (Boston: Houghton Mifflin, 1969); Douglas MacArthur, *Reminiscences* (New York: McGraw-Hill, 1964); Matthew B. Ridgway, *The Korean War* (Garden City, N.Y.: Doubleday, 1967); Mark W. Clark, *From the Danube to the Yalu* (New York: Harper & Bros., 1954); Maxwell D. Taylor, *Swords and Plowshares* (New York: W. W. Norton, 1972); William F. Dean (as told to William L. Worden), *General Dean's Story* (New York: Viking, 1954); George F. Kennan, *Memoirs, 1925–1963*, 2 vols. (Boston: Little,

Brown, 1967–1972); Charles E. Bohlen, *Witness to History, 1929–1969* (New York: W. W. Norton, 1973); John M. Allison, *Ambassador from the Prairie, or Allison Wonderland* (Boston: Houghton Mifflin, 1973); William Sebald (with Russell Brines), *With MacArthur in Japan: A Personal History of the Occupation* (New York: W. W. Norton, 1965); and Karl Lott Rankin, *China Assignment* (Seattle: University of Washington Press, 1964).

4. Harold Joyce Noble, *Embassy at War*, ed. Frank Baldwin (Seattle: University of Washington Press, 1975).

5. U.S., Congress, Senate, Committee on Armed Services and Committee on Foreign Relations, *Military Situation in the Far East: Hearings to Conduct an Inquiry into the Military Situation in the Far East and the Facts Surrounding the Relief of General of the Army Douglas MacArthur from His Assignments in That Area*, 5 pts., 82d Cong., 1st sess., 1951.

6. U.S., Congress, Senate, Committee on Foreign Relations, *Economic Assistance to China and Korea, 1949–50: Hearings Held in Executive Session, Eighty-First Congress; Reviews of the World Situation, 1949–1950: Hearings Held in Executive Session, Eighty-First Congress*, Historical Series, 1974.

7. U.S., Department of State, *Foreign Relations of the United States, 1948*, vol. 6, *The Far East and Australasia* (Washington, D.C.: G.P.O., 1974); *Foreign Relations of the United States, 1949*, vol. 9, *The Far East: China* (Washington, D.C.: G.P.O., 1974).

8. U.S., Congress, House of Representatives, Committee on Armed Services, *United States–Vietnam Relations, 1945–1967: Study Prepared by the Department of Defense*, 12 books, 92d Cong., 1st sess., 1971; see especially book 8.

9. Bernard Brodie, *War and Politics* (New York: Macmillan, 1973), pp. 57–112; Gaddis Smith, *Dean Acheson* (New York: Cooper Square, 1972); James F. Schnabel, *Policy and Direction: The First Year [United States Army in the Korean War]* (Washington, D.C.: G.P.O., 1972); Walter LaFeber, "Crossing the 38th: The Cold War in Microcosm," in *Reflections on the Cold War: A Quarter Century of American Foreign Policy*, ed. Lynn H. Miller and Ronald W. Pruessen (Philadelphia: Temple University Press, 1974), pp. 71–90; Robert R. Simmons, *The Strained Alliance: Peking, P'yongyang, Moscow and the Politics of the Korean Civil War* (New York: Free Press, 1975); Alonzo L. Hamby, *Beyond the New Deal: Harry S. Truman and American Liberalism* (New York: Columbia University Press, 1973).

10. Joyce and Gabriel Kolko, *The Limits of Power: The World and United States Foreign Policy, 1945–1954* (New York: Harper & Row, 1972).

11. Roy E. Appleman, *South to the Naktong, North to the Yalu (June–*

November 1950) [United States Army in the Korean War] (Washington, D.C.: G.P.O., 1961); Walter G. Hermes, *Truce Tent and Fighting Front [United States Army in the Korean War]* (Washington, D.C.: G.P.O., 1966); James A. Field, Jr., *History of United States Naval Operations: Korea* (Washington, D.C.: G.P.O., 1962); Robert Frank Futrell, *The United States Air Force in Korea, 1950–1953* (New York: Duell, Sloan and Pearce, 1961).

12. Lynn Montross, Nicholas A. Canonza, et al., *U.S. Marine Operations in Korea*, 5 vols. (Washington, D.C.: G.P.O., 1954–1972); Richard G. Hewlett and Oscar Anderson, *A History of the United States Atomic Energy Commission* (University Park, Pa.: Pennsylvania State University Press, 1962–1969), vol. 2, Richard G. Hewlett and Francis Duncan, *Atomic Shield, 1947/1952* (1969).

13. Glenn D. Paige, *The Korean Decision, June 24–30, 1950* (New York: Free Press, 1968); David Rees, *Korea: The Limited War* (New York: St. Martin's Press, 1964).

14. John W. Spanier, *The Truman-MacArthur Controversy and the Korean War* (Cambridge: Harvard University Press, 1959); Trumbull Higgins, *Korea and the Fall of MacArthur: A Précis in Limited War* (New York: Oxford University Press, 1960); Martin Lichterman, "To the Yalu and Back," in *American Civil-Military Decisions: A Book of Case Studies*, ed. Harold Stein (University, Ala.: University of Alabama Press, 1963), pp. 569–642; David S. McLellan, "Dean Acheson and the Korean War," *Political Science Quarterly* 83 (March 1968): 16–39.

15. Ronald J. Caridi, *The Korean War and American Politics: The Republican Party as a Case Study* (Philadelphia: University of Pennsylvania Press, 1968); James T. Patterson, *Mr. Republican: A Biography of Robert A. Taft* (Boston: Houghton Mifflin, 1972); Charles A. Lofgren, "Mr. Truman's War: A Debate and Its Aftermath," *Review of Politics* 31 (April 1969): 223–41.

16. Clement Attlee (as set down by Francis Williams), *Twilight of Empire: Memoirs of Prime Minister Clement Attlee* (New York: A. S. Barnes, 1962); Anthony Eden, *Full Circle: The Memoirs of Anthony Eden* (Boston: Houghton Mifflin, 1960); Harold Macmillan, *Tides of Fortune, 1945–1955* (New York: Harper & Row, 1969); Gladwyn Jebb, *The Memoirs of Lord Gladwyn* (New York: Weybright and Talley, 1972).

17. Lester B. Pearson, *Mike: The Memoirs of the Right Honourable Lester B. Pearson*, vol. 2, *1948–1957* (New York: Quadrangle, 1973); Denis Stairs, *The Diplomacy of Constraint: Canada, the Korean War and the United States* (Toronto: University of Toronto Press, 1974); Herbert Fairlie Wood, *Strange Battleground: The Operations in Korea and Their Effects on the Defence Policy of Canada* (Ottawa: Roger Duhamel, 1966); Thor Thorgrimsson and E. C. Russell,

Canadian Naval Operations in Korean Waters, 1950–1952 (Ottawa: Roger Duhamel, 1966).

18. Allen S. Whiting, *China Crosses the Yalu: The Decision to Enter the Korean War* (New York: Macmillan, 1960); Adam B. Ulam, *The Rivals: America and Russia since World War II* (New York: Viking, 1971).

19. Philip D. Lagerquist, "The Truman Papers," *Whistle Stop: Harry S. Truman Library Institute Newsletter* 3 (Spring 1975): 1–3.

20. I am indebted to Capt. Robert H. Alexander, USN (Ret.), director of the MacArthur Memorial in Norfolk, Virginia, for valuable finding aids on the various record groups in the MacArthur Archives.

21. Elizabeth B. Mason and Louis M. Starr, eds., *The Oral History Collection of Columbia University* (New York: Oral History Research Office, 1973); Bemis M. Frank, comp., *Marine Corps Oral History Catalog* (Washington: History and Museums Division, Headquarters, U.S. Marine Corps, 1975).

22. Ulam, *The Rivals*, p. 172.

23. Ruth B. Russell, *The United Nations and United States Security Policy* (Washington, D.C.: The Brookings Institution, 1968), p. 128.

24. Collins, *War in Peacetime*, pp. 306–7; Ridgway, *The Korean War*, pp. 181–82; Brodie, *War and Politics*, pp. 91–97.

25. H. H. Wubben, "American Prisoners of War in Korea: A Second Look at the 'Something New in History' Theme," *American Quarterly* 22 (Spring 1970): 3–19; Richard M. Dalfiume, *Desegregation of the U.S. Armed Forces: Fighting on Two Fronts, 1939–1953* (Columbia, Mo.: University of Missouri Press, 1969).

Discussion

Prof. Robert H. Ferrell (chairman): Professor Leopold's magisterial inventory is not of the kind that one disputes and debates. But among those present are a number of persons who undoubtedly can add to it from their specialized knowledge. I am sure Professor Leopold would welcome their comments as well as any questions from the audience.

Forrest C. Pogue: The reference to Van Fleet reminded me that the Military History Research Collection at Carlisle has an on-going interview project.

Ferrell: Before we go on, have they published a list of those interviews?

Pogue: I do not know. Perhaps General Collins can tell you.

Gen. James L. Collins: No, not so far as I know. But there is an on-going interview program that started with Vietnam which is being extended back. Each year about ten prominent officers, normally retired, have been interviewed. They have in some instances placed certain restrictions on the use of their interviews. There will be, in the coming year, a list published of the interviews made: which ones are open for research, which ones will be opened in 1978, and other restrictions. As of right now there are approximately forty interviews on file.

Daniel J. Reed: I wanted to point out to all those interested in research on the Korean War that I see the prospects, as Professor Leopold does, for declassification through the usual agency channels. I want to call attention, however, not only to the mandatory review provision available through the executive order (11652) on classification but also to the Freedom of Information Act which was amended in 1974 and is now an important means to use for access to classified official records. You may not get everything opened every time you try, but my guess is that you will get most of what you want opened and get it much faster than using the mandatory review provision. The latter is still useful in case of personal papers but in the case of official records, the Freedom of Information Act as amended is the better approach.

225

THE KOREAN WAR

PROF. RICHARD W. LEOPOLD: Dan, could you answer the question about the transcripts of the executive hearings?

REED: No, I do not know.

PROF. JOHN E. WILTZ: They are available; they were declassified during the autumn of 1974.

LEOPOLD: The printed hearings, say, after twelve years—they could be. In other words, if they should be slowed down in the printing of the *Historical Series*, the scholar can go directly to the originals in the National Archives.

WILTZ: In fact you can write the National Archives and they will duplicate 800 pages of deleted testimony at 10 cents a page. They are particularly good for the testimony of the Joint Chiefs of Staff, General Collins's testimony, not very good really for General MacArthur and Dean Acheson.

LEOPOLD: Do you know the answer to the other question with regard to the Senate Committee on Foreign Relations hearings in executive session that have not yet been printed in the *Historical Series*?

WILTZ: I have seen the deliberations in the Armed Services–Foreign Relations Committee just prior to the MacArthur hearings, when they discussed the question of whether the hearings would be in executive sessions. That is available.

AMBASSADOR LUCIUS D. BATTLE: I would like to make a comment that I think is of some interest in light of what has been said. I was in Dean Acheson's office at the time of the war, and on the third day, as I recall it, of that war, Herbert Feis, who was then on the planning staff, said to Dean, "Let's do this time what we have never done before in our history—keep a history of the war as we go along."

It was arranged that a young man from the Historical Office of the State Department, Byron Manville, would come to see me at the end of each day—and they were long days—and he would ask what had been decided that day and in the light of what. That is, what telegrams, what messages, what issues were before the secretary, and, indeed, often the cabinet, because I had a report of what had occurred over there, or elsewhere in town. I would guess that for a year and a half that kind of recordkeeping went on.

In early '53, I was being transferred to Denmark, but I was rather interested in the history of the period. So I called the Historical Office, not having had anything to do with them for some months, and asked,

DISCUSSION

"How are you getting along on our Korean War history?" The response was, "We did brilliantly after we had started doing a day-by-day record, but we have never totally reconstructed that first weekend because nobody kept any records."

Now, all of that will one day be available—whether they ever got the early days straightened out or not I don't know—but I thought it would be of interest here.

NEIL H. PETERSON: I would like to give a report on how the *Foreign Relations Series* is going on the Korean War. Our history has now covered 1950, and with a little luck that should be out in about a year. There is going to be a separate volume for 1951, and, again with a little luck—especially on declassification at the NSC level—we will have that out in about two years. Then there is going to be a three-year volume covering '52 through '54. That is in preparation and we hope will be out in about three years. But I am afraid that 1980 is a fair estimate on when the files for the whole period are going to be open for general research.

The Historical Office project that was alluded to has been relied upon heavily in the preparation of the *Foreign Relations* volumes. The whole project still exists in the Historical Office. It is several cabinets of material, and people who are interested in investigating it ought to contact the Historical Office.

LEOPOLD: Thank you very much. Are there important research projects, or are there important collections that are now open, or soon to be opened, that have not been mentioned here which ought to have been? It is not the easiest thing to keep in mind, although I suppose the Truman Library would know as much as anybody of what some of the research and progress is.

DORIS M. CONDIT: The office of the secretary of defense has begun a small project on this period. The period from 1947 through 1950 is being explored by Dr. Harry B. Yoshpe, and the period between 1950 and 1953 is currently being begun by myself. I believe probably someone else will come in to do the period that immediately follows. This is a long-term project. We will explore the same records that all the rest of the people have to explore but will look at everything from the perspective of the office of the secretary of defense.

LEOPOLD: What are the publication plans?

CONDIT: None at this time. That is very far in the future. I think they hope that the first volume might be out in about six years—but this is not a set date. The publication plan is for declassification and publication in the open domain, if and when declassifiers are willing.

PHILIP LAGERQUIST: I was going to say two things. First, aside from the Truman Papers, the George Elsey Papers are probably, as you mentioned, the best, most valuable collection in the Truman Library.

Insofar as the President's Secretary's File is concerned, we are still processing it, and we are just getting into the files dealing with foreign and military affairs so I can't speak about these in detail. But there is a file relating directly to the Korean War, which consists of well over a filing cabinet of material. In addition, there would be pertinent materials in files of the National Security Council on the conferences of foreign leaders, in the correspondence files between Truman and heads of state in other countries, and in files relating to particular countries and perhaps in other places. Once again, the big problem, of course, is that much of this material is classified. Once we get the material under control we anticipate initiating mandatory review requests on our own, but any such request that could be initiated by interested scholars would be helpful.

LEOPOLD: Phil, on the George Elsey Papers, are those still largely classified materials?

LAGERQUIST: No. We have sent in all of the classified Elsey material pertaining to Korea for mandatory review. All of the Defense Department material has been returned, and I think they only withheld one document. We still have to hear from the State Department.

LEOPOLD: Does someone else have a comment?

GEN. MATTHEW B. RIDGWAY: My name is Ridgway, and my papers were turned over with no restrictions whatever to Carlisle Barracks about three or four years ago, with the exception of my private meetings—and there were several—with the Japanese emperor and many with the Japanese prime minister, Yoshida; those I shall retain until both they and I are dead.

LEOPOLD: Would you be willing, sir, to give the group some indication of the extent of what you turned over to the Carlisle?

RIDGWAY: Well, I don't know; the papers go back long before the Korean War.

LEOPOLD: They cover your entire career?

RIDGWAY: No, not the entire career. I would say probably nothing much before the beginning of World War II.

DISCUSSION

LEOPOLD: Thank you very much. General Collins?

GEN. J. LAWTON COLLINS: My papers will be turned over to the Eisenhower Library. This will involve personal papers and whatever official papers I still have that might be declassified. So far as my personal papers are concerned, there will be no restrictions other than on purely personal matters which would have to be cleared either by me or by my heirs.

LEOPOLD: Thank you very much. Are there any other questions, observations, suggestions?

REED: I was especially intrigued by your suggestion of an administrative history of the Truman administration as a project for the Truman Library, and I will talk to Dr. Zobrist about this. I have in mind the recent experience of the National Archives in doing a great deal towards compiling an administrative history of the Nixon administration. Many people may now think it ironic the way things came out, but the Nixon administration was in many ways—maybe in more ways than you have heard of—extremely well documented. With the administration's encouragement, we did a thorough job of assembling data on who worked for whom, who had what assignments, who changed from this to that assignment, and when. This included organization charts, job sheets, and so forth. We, of course, cannot do all that for the Truman administration but, with the Nixon experience and model, we can now go back while we still have leading contemporaries like Clark Clifford and Charlie Murphy and others who were there . . .

LEOPOLD: George Elsey.

REED: Yes, and George—and get a good deal of the facts together. It would, of course, be of value to the Truman Library and its clientele on many aspects of the Truman period. It is a central body of data that should be recorded for every administration, but, unfortunately, it has not been.

7

Mr. Truman's Way with Crises

W. Averell Harriman

The conference which has brought us together here in Mr. Truman's hometown and in this great library, which he set up for the American people, focuses on one of President Truman's historic decisions: to resist aggression in Korea. I have been asked to talk about a broader and related topic: how Mr. Truman faced crises.

This is, of course, a large assignment. If you are in the White House, it seems that there is a crisis every day. In fact, in the nature of things, issues that are not critical, that do not call for a decision at the highest level, rarely reach the president's desk.

The first crisis that I remember in Mr. Truman's life was when he became president of the United States. I was in Moscow and I came back as rapidly as I could to see him. I was going to try to tell him something about what had been going on in our relations with the Soviet government and how Stalin had been breaking the Yalta agreements, but I found much to my surprise that the president knew as much about Stalin as I did. Mr. Truman had read all the telegrams that had been going back and forth, and, with his extraordinarily retentive memory, he understood them. So there was no reason for me to brief the president: he already knew what I came to tell him. But I was struck by the great humility he displayed at the time. He said to me: "I haven't been elected president; it was Roosevelt. And I want to know as much as I can about what Roosevelt's policies were. I'm going to try to follow them as much as possible."

Let me say here that I was actually worried in the beginning because I thought he was a little too humble. That may be rather strange to say about President Truman, but, as we all know, he gained confidence

230

very rapidly as crises came that had nothing to do with the past and could not be solved by asking what Roosevelt knew or what he would have done.

Mr. Truman's confidence in himself was evident well before the election of 1948. Take the matter of the United Nations Charter. He had the courage to take the position that if we could not get the kind of a charter we wanted, we would get along without the Russians. It may not be fully known that there were several situations where the Russians were holding out. At that time, Stettinius, the secretary of state, was being criticized for opposing that great humanitarian statesman, Mr. Molotov—it is strange today to realize that that was the public feeling then. But Stettinius stood firm, and these matters were not settled until later on when they came to me in Moscow. Fortunately, Harry Hopkins was there, and with his help they were settled. The United Nations became real.

Mr. Truman has been criticized by some revisionists because he was a little rude to Mr. Molotov. Mr. Molotov was rather an expert on rudeness. It was, I think, quite impossible to be as rude to Mr. Molotov as he was to others. But the revisionists forget that shortly afterwards President Truman sent Harry Hopkins to see Stalin. Harry Hopkins was a symbol of the friendship between Roosevelt and Stalin. Remember that Hopkins had been the first Westerner to go to Moscow after Hitler's attack in July 1941. Stalin had great respect for Hopkins and knew that he was close to Roosevelt; and he also knew that Hopkins had done everything he could to get supplies through to support the Soviet position. Mr. Truman knew all this, and by sending Hopkins to Stalin, the message was that we wanted friendship—but also honest dealings.

Mr. Truman hit crises head on. Roosevelt, for whom I also had the privilege to work, tried to avoid crises and tried, if possible, to find ways to get around them, but President Truman met them head on—though always with the most extraordinary amount of care. Before he made up his mind he did all the reading that was necessary—he was an avid reader, as you all know. He talked to the people whose judgment he thought useful. Then when he made up his mind, after he had considered all the facts, he went home and went to bed and went to sleep. He never worried about whether his decisions were right or wrong. He used to say, "Well, I've done the best I can, and there it is." That was a great quality, one of the things that gave him really great strength.

Another thing people don't fully realize is that he was probably one of the best educated men in the White House on the subject of the presidency and on history, American and also world history. He read a great deal and he had a very retentive memory. I was rather embarrassed once by my ignorance when I brought two international labor leaders in to see him, a Britisher and a Dutchman. Mr. Truman said to the Dutchman, "You've had a lot of trouble with the British in the past," and then started to talk about the naval engagements that took place during the seventeenth century between the British and the Dutch navies; and he named the admirals and the ships sunk by the Dutch. The British visitor could not stand it; he said, "Mr. President, we don't write our history that way." The point of the story is that this was not one of those cases where the president had been well briefed. Of course, when a man comes to see the president, the president is given some information on his background and the subject they will talk about. But Mr. Truman couldn't conceivably have been briefed on the history of Dutch-English naval battles three hundred years ago. It was his own knowledge of past world events, and this helped him no end in dealing with problems. He always kept them in the perspective of history.

Let me now report on what was a "mini-crisis": his relation with Jimmy Byrnes. Jimmy Byrnes was always, I think, a little bit envious of Mr. Truman. Byrnes always thought that he should have been Roosevelt's vice-president, and, had that been the case, he would have been in Truman's place. Truman lived with that until there was the case in Moscow when Byrnes attended the Foreign Ministers' Conference. At the end of the first meeting, I said to him, "Jimmy, do you want me to draft a telegram for your approval to send to the president or do you want to do it yourself?" And Byrnes said, "I'm not going to send any telegram." I said, "Well, Jimmy, this is what is usually done." We argued a little bit about it and finally he said, "No, the president has given me complete authority to deal with these matters." He sent only one general summary telegram to the president. Then on his way home he told his press secretary to fix a time on the air for him to report to the nation. When Jimmy arrived in Washington, he was told by the president, "You'd better report to me before you report to the nation." Then there was the discussion on the yacht on the Potomac; no one ever knew quite what happened there. Each had a somewhat different point of view in his report of the discussion. In any event, what came out of it was that Byrnes took orders from then on and served, in many ways, well.

Mr. Truman had a reverence for General Marshall, Byrnes's successor, and it was one of the most interesting relationships I have ever known between two men. Truman thought that Marshall was one of the great men of our nation and of all time. He respected him enormously and depended a great deal on him as secretary of state and later as secretary of defense. Clark Clifford will bear me out that it was President Truman who named the Marshall Plan, partly because the Truman Doctrine already bore his name and partly because he had enormous respect for General Marshall.

It is important to remember how severe the crisis was in Europe at that time. Not only were the people hungry, but there were not enough raw materials to get industry moving again. President Truman had the foresight to see that our own future depended on the rehabilitation of Europe. There is no doubt in my mind that Stalin would have moved toward domination of Europe had it not been for the action President Truman took at that time. The Communist parties in Italy and France were so strong then that I am sure Stalin figured that Europe, with hunger and unemployment, was ripe for his brand of communism. And this, I believe, is one of the reasons why Stalin decided to break the agreements made at Yalta.

Since Korea has been discussed at length during this conference, I will not spend much time on it. Dean Acheson helped the president a great deal by the rapid manner in which he took the situation to the United Nations and achieved what President Truman wanted, which was to get United Nations support. President Truman understood that in that situation it was absolutely necessary for the United States to have the support of the world, or else we could not succeed.

On Mr. Truman's relations with MacArthur, I will say only that the stories of a disagreement on Wake Island just are not true. After the meeting was over, MacArthur indicated his satisfaction with the talk. President Truman said as he closed it, "This has been a most satisfactory meeting. We've covered a great deal of ground."

People forget that Truman gave General MacArthur the highest decoration a president can give a soldier. But President Truman was gravely concerned that MacArthur was not paying enough attention to reports of a Chinese build-up in Manchuria and the possibility of Chinese intervention. In fact, as early as the first part of August he sent me out to talk to General MacArthur; I went with General Ridgway and General Norstad. The president asked me to tell General MacArthur that he did not want any involvement with Chiang Kai-shek which would get us into a war with mainland China. That was the first week in August, and Mr. Truman was already concerned. He had the foresight to see that a conflict with mainland China could be disastrous. Mac-Arthur did not see it that way, but he said that he would take orders from his commander-in-chief. I had to report to the president, however, that I was not convinced MacArthur fully accepted the president's position. That was the beginning of the later difficulties.

The MacArthur crisis was perhaps typical of the manner in which

ACME Newspictures—UPI

President Truman and General MacArthur on Wake Island—October 14, 1950.

Truman dealt with crises. There had been two incidents: one, the speech to the Veterans of Foreign Wars, and then, the famous letter to Representative Martin which offended all sense of propriety and clearly indicated that he had ideas which were not in conformity with the president's. MacArthur wanted a military victory instead of accepting the situation as President Truman saw it, namely that we had achieved our objectives.

I happened to be sitting with the cabinet in those days, as special assistant to the president. After this cabinet meeting, on Friday morning, the president asked four of us—General Marshall, General Bradley, Dean Acheson, and myself—to come to his office. He discussed the question of the relief of General MacArthur. He asked each of us what we thought about it, and each one made certain observations. I think in his memoirs Mr. Truman recorded that, when it came to me, I said, "Well, you should have fired him two years ago." Actually, what I said was, "Mr. President, this was a problem which you faced last August and which you decided you would not deal with until later." He held two or three meetings with the four of us during the next two days. He gave each one of us a chance to review the questions in our minds: what would be the public reaction; what would be the reactions of the Joint Chiefs; what would be the impact on the morale of the military, etc. I have always felt that the president consulted Fred Vinson, the chief justice of the Supreme Court, on Sunday. I cannot prove that but it would have been typical of Mr. Truman, because he had great respect for Chief Justice Vinson's judgment and opinion. Anyway, on Monday the president announced that he made his decision; and then, of course, Frank Pace was asked to bear the news to MacArthur. But unfortunately he was in Korea rather than in Tokyo, and, regrettably, General MacArthur heard the report first on the radio.

The interesting thing about the decision was the care with which Mr. Truman proceeded—that was typical of the way in which he considered important questions. He has been pictured as a man who acted by impulse. That was not true. He did act on instinct; he did act on his concepts of what was right and wrong. He never asked, "What are the options?" but, "What's the right thing to do?" He wanted to know what your judgment was, not what the alternatives were.

The MacArthur case is interesting because the problem with General MacArthur was that he was senior to all officers in the army. He had been chief of staff before he went to Manila. All the members of the armed services were junior to him and he took advantage of that. I think it is fair to say that President Roosevelt handled MacArthur with caution; General Marshall was cautious in his dealings with him; General Bradley was also cautious in his dealings with him. Harry Truman dealt with him as the president of the United States would deal with a subordinate who was not carrying out the president's orders. This was not, as some people have called it, a crisis with the military. It was a constitutional crisis: whether the president or a military proconsul would decide foreign policy. It was not a conflict with the military; it was a conflict with one individual. President Truman was the one man who had the courage to step up and deal with it. It was one of the most courageous acts that any president did.

I will close with the question of the use of the atomic bomb. A lot of nonsense has been written on the subject. There was one reason why Mr. Truman ordered the dropping of the bomb and that was to save an infinite number of lives. The advice he had from the Chiefs of Staff at Potsdam, or only a short time before, was that it would be an eighteen-month campaign to end the war in the Pacific, that we would have to land on the main islands of Japan. It seemed very clear that there would be a desperate battle right through to the plains of Tokyo, in which the casualties would total in the hundreds of thousands. Mr. Truman took the decision to drop the A-bomb for one purpose: to end the war and to save lives. There is no evidence that the Japanese would have surrendered; on the contrary, the evidence I have seen since that time confirms the fact that President Truman's decision ended the war far earlier than it otherwise would have. All this talk of some ulterior motive in dropping the bomb is nonsense; he did it to end the war and save American lives.

Now we are in a period, it seems, when feelings for President Truman are coming to life again. One sees it in so many different ways, even in popular songs. The American people are beginning to long for his straightforward, forthright way, for the integrity of Harry S. Truman. His image can keep alive some of the most precious and greatest inspirations that our nation has.

8

Has America Lost Her Way?
A Retrospect on Mr. Truman

Clark M. Clifford

As we recall Korea, we should also pay tribute to an illustrious period in American history. The accomplishments of the years following the Second World War gave added meaning to the sacrifices of that war. It was a period of international tension and suspicion, and yet a time also of extraordinary innovation and growth. My memories of those times and of the president we loved so deeply seem all the more poignant to me today, when I think of the current state of our relations with the world and of Americans' relations with each other.

It is not surprising that public expressions of respect and affection for President Truman should be increasingly evident in a wave of books, articles, and dramatic presentations. Americans now seem confused about our national goals and cynical about our institutions. They wonder what meaning can be given to the agony of Indochina and how the wounds of Watergate can be healed. When our national spirit seems to have been replaced by a national malaise, we remember with all the more pride a man who symbolized those fundamental national virtues of courage, honesty, and a sense of high purpose.

President Truman recognized a basic truth about American leadership in the world. He knew that the foundation of our leadership was the ethical and moral concepts to which we adhered, together with the example of our domestic system and the character of our foreign policies, rather than our economic or military strength. This concept was an abiding one with Mr. Truman. In his inaugural address of 1949, he stated his own faith in proclaiming,

> The American people stand firm in the faith which has inspired this nation from the beginning. We believe that all men have a right to equal justice

under law and equal opportunity to share in the common good. We believe that all men have the right to freedom of thought and expression. We believe that all men are created equal because they are created in the image of God. From this faith we will not be moved.

The founders of our nation established the free institutions that gave substance to these beliefs. Thomas Paine extended this vision in his famous work, *The Rights of Man.* "What Archimedes said of the mechanical powers," Paine wrote, "may be applied to reason and liberty: Had we . . . a place to stand upon, we might raise the world. The Revolution in America presented in politics what was only theory in mechanics. . . . She made a stand, not for herself only, but for the world. . . ."

During our first century of nationhood, we avoided heavy involvement in international political affairs, but we were not separate from the world. Our freedom and our growth provided a beacon for the poor, the hungry, and the oppressed who flocked to our shores. Our people were also generous with their own wealth in times of human tragedy abroad. For example, in 1847 American citizens raised and sent to Ireland $1 million for the victims of the great hunger—a huge sum in that day.

A similar strain of American idealism shaped our entry into World War I. Our purpose was not to acquire foreign territory, but to aid freedom and to create a better international system. Disenchantment and domestic divisions prevented our fulfilling the role we should have played in the peace that followed.

A generation later, we entered World War II to protect ourselves from attack and to help free men stay free. We then took the lead in building new international institutions, to create rather than to retreat again from responsibility. That we did so is testament to the moral force, no less than the statesmanship, of President Truman. In his first comprehensive foreign policy speech, on October 27, 1945, he warned that "the immediate, the greatest threat to us is the threat of disillusionment, the danger of an insidious skepticism—a loss of faith in the effectiveness of international co-operation."

This is my fondest memory of President Truman, a man who stood firmly against our being less than we could be, a man who made the most of himself and of the nation he loved. The result was a period of unparalleled accomplishment: the firm establishment of the United Nations; American leadership in promoting relief in Europe and elsewhere; the development of the Marshall Plan, the Truman Doctrine, NATO, and Point Four; and the creation of new foreign policy mechanisms within the American government that gave central direction to this creative era of progress. The American position was more than one of generosity; we were, by example and by policy, the moral as well as the political leader of most of the world.

I cherish, too, the memory of another quality of President Truman's: his refusal to bend his foreign policies to the advancement of his domestic political fortunes. Some of his international policies were unpopular at the time. Their motives and effects are still debated. But the force of his beliefs and his deep convictions allowed him to endure the criticisms of his opponents. He was, of course, a man of strong partisan political views. As he said in 1962, with a smile, "I don't like bipartisans. Whenever a fellow tells me he's bipartisan, I know he's going to vote against me." But he was able to obtain bipartisan support for his policies because he so obviously believed that foreign policy transcended politics. He once said that "if the president wishes a bipartisan foreign policy, it is his responsibility to make one possible."

President Truman made a practice of consulting with congressional leaders in advance, seeking their agreement to new departures, and then weathering the attacks of the minority who would not be persuaded. This is precisely the pattern he followed with regard to the North Atlantic Treaty. The candor of the administration in consulting with the Congress, well before the formal negotiations on the treaty, was right in principle and effective in practice. Confident of key congressional support, American negotiators were all the more effective; and the Senate approved the treaty by a healthy margin.

It was in the same spirit that the president, in October 1948, decided not to send Chief Justice Vinson on a mission to Moscow, lest it complicate the position of Secretary of State Marshall at the foreign ministers' meeting then being held in Paris. It would have been good politics. The president was under attack from the Left as well as the Right for his foreign policies, and headlines about such a journey for peace would have helped the campaign. But President Truman overruled his political advisers—and still won the election by the same force of character he had shown in making his decision.

This character, translated into the moral character of American foreign policies, earned the world's respect. I recall the words of Arnold Toynbee, when he stated that it was "not the discovery of atomic energy but the solicitude of the world's most privileged people for its less privileged as vested in Truman's Point IV and the Marshall Plan . . . this will be remembered as the signal achievement of our age." In his extraordinary memoirs, *Present at the Creation*, Dean Acheson recalled another tribute to American leadership. In January 1950, the Norwegian ambassador spoke on behalf of the other members of the NATO Council in paying what was recorded as "a warm tribute to the initiative, the

239

vision, and the constructive statesmanship of America ever since the inception of the idea of an integrated defense of the North Atlantic Area."

These words echo sadly when I recall the words I heard from another Norwegian official, an old friend of our country, whom I was visiting in 1972. It was May, and the American government had just mined the harbor of Haiphong while escalating the bombing of North Vietnam. My Norwegian friend made a comment that has deeply concerned me ever since. He said, "America seems to have lost its way."

I asked him what he meant. He said, "America has always stood for what was right, what was decent, what was highminded. Many of us don't understand the picture we now see, of a country that seems confused and uncertain at home, and at the same time is blockading and bombing a small Southeast Asian nation back into rubble."

I did not reply. I did not wish to speak critically of my country's policies while abroad. But, in honesty, I could not disagree with him. There was a brief, sad silence, and the conversation then turned to other subjects.

But the question remains with me. Why, with our traditions, with the legacy of the magnificent accomplishment of the Truman years, should we be told that we seem to have lost our way? I believe that the most important reason is unhappily clear: it is because our recent international behavior does not display that strong sense of moral purpose so evident in the past. It was not only the brutality of our actions in Indochina, including the terror bombings of 1972 and the invasions of Cambodia and Laos, that brought us to this pass. It has been a continuing pattern of recent behavior.

For example, our government is now in the position of threatening, through statements by our secretary of state and president, that under certain conditions we would consider military action in the Middle East to gain access to a natural resource of which we are running short. Let us pass over the obvious military and diplomatic disadvantages of such folly. Let us step back for a moment and see what it reveals about the character of our current foreign policies.

No threat of aggression is justified by a claim of economic hardship. This is what aggressors in other times have claimed. The leaders of the Third Reich coveted the assets of their European neighbors; they wanted space. So they took what they wanted, by force of arms. Stalin behaved in similar fashion. The nations on his western border had something he wanted, and he took it. Of course, the United States is very different from Nazi Germany and Soviet Russia. But should we lower ourselves to making threats that may recall their actions?

A RETROSPECT ON MR. TRUMAN

We, ourselves, have refused to sell economic assets to other nations, without assuming it justified military action against us. I refer not only to the history of our complete or selective embargoes of exports to Cuba and other Communist nations. In July 1941, the United States froze Japanese assets in this country. Thus Japan could no longer purchase badly needed oil from America. Japanese leaders decided that it was necessary to neutralize our Pacific fleet before they could seize the economic resources, including oil, of Southeast Asia. I do not recall any American who believed then that the Japanese attack on Pearl Harbor was justified; I do not know of any Americans who think that now. And I do not believe that we can claim to act with ethical responsibility, and thus to lead through the force of our example, when we allow ourselves different standards of behavior from those to which we hold others.

Coupled with this very damaging loss of the moral compass which helped President Truman shape his approach to the world is another shift from those days: the use of foreign policy by the administration for short-term political gains.

We all remember the stunning announcement on July 16, 1971, that President Nixon would visit China during the following year. It was a tremendous, and politically very effective, surprise to the American public. It was also a tremendous, and diplomatically very damaging, surprise to our allies, especially Japan. Once agreement with Peking had been reached, the only reason for such secrecy could have been to guarantee the maximum political effect of the announcement. This was given priority over the obvious humiliation it would cause the Japanese government. I cannot help but remark on the stark contrast with President Truman's decision not to send Chief Justice Vinson to Moscow in 1948—or President Johnson's decision not to run again in 1968, taken in part lest a reelection campaign damage the prospect of negotiations on Vietnam.

That decision by President Johnson also stands in stark contrast to the events of October 16, 1972. On that day, less than two weeks before our presidential election, Dr. Kissinger made the exhilarating pronouncement that "peace is at hand." With "peace at hand," the stock market quickly rose, together with Mr. Nixon's prospects for a landslide victory. He immediately took up the refrain. On the same day that Kissinger made his statement, Mr. Nixon traveled to Huntington, West Virginia, and Ashland, Kentucky, to make campaign speeches on the theme of peace. He spoke of the details of the agreement that remained for negotiation and of his conviction that they must be resolved in a way that would "deter aggression" and thus help provide more than a single "generation of peace." But he left no doubt that the war would soon be over. He recalled his memories of the ends of other wars: Armistice Day, 1918, when he was a five-year-old in Yorba Linda, California; V-J Day, when he was in Times Square, New York; the end of the Korean War. And now, Vietnam would soon be over.

The American public, and many abroad, believed that peace was at hand. It was not. Two months later, American bombers were carrying out the most savage air raids of the war against innocent civilians in Hanoi. Once again, the confidence of the world and the confidence of the American people in either the word or the decency of our government deteriorated. When we needed unity, we got divisiveness; when we needed honesty, we got duplicity; when we needed candor, we got deception.

President Truman used our power for the sake of principles in which he deeply believed; during those great years after World War II, he used it to create, not to destroy. Now, we may be seen to seek power as an end in itself, as part of an abstract international balancing act more suited to the nineteenth century than to our own. During the Truman years, as now, we were emerging from a period of war and were confronted by new international developments of great uncertainty. Then, American diplomacy took the lead in creating new international institutions to match the new times. Now, lacking a sense of clear direction, American diplomacy relies on ad hoc arrangements and the secret maneuverings of one man. During those years of challenge, as now, the American people needed to believe in their governmental institutions. Then, the foreign policy bureaucracy was reorganized and used to serve high purposes. Now, it is disregarded and misused. And faith in our institutions declines. President Truman built a consensus by including the Congress in his hopes and plans. Now, despite the administration's rhetoric about bipartisanship, the Congress is not consulted before decisions are made, and it has been blamed, unfairly, for the inevitable disaster in Indochina.

In short, then we inspired others. Now, others say we have lost our way. It need not be like this. With vigorous moral leadership, with a return to caring about what is right and what is wrong, we can recapture our greatness. I do not share the self-damaging despair of those officials and observers who proclaim to the world that our coming to our senses over Indochina is a sign of inherent American weakness. These tend to be the same people who equate national strength only with the will to use military power, even when that power is being substituted for common sense. Such hand-wringing in public makes the world sound more dangerous for the United States than it is and promotes the erroneous view that, if anything goes wrong in the world, it is somehow our fault.

A RETROSPECT ON MR. TRUMAN

Circumstances change. In seeking to find our way again, we should not try to regain the dominant responsibility for events we neither can nor should control. But we must bring to our policies the ethical concerns that President Truman brought to his decisions, as we define those issues that require our continued, strong involvement and those that are not our business.

At the end of his term in office, President Truman gave us some ringing advice. It has never been more appropriate. "To beat back fear," he said, "we must hold fast to our heritage as free men. We must renew our confidence in one another, our tolerance, our sense of being neighbors, fellow citizens. Our ultimate strength lies not alone in arms, but in the sense of moral values and moral truths that give meaning and vitality to the purposes of free people. These values are our faith, our inspiration, the source of our strength, and our indomitable determination."

Index

INDEX

INDEX

INDEX

INDEX